NONVOTERS

Voting is our most precious right as citizens. For more than two centuries, good people have been fighting and dying to protect that right. This year, be sure you vote to help determine the nation's future.
—*Atlanta* Journal and Constitution editorial titled
"Clock Ticks on Voter Registration," October 1, 1996

I still get excited when I go to vote. It makes me feel important and patriotic, much more so than watching parades and fireworks on Independence Day. I don't think I'm alone here. My neighbor says it makes her feel like she's really part of the greater whole that is our country. I got a thrill hearing my oldest son talk about participating in mock elections at school, and I loved teaching my six-year-old about the electoral process as part of his homework assignment Tuesday night. I guess I'm not alone. My mother, who was an election judge, reported with a smile about the young woman she met at the polls who admitted she was scared and excited because it was only her second time voting. Voting should be exciting and scary, insofar as it is our voice in how our government runs.
—Opinion piece by Caroline Schomp in the *Denver Post* titled
"Should We Force People to Vote?" November 8, 1996

I believe if you vote, you have no right to complain. People like to twist that around, I know. They say, well, if you don't vote you have no right to complain, but where's the logic in that? If you vote and you elect dishonest, incompetent people and they get into office and screw everything up, you are responsible for what they have done, you caused the problem, you voted them in, you have no right to complain. I, on the other hand, who did not vote, who, in fact, did not even leave the house on Election Day, am in no way responsible for what these people have done and have every reason to complain as loud as I want about the mess you created that I had nothing to do with.

—Comedian George Carlin

Producer Stanley Motss: Would you vote for that person based on that commercial?

Fad Queen: You know I don't vote.

Motss: Why don't you vote?

Fad Queen: The last time I voted, I voted that one time, major league baseball when they started the fans voting. I think I voted for Boog Powell, the first baseman. He didn't get in and it just disappointed me. It stayed with me. It's futile. That was it.

Motss: You've never voted for president?

Fad Queen: No. Do you vote?

Motss: No. I always vote for the Academy Awards, but I never win.

Fad Queen: Liz, Liz, do you vote?

Liz Butsky: Nah, I don't vote. I don't like the rooms. Too claustrophobic. I can't vote in small places.

> —Conversation in *Wag the Dog*, the satirical film
> that stars Robert DeNiro and Dustin Hoffman.
> The conversation occurs as the Hollywood film producer
> played by Hoffman and his crew, while planning a phony
> war to save the president's reelection campaign,
> react to an ad by the opponent.

A statesman is an easy man,
He tells his lies by rote;
A journalist makes up his lies
And takes you by the throat;
So stay at home and drink your beer
And let the neighbours vote.

> —William Butler Yeats's *The Old Stone Cross* (1938)

JACK C. DOPPELT / ELLEN SHEARER

NONVOTERS

AMERICA'S NO-SHOWS

Sage Publications, Inc.
International Educational and Professional Publisher
Thousand Oaks ■ London ■ New Delhi

For information:

Sage Publications, Inc.
2455 Teller Road
Thousand Oaks, California 91320
E-mail: order@sagepub.com

Sage Publications Ltd.
6 Bonhill Street
London EC2A 4PU
United Kingdom

Sage Publications India Pvt. Ltd.
M-32 Market
Greater Kailash I
New Delhi 110 048 India

Printed in the United States of America

Library of Congress Cataloging-in-Publication Data

Doppelt, Jack C.
    Nonvoters: America's no-shows / by Jack C. Doppelt and
Ellen Shearer.
        p.   cm.
    Includes bibliographical references and index.
    ISBN 0-7619-1900-7 (cloth: alk. paper)
    ISBN 0-7619-1901-5 (pbk.: alk. paper)
    1. Voting—United States—Case studies.   2. Political participation—United
States—Case studies.   3. Presidents—United States—Elections—1996—
Case studies.   4. United States. Congress—Elections, 1996—Case studies.
    5. Alienation (Social psychology)—United States—Case studies.
    I. Shearer, Ellen, 1952–   II. Title.
    JK1968 1996g
    324.973′092—dc21   99-6630

This book is printed on acid-free paper.

99   00   01   02   03   04   05   7   6   5   4   3   2   1

Acquiring Editor:	Margaret Seawell
Editorial Assistant:	Renée Piernot
Production Editor:	Denise Santoyo
Editorial Assistant:	Nevair Kabakian
Typesetter:	Lynn Miyata
Cover Designer:	Candice Harman

Contents

Introduction

Why Hear From Nonvoters?

This book began in 1995 as an inquiry into the politically and culturally disaffected in America, a subject that intrigued Northwestern University's Medill School of Journalism, Chicago public television station WTTW, and the John D. and Catherine T. MacArthur Foundation. We wanted not only to study and report on the phenomenon of disaffection but to get to know the people who fall under this often-used but ill-defined rubric.

We decided early on that it was not our mission to change disaffected Americans but to investigate the subject in ways and in media that also would engage them in the inquiry. We wanted to hear from them and report back what we learned—to them as well as to the rest of America. We wanted to give voice to the alienated themselves.

One of the threshold conundrums was how to define the "politically and culturally disaffected" for the purposes of our project. We resolved to use voting as the minimum measure of involvement in the political process and therefore focused our work on those whom we could predict with a high degree of accuracy would *not* vote in the November 1996 elections. Our decision proved remarkably prescient: In the 1996 presidential election, the United States experienced the lowest national voter turnout since 1924, with less than half of those old enough to vote actually casting ballots.

As we started our exploration, we found that almost every dimension of nonvoting and nonvoters opened a Pandora's box of dueling realities. Some observers claim the phenomenon strikes at the heart of democratic legitimacy; others write it off as trivial. There is plentiful evidence that nonvoters are virtually ignored, particularly during election years, yet the topic elicits angry responses that there is too much hand-wringing about nonvoters.

We observed that during the 1996 election campaign year as well as during previous preelection periods, political parties and campaigns and the news media targeted likely voters, ignoring to a large extent the predictable nonvoters and, with them, the nonvoting phenomenon itself. We found little in-depth information available about the millions of Americans not counted on Election Day; most of the data involved gross characterizations of the group as a whole with little differentiation among its many members.

To tell the story of nonvoters, then, we decided first to conduct a scientifically designed poll—to create a new body of knowledge based on a deeper understanding of those people pushed out of most other polls. With the help of graduate students in Medill's Washington program and Dwight Morris, president of the Campaign Study Group and a polling expert, between July 8 and July 21, 1996 we surveyed by telephone 3,323 adults, 18 years of age and older, living in the continental United States. We screened the respondents to distinguish between the likely voters and the likely nonvoters and asked the resulting group of 1,001 likely nonvoters 64 questions. (The survey methodology and survey results are included as appendixes.)

When we released the findings of our survey on August 19, 1996, which fell between the Republican and Democratic national conventions, the information was so compelling that more than 50 news organizations covered the story. News organizations reported and in many cases adopted the subgroup nomenclature—"Doers," "Unpluggeds," "Irritables," "Don't Knows," and "Alienateds"—that we created. The subgroups themselves emerged from the cluster analysis of the project's polling, and we use them as an organizing tool in this book. In addition to the reporting by other news outlets, Medill's graduate students provided stories for television stations and newspapers around the country that subscribe to the Medill News Service, the school's student-staffed wire service in Washington, D.C.

The students, in fact, named the five subgroups as well as the overall project: "No-Show '96: Americans Who Don't Vote."

Through our survey and the Medill News Service stories, we wanted to put faces to the people who don't show up on Election Day to create a better, more accurate picture of the other half of Americans, those who choose not to participate in the most fundamental right of a democracy, the right to vote.

The stories, both those produced by Medill students and those reported by other news media, generated strong public reaction. We appeared on at least a dozen call-in radio shows in which a number of voters expressed anger at their nonvoting fellow citizens. But nonvoters were just as vocal, saying no one talks to them or takes them into account except as a statistic that is alarming on Election Night and then forgotten.

We followed up the survey with a series of in-person profiles conducted on November 5, 1996. We dispatched five Medill graduate students to different cities to spend Election Day with one member of each of the five types of nonvoters. The students wrote a series of stories that was distributed to the more than 20 newspaper subscribers of the Medill News Service; they are quoted at length in the book. It was clear from their stories that nonvoters' voices and ideas had not been heard often enough or in enough depth to fully appreciate the philosophies and emotions behind their decisions, quite deliberate in several cases, to stay away from the polls.

The collaboration between Medill, WTTW, and the MacArthur Foundation also yielded a 90-minute video documentary, *None of the Above,* which featured lengthy profiles of six nonvoters and a conversation between them and two former members of Congress. At times galling, exasperating, and annoying but at other times wise, insightful, and defiant of conventional wisdoms, the six people profiled in the documentary cut to the fault line in the divide that separates the participatory from the disaffected in American society. The documentary, hosted by WTTW senior correspondent John Callaway and produced by Tom Weinberg, debuted in Chicago on October 29, 1997, and aired in 15 cities thereafter.

This book caps the collaboration with in-depth profiles of 30 nonvoters, systematically selected from the initial survey group of 1,001 likely nonvoters to represent the five groups that characterize nonvoters in America. For the book, we have added a sixth group—"Can't Shows"—to account for the more than 17 million age-eligible people who live permanently in the United States but who cannot vote because they are ineligible as aliens or convicted felons.

We traveled to 15 states to visit 30 nonvoters in their homes or their workplaces, mainly within months of the 1996 elections. Therefore, the stories of these 30 people are written as of November 5, 1996—Election Day. Their lives and the world around them—ages, time elements, and events—are depicted in that year. However, we have returned to them to update their lives—and their voting decisions—through the November 3, 1998 election.

In this book, as among the 100 million nonvoters in America, there are Doers, such as Dr. Robert Wolkow, Claudine D'Orazio, and Gene Tencza. They tend to be educated, financially secure, active, and news consumers. People who vote for the lesser of two evils offend Wolkow, who has voted only twice in his life. D'Orazio, a hotel employee in the thick of Savannah's thriving tourism and convention industry, feels she does not know enough about candidates but is embarrassed to be among the nonvoting majority. Tencza is content to let those interested in politics carry the load while he exercises his right to pursue ordinary happiness on his Massachusetts farm.

Unplugged nonvoters tend not to have as much formal education and do not interact much with their communities. Jazz musician Jack Daniels's interest in politics is fixed on the heightened dramas of President Kennedy's assassination and Watergate. Barbara Beth tends bar and ignores discussions of politics, Iris Llamas tends to her nephew and her job, and Janet Shepherd tends to leave her mobile home mostly to sit at the pub across the road. They feel politicians do not tend to them, and they return the sentiment in kind.

Irritable nonvoters are inclined to believe their vote does not matter no matter who is running. Michael Keegan has not seen a politician yet who deserves his vote. Melody Lewis sees them all as empty suits on parade and has no idea what they really do with their days.

Don't Knows know they don't know. George Perez watches television news every night and realizes he doesn't know a Democrat from a Republican. Erica Smith didn't know until the last minute that Hillary Clinton was coming to her son's school, and when she saw the event with her own eyes, she just got mad.

Alienated nonvoters, such as Kathy Smith, are among the hardest core of the nonvoters. She has lost faith in the system. Although her father voted as a lifelong Democrat, she has never voted and never will.

Although the bedrock of this book is the actual voices of the nonvoters provided through the profiles, we also felt it was important to frame their perspective by a critical review of the conventional wisdom that has percolated through the news media about the nonvoting phenomenon.

The book addresses a natural limitation in our and other national surveys: that nonvoter respondents do not have a firm grasp themselves of why they do not vote, often clinging to rationalizations that they do not fully believe or that are internally contradictory. The answers reveal multiple truths and observations, conflicting and almost always susceptible of deeper answers beneath the surface.

Knowing more about the "No-Shows" can help illuminate the discussions of the future of a democracy without the active participation of half of its members. Beyond that, as the 30 people featured in the book tell us about themselves, they provide insights not only into why they do not vote but into our society and its ambivalence in the dual meaning of *body politic*—as a synonym for American society as well as a definition of Americans' responsibility, as a group, for public policy. They point us to a two-way disconnect, from nonvoter to the political process and from the political process back. We hope this book gives voice to a disaffection that prompts us to address a disturbing question as we move into the 21st century: Is American democracy half full or half empty?

Acknowledgments

This book is the result of both a literal and a figurative journey across America. As we visited with 30 nonvoters who gave generously of their time to help us understand their nonvoting status, we were buoyed by colleagues, students, friends, and family.

The No-Show project began in 1995 as a collaboration among more than half the graduate faculty and students at the Medill School of Journalism at Northwestern University. As a group, we engaged in an ongoing, intensive investigation of the many aspects of disaffection in America, eventually settling on nonvoting as the barometer for taking the temperature of Americans' alienation from the democratic process. The project could not have been conducted without the generous financial support of the John D. and Catherine T. MacArthur Foundation and the early and devoted nurturing of Medill's former dean, Mike Janeway.

The collaboration also extended to a unique partnership with Chicago public television station WTTW; its former president and general manager Bill McCarter; one of its vice presidents, V. J. McAleer; and its senior correspondent and spiritual force, John Callaway, whose search for the meaning behind the disaffection of nonvoters helped steer the research. Callaway's documentary on the subject, *None of the Above*, created in conjunction with producer Tom Weinberg, is a cornerstone of the final results.

Creating empirical data on which to base our reporting was crucial to the effort. Dwight Morris, president of the Campaign Study Group, and his partner, Murielle Gamache, guided us in devising and executing a survey that would shed new light on the views of nonvoters. Their extensive analyses of the polling data, continuous efforts to ensure the accuracy of our reporting, and commitment to teach and guide our students are greatly appreciated.

At Medill, special thanks go to our faculty and staff colleagues Earl Barriffe, Jan Boudart, Neil Chase, Mary Coffman, Pat Dean, Mary Dedinsky, Sharon Downey, Mary Ann Gourlay, Ava Greenwell, Peter Miller, Gina Nolan, Rick Rockwell, Jean Shedd, Frank Starr, Larry Stuelpnagel, Mindy Trossman, Marcie Weiss, Jim Ylisela, and Jon Ziomek, whose energy and spirited team-work during the spring, summer, and fall of the 1996 presidential campaign created an infectious enthusiasm that carried us through completion of this book.

The summer 1996 students of Medill's Washington program, who undertook the No-Show survey and series of stories and who named the categories of nonvoters we found, deserve special recognition: Stacy Adams, Delia Blackler, Lisa Bowman, Stephen Coplan, Nicolle Devenish, Mary Dittrich, Eric Dyer, Crystal Edmonson, Michelle Gallardo, Jennifer Hamilton, Allison Haunss, Keith Huang, Courtney Jamieson, Nanci Kulig, Michael Lazerow, Shannon Luckey, Dawn MacKeen, Kelly McEvers (who also created the Web site), Holly Miller, Carmen Nobel, Brad Rubin, John Shea, Hannelore Sudermann, Carolyn Tang, Patricia-Anne Tom, Christine Van Dusen, Lisa Wirth, and John Zelenka. Special mention also goes to Michael Fielding, Julie Fustanio, Rod Hicks, Siobhan Hughes, and John Shea, the students who spent Election Day 1996 with five nonvoters around the country.

Several other students provided research help for this book: Bridget Clingan, Dana Damico, Sarah Freeman, Michael Hershaft, Bridget Horan, Ben Dae-Young Huh, and Victoria Needham. Many thanks along the way to others at Northwestern—John McKnight and Ken Janda for inspiration, Medill Dean Ken Bode for allowing us time to finish the book, and Wendy Leopold and Audrey Chambers for spreading the word; the election officials who make voting their life's work and who encouraged us to continue our research; Isabel Wilkerson and Alex Kotlowitz for their advice on how to capture the context without losing the people; our agent Deborah Schneider for the fine print; and Margaret Seawell, our editor at Sage, who liked the project from the beginning and never wavered.

Even before we began the project and book, Jack was commissioned by David Orr, the newly elected clerk of Cook County, Illinois, to produce a report as part of a comprehensive effort to increase voter registration and participation in the county. It was that report and continuing conversations with Orr, an official dedicated to the ideals of universal registration, that stoked an interest in core nonvoters, the people whom election officials treat, we believe mistak-enly, as those who are getable if only more proactive voter registration proce-dures are put in place.

Most of all, our thanks go to the 30 people who let us into their lives. They put up with our regular intrusions into their homes and opinions as we tried to understand and accurately portray them as people and as part of American democracy. From the 1996 presidential campaign through the 1998 off-year elections, we were welcomed into the lives of people whose failure to vote, had we not been exposed to more than their initial survey answers, would have said little about them or about the nonvoting phenomenon.

We listened and learned from what they had to say and what they allowed us to observe. We offer unrestrained thanks here to those 30 individuals, whose lives beyond the electoral process involved, among so many other things, working to keep a daughter alive, recovering from a stroke, getting married, getting a new job, losing a job, losing a son to gang violence, and introducing us to a newborn son the day after his birth.

During our travels and time at home spent on research and writing, our families motivated us by believing in the value of our undertaking. Our spouses took on added work, including editing, and our children tried to miss us when we felt the need to be missed.

Alan Shearer and Margie Schaps were constant sources of encouragement, emotional strength, and editorial judgment. Zack Shearer helped care for young Nathan and vows to vote in the presidential election in 2000, the year after he turns 18. Nathan provided inspiration by becoming a voter himself at age 5. After mom voted on Election Day 1998, Nathan used an educational ballot machine to punch holes in his ballot for such candidates as Bertram Bronze and Charles Cinnamon. But he didn't consider it a game and demanded to vote for a real candidate for Maryland governor—Parris Glendening. Sylvie and Noah Doppelt, writers both, probed and kept probing until they got the full treatment from dad on what voting is about. Both appreciate why people do not vote, yet both say they will when they grow up. Hard to tell, though, at 8 and 6 years old, what is more ingrained, the commitment to vote or to write about it.

Without the help of all of those mentioned, our journey would have faltered.

1

The Conventional Wisdom About Nonvoters

When Henry Montoya walked into his neighborhood polling place in west Denver on November 5, 1996, as he had for the previous 10 years, he signed in to record his presence. Democrat Bill Clinton, Republican Bob Dole, Reform Party candidate Ross Perot, and Libertarian Harry Browne were on the ballot for president of the United States. The ballot also afforded an opportunity to vote for candidates for the U.S. Senate and House of Representatives, the state senate and house, and the University of Colorado regents, among other offices, and for four citizen-initiated referenda.

Montoya went behind the curtain and pushed the exit button at the bottom, having deliberately voted for no one. His reason? "In any election, there's no one worth my vote." Montoya's disaffection is common, his method of voicing it unusual. But in him lie two distinct political species: Americans who vote and those who don't. Those who don't now outnumber those who do. In presidential elections, the numbers are close, with 51% of the voting-age population—about 100 million people—not voting in November 1996. In off-year elections, such as the November 1998 congressional elections, they're not even close.

A front-page story in the *Denver Post* two days before the 1996 presidential election predicted a low voter turnout despite objective indicators, it noted, that would point to the contrary. "There were surprise candidacies and noncandidacies, a big turnover in the Colorado legislature, a presidential primary in March and almost weekly visits from the two major contenders in the final weeks," the daily newspaper reported. "But somehow Colorado voters never really got all that fired up." The *Post* reported that about 80% of Colorado's *registered* voters went to the polls in 1992, whereas the prediction for the impending election stood at 69% to 72%. The story quoted experts and politicians attributing the expected low turnout to the usual laundry list trotted out after each election: negative campaigning, the turnoff of big money, apathy, a sense of powerlessness, the remoteness of government, the public's thoughtful pragmatism, and the uninspired presidential race.

The day after the election, a team of reporters for the *Denver Post* reported "an unexpected healthy turnout" in a story about the tics, quirks, and offbeat behavior that accompany the American voting process. The following day, the *Post* dramatically adjusted its postmortem. Its headline over a story datelined Washington, D.C., read, "Pilgrimage to the polls is lowest in 72 years." The jarring reality of that story and of the phenomenon of nonvoting in the United States is that in November 1996, for the first time since 1924, less than half of the nation's voting-age population voted in a presidential election. Yet the *Post's* schizophrenic analysis of the phenomenon is indicative of how the American political environment addresses the issue by fixating on incremental shifts in Election Day turnout figures.

Through that lens, one sees that 49% of voting-age Americans voted in 1996, a significant 6% drop-off from the 55.2% who voted in 1992. In real numbers, 96,277,872 people voted in 1996, more than 8 million fewer than the 104,428,377 who voted 4 years before. Understandably, the story around Election Day is the 6%, the potential voters who turned off from the electoral process somewhere between November 3, 1992, and November 5, 1996, despite government efforts, such as the National Voter Registration Act of 1993 to ease the registration process, and partisan efforts from every quarter to draw more Americans to the polls.

In a story 10 weeks before the 1996 election, the *Christian Science Monitor* reported, "From MTV's Rock the Vote to appeals over the Internet to state motor-vehicle offices and traditional outreach campaigns, the United States is witnessing the most extensive voter-registration efforts ever mounted for a national election." The side of the "Choose or Lose" campaign bus that MTV dispatched for a nationwide swing read, "You might as well pull the lever. What 'chu afraid of?" MCI and the nonprofit Rock the Vote group collaborated to launch an online voter registration effort that they called "the most convenient in America's history." The Southwest Voter Registration Education Project introduced its "Su Voto Es Su Voz" (Your Vote Is Your Voice) program, supported by Budweiser, to register new Latino voters and get them to the polls on Election Day. Two weeks before the election, the Christian Coalition's executive director, Ralph Reed, announced plans for "the most ambitious, aggressive and expensive get-out-the-vote effort in our history." Human Serve, a New York-based voter advocacy group, issued a report prepared in 1996 for the League of Women Voters and the NAACP, documenting that 20 million Americans signed up to vote or updated their voting addresses over an 18-month

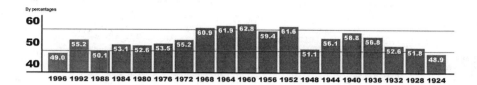

Figure 1.1 National Voter Turnout by Election Year

SOURCE: Committee for the Study of the American Electorate (CSAE), dividing the total vote for the presidential candidates by the number of eligible Americans, a number based on Census Bureau estimates of the age-eligible population as of November of that election year.

period after enactment of the National Voter Registration Act. The report touted the effort as "the largest increase in voter registration since the practice of registration was established in the closing decades of the nineteenth century" and projected an increase in turnout from 1992.

The 1992 turnout figure had been cause for optimism because it had disrupted, if only temporarily, a steady trend downward from 1960, when 62.8% of voting-age Americans voted in a presidential election that resulted in a narrow victory for John Kennedy over Richard Nixon. The 1960 figure also was noteworthy because it represented the end of an equally long upward trend in voter participation from the 48.9% who voted in 1924.

A slightly different lens, fixed not on the marginal shifts from election to election but on the core nonvoters, reveals a more profound, entrenched phenomenon; that is, as the number of voters in America is increasing as a function of an increase in the number of adult Americans, the number of nonvoters is increasing at a faster rate to the point that in the 1996 presidential election, two major milestones occurred. One hundred million voting-age Americans did not vote, and more people did not vote in a presidential election than voted, the first such statement of majority disaffection since 1924.

The nonvoting phenomenon crosses state lines indiscriminately. Only five states—Maine, Minnesota, Montana, South Dakota, and Wyoming—had more than 60% of their adult populations show up at the polls in November 1996, according to the Committee for the Study of the American Electorate. More people failed to vote in the 1996 presidential election than did vote in 25 states, including California, Texas, New York, Florida, Pennsylvania, and Illinois, the 6 states with the largest adult populations. Nevada had the highest percentage

TABLE 1.1 Comparison of U.S. Voters and Nonvoters by Election Year

Election Year	Voters	Nonvoters
1996	96,277,872	100,229,128
1992	104,428,377	84,615,623
1988	91,594,805	91,033,195
1984	92,653,000	81,814,000
1980	86,497,000	78,098,000
1976	81,603,000	70,705,000
1972	77,625,000	63,152,000
1968	73,212,000	47,073,000
1964	70,645,000	43,445,000
1960	68,838,000	40,834,000
1956	62,033,908	42,481,092
1952	61,551,919	38,377,081
1948	48,833,680	46,741,320
1944	48,025,684	37,628,316
1940	49,815,312	34,912,688
1936	45,646,817	34,707,183
1932	39,816,522	35,951,478
1928	36,879,414	34,305,586
1924	29,091,417	30,412,049

SOURCE: Committee for the Study of the American Electorate (1998a, 1998b, 1998c) for the total number of eligible Americans, a number based on U.S. Bureau of the Census estimates of the age-eligible population as of November of that election year. The authors calculated the nonvoter count by subtracting the total vote for the presidential candidates from the total number of eligible Americans.

of no-shows and was the only state in which less than 40% of its potential electorate voted in 1996. Interestingly, Nevada is the only state that, since 1975, provides on its ballots for state office the option of choosing "none of these candidates."

CIVIC EMBARRASSMENT

Just as voting traditionally has been a matter of civic pride, nonvoting has become a source of state, regional, and local embarrassment. Newspaper stories from across the country tell the story vividly. In Virginia, the *Roanoke Times & World News* published a front-page story on April 12, 1998, a month before the city council election, in which it characterized Roanoke's chronic nonvoting behavior as "the Big Shrug." "Welcome to Roanoke," the story told its readers, "the 'All-American' city where most people can't be bothered to vote. The city where government officials boast so often of the 'All-American' designation that it sounds like a mantra—but about 80 percent of eligible voters do not cast local ballots."

The newspaper reported that political analysts were at odds in trying to explain why. It noted that nationwide, "Voter turnout typically is lower in local elections because people consider the issues, although closer to home, to be more complicated and thus easier to ignore than in state and national elections." And why are so many people choosing to not vote in almost every election, national or local? The story reported,

> Many factors affect voter turnout—a populace's penchant for political activism, whether issues are controversial or mundane, whether candidates are well known or unknown, whether Democratic and Republican party-supported incumbents face a serious challenge from outsiders, the weather on voting day, among others—but participation often hinges on whether people believe their vote will make a difference.

The reporters talked to residents.

> Some people said Roanoke's turnout is low because residents are satisfied with city government. Others accused City Hall of doing nothing to encourage voter turnout so the citizenry does not get fired up and start scrutinizing every action by council members and administrators. Some people faulted the news media for not providing more coverage. Some pointed the finger at both citizens and politicians.

In an editorial titled "Voting With Pride," the *Boston Globe* on September 14, 1998, tried to stir up its readers' competitive civic juices:

> New Hampshire, which prides itself on being the soul of civic spirit, had only 15 percent of its voters exercising the franchise in last week's primary—a record low. Vermont had an 18 percent turnout, and in Maine just 11 percent of eligible citizens voted instead of the 25 to 30 percent that usually participate in June primaries.

Why? the editorial asked. "The pundits point to voter cynicism over political scandals, the power of big money and the feeling that the little guy doesn't count." The answers didn't satisfy the *Globe*:

But these are tired excuses that have become cliches and a national self-fulfilling prophecy: "I won't participate because politics is so bad." Politics wouldn't be so bad if more people participated. So, vote. Consider it a matter of state pride to beat New Hampshire, Maine, and Vermont.

In Texas, the headline to an April 19, 1998, story in the *Dallas Morning News* read, "Small voter bang for the electoral buck draws concern." The bang, the paper noted in its lead, was that "the combined turnout for two statewide elections," the March 10 primary and a runoff earlier that week, was "a pitiful" 1.6 million of the 11.1 million registered voters in the state. "In the wake of the 3 percent turnout for the runoff election," the newspaper reported, Texas Secretary of State Al Gonzales called a news conference "to announce that he was willing to try almost anything to get voters to go the polls."

In Nebraska, a weekly newspaper tried to help. According to the *Omaha World-Herald,* a weekly newspaper in Sarpy County took on its readers after what the weekly called a "pathetic" turnout of 24% in the state's May 1998 primary election. It adopted a new letters-to-the-editor policy under which it would not print any letters addressing a political issue from readers who were not registered voters.

In Michigan, after local elections in 1997 in which the Flint City Council primary attracted only 8.5% of eligible voters, the *Flint Journal,* the city's daily newspaper, and Channel 12, the local ABC affiliate, collaborated to poll residents and conduct a focus group for a continuing series on voter apathy. The series that ran and aired on consecutive Sundays in June 1998 concluded that people don't vote for many reasons, many because "they feel their vote doesn't make a difference," some because they distrust government, some because voting is too inconvenient, and some because they just don't care. The poll, however, surveyed only registered voters and included only those who vote regularly and those who vote infrequently. The core nonvoters, the people who comprise the vast majority of the disaffected—those who have never voted or who seldom vote—were not heard from.

In Oklahoma, the *Daily Oklahoman* reported on July 10, 1998, about 6 weeks before the state's primary election, that "they come from all walks of life and often have specific reasons for shunning polling places. Nonvoters are rampant in the United States—and in Oklahoma." That day, the newspaper asked its readers in its weekly Your Turn feature, "Do you plan on voting in this year's election?" The following week, it reported the phone-in results: 359 yes, 52 no, or 87.35% saying they would vote. Six weeks later, immediately after the primary election, the *Oklahoman* reported that "voters avoided the polling places in Tuesday's primary election like they were filled with fire ants." Eleven percent of the eligible voters had shown up.

DISGRACE IN THE EYES OF
OTHER COUNTRIES

Beyond local pride, there is the matter of America's global image. On National Public Radio's *Talk of the Nation,* host Ray Suarez opened the call-in program on April 14, 1998, by putting the American nonvoting phenomenon in a global context:

> American diplomats, human rights campaigners, NGOs [nongovernmental organizations]—they cast their eyes around the world and divide the globe into two kinds of places: those places where the government operates with the consent of the governed through the electoral process; and those places where there is no vote—no democracy. The United States is increasingly a country where people have a vote, and it's a vote that they choose in the millions not to use. It's a kind of consent that's being given, or a passive assent, to who it will be that ends up in the 435 seats in the House of Representatives, the 100 chairs in the United States Senate, as county commissioners and mayors, state delegates and governors.

Suarez asked, "What can we conclude about America—its various governments and its citizens—based on the voting habits of the last 30 years?"

Andrew Marr, who covered the 1996 presidential election for the *Independent* in London, wrote the following the day after the reelection of Bill Clinton:

> So, as the political class [in the United States] gazes admiringly at the latest glittering example of a great campaigner or a great party-manager at work, the rest of the world turns quietly away. Look at the pathetic voter turnout achieved in yesterday's election in America; or the worryingly low rates of registration and intention to vote among younger adults here. A decade or so more of this and the essential base of center-leftish voting—the very mechanism on which Clinton and [Britain's Prime Minister Tony] Blair depend—will have been eaten away.

From the other side of the globe, reinforcing the poor regard in which U.S. voters are held, the headline in a story in the Singapore-based *Straits Times* the week before the 1996 presidential election read, "Voter turnout the issue as US heads for presidential polls." The news account referred to the campaign as Election Yawn '96 and predicted that the turnout would be fewer than 50% of eligible voters, not so much due to the soporific campaign as to the chronic phenomenon itself. "Voter turnout is always low in America," the story reported.

The American benchmark of 50% voter participation is often the standard by which democratic governance in other nations is gauged. In a story on

Hong Kong's first election under Chinese rule in May 1998, the *South China Morning Post* reported that voter participation in local elections is about 68% in France, 72% in Germany, and only 33% in England, making the British "the least enthusiastic voters in Europe." Recognizing that American voter participation in local elections is as low, often lower than Britain's, the *Morning Post* reported that the United States in 1998 was still "reeling from the realization that voter turnout for its last presidential race in November 1996 had fallen below 50 per cent."

Speaking before the U.S. Chamber of Commerce in Washington, D.C., in December 1997, Mesut Yilmaz, the prime minister of Turkey, wanted the gathering to know that Turkey's democracy was strong. "Consider this," Yilmaz said in calling politics Turkey's number-one spectator sport. "Since 1961, voter participation in national elections has never fallen below 64 percent. In 1995, voter turnout was 85 percent. Turks make their voices heard."

Even some of America's largest foundations have found that low voter participation in the United States puts their global mission in a compromising position. "There's a tendency among the people you're trying to help overseas to ask: 'How's your election going?' " Paul Light, director of the Pew Charitable Trusts' Public Policy Program, told the *Los Angeles Times* shortly after the 1996 election. "As you're working on strengthening democracy in Central Europe, it may sensitize you to the fact it's not working so well in the United States."

The day after the 1996 presidential election, the *Chicago Tribune* offered a modest, satiric proposal. "All registered voters in Chicagoland who did not cast ballots Tuesday, and all who are eligible to vote but did not register, should be gathered together in Grant Park at dawn and flogged." The newspaper was embarrassed for the nation:

> Here in America, the decline in the number of voters has dropped even below the level of apathy. From a respectable 64 percent of the potential electorate in 1960, voter turnout declined to 50 percent in 1988 before climbing a few points in 1992. That is a humiliatingly low number among democracies. Greece, Australia, South Africa, Denmark and Indonesia post turnouts above 80 percent; Brazil, Norway, Germany, France, Poland, Canada and, yes, even Russia, have voter turnouts above 70 percent.

The solution? The editorial considered but rejected compulsory voting, backed up by fines, as is the law in Greece, Australia, and Brazil. Instead: "You know those little white ballot stubs that they tear off and give you after you've voted? From now on, anyone who complains about the country or the government ought to be required to show his stub—his license to gripe—or be ignored," the newspaper fumed. "Or they could choose flogging in Grant Park."

The late syndicated columnist Mike Royko ridiculed CBS news anchor Dan Rather for announcing during the network's 1996 Election Day coverage that the low voter turnout was a "national disgrace." "My belief is that someone who must be nagged into voting hasn't been paying attention and doesn't have any idea what the issues are or what the candidates will or won't be trusted to do. In other words, a civic klutz," wrote Royko. "So why is it important to the future of this nation for a klutz, or millions of klutzes, to go punch holes in a ballot?" Voters at least know enough to "bother to say eenie, meenie, miney, mo" when they go to the polls, he argued.

A VITAL DEMOCRACY?

Others perceive the issue as vital to democracy itself. In a 1988 report for *Congressional Quarterly,* titled "Why America Doesn't Vote," Robert Landers asked if American democracy is in a dangerous state of decay. Landers saw it the way former President Jimmy Carter saw it when he made his famous "malaise" speech in 1979: that nonvoting is symptomatic of a crisis in the American spirit. Walter Dean Burnham, political science professor at the Massachusetts Institute of Technology, argues that the nonvoting phenomenon saps the authority of the political order. Burnham views the problem as class based, with the "party of nonvoters" disproportionately concentrated in the bottom half. Frances Fox Piven and Richard Cloward, who coauthored the 1988 book *Why Americans Don't Vote,* have argued for years that the reason poorer people and those with lower levels of education vote less in the United States is because the political system tends to isolate them, to cause and entrench apathy. In a January 25, 1998, *New York Times Magazine* article titled, "Whatever Happened to Politics?" author Garry Wills of Northwestern University pondered whether Bill Clinton had become America's first postpolitical president in that whether the public is disaffected or complacent, the results seem the same: "stasis and dead air" or, more acutely, "a failure of politics."

Larry Sabato, director of the Center for Governmental Studies at the University of Virginia and author of the 1991 book *Feeding Frenzy,* was quoted in the *Roanoke Times & World News* as characterizing the low voter participation as a national crisis. "Most people don't see it as a crisis because it's occurred gradually, but it's a major problem when a sizable majority of your community doesn't even fulfill the minimum requirement of citizenship: Voting."

Harvard Professor Robert Putnam, who has made the case in articles such as "Bowling Alone: America's Declining Social Capital" that the United States is experiencing an epidemic of civic disengagement, sees the nonvoting phenomenon as symptomatic of a deeper illness in the body politic. It is "like a temperature in a child," Putnam was quoted as saying in the *National Journal.* "If your child gets a high fever, you need to get it down because the fever itself is bad. But the fever is also a symptom of something else that is wrong in the body." The *National Journal* article by Eliza Newlin Carney, titled "Opting Out of Politics," depicted the conventional wisdom about nonvoters as citizens who are "disgusted with money-grubbing candidates, televised air wars and cynical, conflict-driven media coverage." The article countered that the problem with the conventional wisdom is that it assumes that nonvoters are more alienated than voters are, an assumption based more on myth than data.

"So what's with American citizens, and what might lure them to the polls?" the article posed. "It's a question that's puzzled political scientists, pollsters and civic leaders for decades. If anything, experts disagree more than ever," the article answered. "And without a clear diagnosis, no one knows the remedy."

Some political observers see nonvoting as understandable complacency in a democracy that works, particularly during healthy economic times. David Shribman, Washington bureau chief of the *Boston Globe,* referred to it as "hapathy," a peculiar combination of happiness and apathy, in his article "The Anesthetic of the Masses," in the September 28, 1998, issue of *Fortune* magazine. Syndicated columnist Charles Krauthammer called low turnout "a leading indicator of contentment" in a 1990 essay in *Time* magazine. Conservative columnist Ken Adelman wrote, "It probably indicates high voter satisfaction— if not in politics, at least in life." And Robert Kaplan wrote in a cover story titled "Was Democracy Just a Moment?" in the December 1997 issue of *Atlantic Monthly* that "apathy, after all, often means that the political situation is healthy enough to be ignored. The last thing America needs is more voters—particularly badly educated and alienated ones—with a passion for politics."

Nonetheless, Kaplan concluded that the political disconnect in the United States may have crossed the line:

> When voter turnout decreases to around 50 percent at the same time that the middle class is spending astounding sums in gambling casinos and state lotteries, joining private health clubs, and using large amounts of stimulants and anti-depressants, one can legitimately be concerned about the state of American society.

Chicago Tribune columnist Steve Chapman sees the same line as an indication of societal maturity in which millions of citizens

> have made a rational decision to devote their energies to pursuits other than the rituals of self-government. Is that a tragedy? John Adams said he studied politics and war so his children could study commerce and agriculture and their children could study poetry and music. . . . It's no disgrace for many Americans to behave

as though politics is not among the most important activities in life. As it happens, they're right.

Others see the nonvoting phenomenon as a reaction by the public to contemporary flaws in the political environment. Conservative columnist George Will wrote the week before the 1996 presidential election, "Nonvoting is a sensible way for people who feel soiled by contemporary campaigning to express disgust." In their postelection article, "Why Americans Don't Go to the Polls" in the *National Journal,* Washington correspondents Jack Germond and Jules Witcover wrote, "A strong possibility is that eligible voters stay home on Election Day because they're turned off by negative campaign advertising." Thomas Patterson, author of *Out of Order,* a book on media coverage of political affairs, sees the problem as one in which the news media contribute to the perception that politics is not for them: "If politics is a mess and not to be trusted, why pay attention to the darn stuff?"

In a January 1998 story, the Gannett News Service enumerated the contemporary flaws most often cited to explain the nonvoting phenomenon:

- Few real choices, in that in the November 1998 elections for the House of Representatives, for instance, only about 75 of 435 races would be truly contested and in that incumbents' money advantages make a viable alternative candidacy less likely.

- Time, in that polling places are not open long enough during the day to accommodate busy people.

- Too many elections and jurisdictions, in that people recognize they don't know or aren't interested in many candidates and their races.

- Elections on the wrong day, in that weekend voting would likely increase participation.

- Inadequate civics, in that the failure of schools to teach the basics has left citizens intimidated and uninterested.

- The tone of campaigns, in that they instill distrust in public officials.

- Media focus on the horse race, in that citizens are left feeling like outsiders whose problems are trivialized.

- The decline of political parties, in that the public is left less connected to the process.

- A reluctance to serve on juries, even though the majority of states now use driver's license lists rather than voter registration lists to select jury pools.

"What we are witnessing is a progressive meltdown in civic engagement, a major danger to American democracy," says Curtis Gans, the most vigilant and most relied-on authority on the nonvoting phenomenon. As director of the Washington-based Committee for the Study of the American Electorate, Gans releases periodic reports that not only document and analyze the phenomenon but have become the authoritative source of the data that provide the larger context for the raw election returns.

In the committee's September 1998 report issued between the primaries and the November 1998 general election, Gans offered an expansive list of causes and conditions that have undermined citizen participation, including

> the decay and misalignment of political parties, the conduct of our campaigns, the lack of civility in our political dialogue, the inadequacies of our educational system when it comes to training citizens, the fragmenting effects of the coaxial cable and computers, and our increasingly anti-engagement, anti-government, self-seeking and libertarian values, among other things.

The danger to American democracy, according to Gans, is "the nation that prides itself as being the best example of government of, for and by the people, will continue to drift towards a government of, for and by the interested few."

In a report a few months earlier, in June 1998, Gans argued that the entrenched nonvoting phenomenon is neither a picture of a "satisfied electorate" nor one of procedural disincentives to registration or voting. He concluded that the problem is motivational, one in which there are no quick fixes and in which "we are progressively driving out the civic impulse to participate."

The years of respectable voter participation in the middle of the 20th century had passed, Gans noted, because so had

> a commitment to civic values; strong political institutions; educational institutions committed to developing the person as a citizen; a politics governed by minimal bounds of civility, comity and common purpose; major and central mobilizing issues; a media committed to informing; and a general belief in the honor of the political enterprise.

CHANGING SYMBOLISM OF VOTING

In a 1996 report on voter participation commissioned for the Michigan legislature, the authors concluded that "citizens appear to cherish the American flag, a symbol of democracy, more than they value the vote, the actual exercise of democracy." In the face of a generation of consistently declining voter participation, others are coming to view voting as something other than the societal reinvestment in democracy. In his 1995 book, *The Two Faces of Political Apathy,*

Tom DeLuca contends that chronic low voter participation is "powerful evidence that the ideal of democracy needs to be tempered, is unrealistic and out of character with human nature at this point in history." Similarly, sociologist Michael Schudson wrote in his article "Voting Rites: Why We Need a New Concept of Citizenship" that the problem is with "our contemporary conception of how democratic citizenship ought to work." In the article, published in the fall 1994 issue of *The American Prospect,* Schudson wrote that in an experiment involving his students, they reported a letdown when they voted in 1992. They felt inadequate to the task. Schudson came to their defense:

> Whatever else we learn from elections, we are tutored in a sense of helplessness and fundamental inadequacy to the task of citizenship. We are told to be informed but discover that the information required to cast an informed vote is beyond our capabilities.

In a series in late October 1997, titled "Beyond the Ballot Box," *The Portland Oregonian* reported that the "steadily swelling ranks of nonvoters haven't abandoned citizenship, they are finding it in places beyond the polls." In a study of Oregon residents, the newspaper found that 8 of 10 nonvoters were active in their communities and that whether people voted or not, the majority thought voting meant choosing the lesser of two evils. The *Oregonian* coined a new model of citizenship, which it called "shirt-sleeve citizenship," that compensates for the loss of faith in what had heretofore been the fundamental virtue of voting. "Voting doesn't matter much anymore to a lot of people who consider themselves good citizens," the *Oregonian* reported.

From pundits to politicians and from scholars to people on the street, Americans can be quite impassioned about the nonvoting phenomenon. They may divide on whether it matters, what's causing it, who's to blame, and what can be done about it. But the fallacy in much of the conventional wisdom, even in the passion that accompanies it, is that it is based on the stereotype of the homogeneous nonvoter, as if nonvoters all are infected with the same no-show virus.

2

Profiling America's Nonvoters— Their Voices

The weekend before the 1996 presidential elections, seven national polls were conducted. All were quite accurate. When averaged, according to an article in *The New York Times,* they showed President Bill Clinton with 49% support. Clinton emerged on November 5 with 49% of the popular vote.

All seven polled probable or likely voters. Earlier in the campaign, national polls used looser screens to separate probable voters from the likely nonvoters. Nonetheless, the goal was the same: to hear from those likely to vote in an effort to predict as accurately as possible who would win the election.

More and more, political strategists, candidates, parties, and the news media are ignoring the half of America that isn't likely to vote.

In a front-page *Wall Street Journal* article on July 13, 1998, reporter John Harwood explained how the political parties and candidates, with the help of polling experts and strategists, not only avoided wasting any time on likely nonvoters but also avoided many likely voters in favor of wooing "ideologically motivated groups."

These efforts to push the partisan groups toward the election booth while either ignoring the half of the adult population that doesn't vote or, in a more active role, aggressively but subtly pushing political moderates away from the voting booth confirm what many nonvoters believe—that politicians and elected officials don't care what they think.

It was precisely because they were ignored that we decided to talk to likely nonvoters. The need for more quantifiable information to dispel—or confirm—conventional wisdom was apparent.

What we found in talking to 1,001 likely nonvoters in the summer of 1996 was as simple as common sense—that they don't fit one stereotype of politics, race, age, or income. When finally asked for their opinions, they are as opinionated and their views are as varied as those of voters.

As reporter Hannelore Sudermann wrote in the Medill News Service series, which was published in 30 newspapers, from the *San Francisco Examiner* to the *Delaware State News,*

> Some are poor. Some have incomes over $75,000. Some are educated. Some haven't finished high school. Some are plugged in to government and write their congressmen. And some just don't care. But the likely nonvoters who participated in the poll generally fit into five different groups based on their ages, incomes, education and responses to the poll. And it's the smallest group that most closely matches the stereotype of nonvoters as a monolithic group of lower-income, less-educated and less-informed Americans. What made this study unique is that it surveyed enough nonvoters to analyze the differences among them.

Our goal as we created the survey structure and sample was just as Sudermann wrote: to be able to look at nonvoters as individuals and to find patterns in their thinking. To do so, we decided to survey only nonvoters so that the sample size would allow for scientifically valid cluster analysis. From the 2,322 likely voters we reached in our polling, we asked for demographic information only to provide a gross comparison to likely nonvoters.

In the nonvoters we found an incredibly diverse group of people with highly divergent views. However, their disaffection for and disconnection from the political process was a unifying force.

A sampling of their opinions, from one of the Medill News Service stories by Nanci Kulig, shows the range from disconnection to dissatisfaction as well as a second range of those holding themselves accountable for their nonvoting to those who blame the system: "I just don't care nothing about politics." "I didn't think it made a difference either way." "We have no control over what's going on." "I don't like anybody they've got up for it." "I don't really think any of the candidates are interested in the issues that I am."

Although they do fit the stereotypical view of nonvoters in many ways, it is a mistake to consider the 100 million Americans who stayed away from the polls in 1996 as a unit. The Medill poll identified five distinct groups within that population whose members view government, elected officials, political parties and other institutions, and the news about those institutions and officials quite differently. The Medill News Service students named the groups Doers, Unpluggeds, Irritables, Don't Knows, and Alienateds. The Doers, the largest of the clusters, look startlingly like voters and represent the largest single segment of nonvoters—nearly one third of the total. The Alienateds most closely capture the stereotypical nonvoter profile but represent only 12% of all nonvoters.

REFLECTING THE STEREOTYPE

We are told repeatedly that nonvoters are alienated, less affluent, less educated, younger, and more likely to be members of minority groups than their voting counterparts. We should pay attention to these facts: They're true. In fact, the Medill survey reinforced them.

But it also highlighted what those facts obscure: 18% of the nonvoters earned $50,000 a year or more, 44% had attended at least some college or had obtained a degree, and 25% were at least 45 years old.

Nevertheless, age is the biggest difference between nonvoters and voters: 73% of nonvoters were 18 to 44 years old compared with 48% of voters. More telling, 39% of likely nonvoters were under age 30 compared with 16% of voters. Age clearly was a dominant factor in 20-year-old Ryan Gerali's nonvoting status. Gerali, a student whom we interviewed in his Itasca home west of Chicago, missed the deadline to register in 1996 so he could not vote in the first presidential election for which he was eligible, but he admits that, at this stage of his life, he wasn't interested. He will be more interested when he's older, he says, and paying taxes, which would provide a connection he can see between his life and Washington.

Nonvoters also tend to have lower household incomes, with 48% reporting incomes of less than $30,000—much lower than among voters at 33%.

Only 18% of the nonvoters had at least a bachelor's degree from a college or university compared with 37% of voters. Among nonvoters, 55% had a high school diploma or less schooling, whereas only 37% of voters had achieved no more than a high school education.

Thirty percent of nonvoters identified themselves as minorities; the comparable number among voters was 18%. Although African Americans were more likely to say they were registered to vote than other minorities or Whites, race is not a major factor in distinguishing among nonvoters. Statistically significant differences on policy issues are nonexistent except on the issue of race relations; African Americans were more likely than others to consider it the most important issue facing the country.

Henry Montoya, whom we interviewed in the Denver apartment building he manages, personifies the alienation from elected officials felt by many nonvoters. Of those surveyed in the Medill poll, 64% said they either completely or mostly agreed that "most elected officials don't care what people like me think." Montoya demonstrates to whoever wins that he doesn't care about them either by pulling the lever on an empty ballot. When Erica Smith, the mother of an elementary school child in Lynn, Massachusetts, saw her child and others waiting outside in the winter cold for security reasons during a visit to the school by First Lady Hillary Rodham Clinton, she knew the school was an election prop, nothing more.

TABLE 2.1 A Demographic Comparison of Likely Nonvoters and Voters
(in percentages)

	Likely Nonvoters (Base = 1,001)	Likely Voters (Base = 2,322)
Gender		
Male	46	48
Female	54	52
Age		
18-29	39	16
30-44	34	32
45-64	18	30
65 and older	7	21
Race		
White	68	81
Black	13	9
Other	17	9
Education		
Less than high school	17	10
High school graduate	38	27
Some college	26	26
College graduate	18	37
Income		
Under $30,000	48	33
$30,000 and over	43	60

NOTE: Percentages may not add to 100% due to rounding and the exclusion of those who refused to answer.

But the gross characteristics of nonvoters can undermine a deeper under-standing by assuming that the group's demographic differences compared with voters mold this half of the population into a single group.

Instead, a closer look at the data, using the statistical technique of cluster analysis to move the survey respondents into the most homogeneous, mutually exclusive groups possible, reveals five distinct subgroups. No one answer or specific set of answers results in the assignment of respondents to a particular group. Clustering takes the range of answers and respondent characteristics and determines where any given person "best fits." What was clear in the creation of our five groups of nonvoters is that only the smallest group fits the description of alienated, less affluent, and less educated.

TABLE 2.2 A Demographic Profile of Nonvoter Clusters (in percentages)

	Doers (Base = 288)	Unpluggeds (Base = 250)	Irritables (Base = 177)	Don't Knows (Base = 146)	Alienateds (Base = 121)
Gender					
Male	46	50	50	33	48
Female	54	50	50	67	52
Age					
18-29	48	46	29	33	26
30-44	32	35	36	38	35
45-64	17	16	22	15	24
65 and older	3	3	11	12	14
Race					
White	74	65	65	74	71
Black	12	11	19	11	14
Other	13	24	15	13	15
Education					
Less than high school	8	24	14	22	26
High school graduate	37	40	36	41	41
Some college	32	24	26	20	22
College graduate	23	13	25	16	11
Income					
Under $30,000	40	55	44	52	63
$30,000 and over	55	39	48	32	29

NOTE: Percentages may not add to 100% due to rounding and the exclusion of those who refused to answer.

DETACHMENT AND CYNICISM BELIE
GOOD VOTING INTENTIONS

As was shown in the 1996 election, higher levels of voter registration will not solve the no-show problem: The Committee for the Study of the American Electorate reports that registered voters increased by 3.5 million from 1992 to 1996 due largely to the implementation of the 1993 National Voter Registration Act—the so-called "motor-voter law"—but the number of voters casting ballots dropped 8 million to 49% of eligible voters.

In the Medill poll, 36% of likely nonvoters said they were registered, but 80% of them did not vote in 1992 and 25% said they definitely would not vote in 1996.

Alma Romanowski is an example of the difficulties in the 1993 law. Its intent was to make registering to vote easier by requiring states to provide voting information along with driver's license forms.

Romanowski is one of those profiled in this book. She registered in 1996 because the registration material came by mail with her driver's license renewal form. It was easy to register, so she did. But she didn't vote.

Mobility and difficult registration procedures have been viewed by many as prime factors in suppressing voter turnout. Our study suggests that the impact on registration and voting of a recent move is minimal. And the nonvoters we interviewed more often criticized the political process than the registration process.

Among those who were not registered, 14% cited a recent move as the reason, and roughly one out of five said they didn't care much about politics.

Two thirds of nonvoters surveyed had lived at their current address for more than 2 years, yet 61% of that group had not been motivated to register.

Michael Keegan, an Irritable nonvoter, told us that politicians have to earn his vote. He registered to dangle the possibility of his vote before politicians, but he didn't find any candidate he considered worthy: "By not voting, you should be saying something." Like Keegan's 1996 decision, 45% of nonvoters said they simply *chose* not to vote in 1992.

Belying their status as nonvoters, 53% said in July 1996 that they would definitely or probably vote that year. And the reasons they gave were right out of a civics textbook: Among those who definitely intended to vote, 21% said it was because they "want a say in who's elected." Another 21% gave responses such as "It's my right," "It's my duty," or "It's the right thing to do." And 12% said, "My vote counts/makes a difference," "You can't complain if you don't vote," and "Because it is important."

However, 53% of the "definite" voters also acknowledged they were not registered, and the rest did not vote in 1992, even though they were old enough. Doers are a perfect illustration of this reality disconnect: 75% had good voting intentions, but 62% weren't registered.

Terril Printy, an Irritable and the subject of one of the Medill News Service stories, had resolved never to vote again, but our calls to her were part of the reason she returned to the election booth in 1996, when she did, in fact, vote. She's one of the minority of nonvoters who move in and out of the system, a characteristic more often associated with Doers and Irritables.

"Everybody in politics has lost the reality that the public wants to hear the truth and not the bull," says Keegan. "I want an individual in there who will take responsibility for what they do."

Dr. Robert Wolkow, one of the Doers we interviewed, also is resigned to elected officials who are unethical: "There's too much glad-handing and compromises that cause them to lose sight of the principles they may have had."

Unplugged Elizabeth Baxley told us that she avoids learning about politicians because she figures that the winning candidate is simply the best liar.

They reflect the anger, cynicism, and detachment that many nonvoters feel about much of what they see in the political arena, particularly at the national level. When asked whether they felt that "things in this country are generally going in the right direction" or had "pretty seriously gotten off on the wrong track," 58% of all likely nonvoters took the pessimistic view.

Nearly two thirds of the nonvoters agreed to some degree that elected officials generally don't care what they think. Among those we tracked for this book, Don't Know cluster member Erica Smith offers this: No one would respond to her repeated attempts to talk to campaign offices about candidates' positions on domestic violence. Claudine D'Orazio, a Doer who is also profiled later in the book, believes that "what I say doesn't really matter." Says Karen Pelling, an Unplugged nonvoter, "We don't have the money, so why should they care what we think?"

Steve Gordon, another Unplugged nonvoter who, like Pelling, appears in Chapter 4, is so convinced that the actual person elected is irrelevant that he favors having a lottery. "At least it's something different," he said during our interview. Slightly more than half of the nonvoters, 53%, agreed to some extent with the statement "It makes no real difference who is elected—things go on just as they did before." D'Orazio, like Gordon, is among them: Affirmative action has hurt hiring practices at her hotel, she told us, but it's outside the ability of politicians to change it.

However, nonvoters are not entirely disenchanted with the political process: 52% agreed to some degree with the statement "The federal government often does a better job than people give it credit for."

In fact, most nonvoters think the government should have a major policy role, at least in the realms of health care, housing, and education—83%.

But they don't want elected officials to stay in Washington indefinitely—74% supported term limits for Congress.

Anger and alienation vary significantly from cluster to cluster, with Doers showing few signs of alienation from their elected officials or governmental institutions. They are the most likely to feel that elected officials actually care what they think—53% of them agreed with that idea. And they are the most likely to believe that the country is headed in the right direction, although those with that optimistic view still only represent 39% of all Doers.

Doer Nancy Smith, profiled at length in Chapter 3, says that the right elected officials can change things. "We definitely need to vote to get people in there to represent you and who have a proven track record."

At the opposite end of political cynicism are the Alienateds. Although majorities in every nonvoter cluster said they felt the country had "pretty seriously gotten off on the wrong track," the Alienateds were the most pessimistic, with 65% stating that view.

AVOIDING POLITICAL PARTIES

One of the most significant findings in the survey is the affinity for the Independent label among nonvoters. Nearly half, 46%, called themselves Independents. Dottie Turner, a Rio Linda, California, mother of two grown children, was quoted in the Medill series as saying she hasn't voted since 1972 and considers herself an Independent. She reflects the definition of Independent for many nonvoters: independent of the political system.

Another nonvoter interviewed for the Medill series, Adrian Perry of Culbertson, Montana, sees no difference between the two parties and no connection between them and his life.

After Independent, Democrat was the next most popular political label—but only 24% identified themselves as such, and 17% called themselves Republican.

Doers were most likely to align themselves with the GOP or Democrats, Irritables least likely. Retired musician Jack Daniels, profiled in the Unplugged chapter, grew up in a household of voting Democrats whose hero was Franklin Delano Roosevelt. He voted the Democratic ticket in a local election or two because party workers provided him an incentive.

Overall, nonvoters are not a liberal group, with 39% of those we surveyed saying they were politically moderate, 30% conservative, and only 19% liberal. Doers were the most likely to label themselves liberal, at 25% of their cluster.

Although 46% of nonvoters believed in the need for a third political party, 56% said they could see at least "a fair amount of difference" between Democrats and Republicans. Among those nonvoters we tracked, Ross Perot was praised frequently for offering an alternative point of view in his bid for the presidency in 1992. Not surprisingly, self-described Independents had considerably more difficulty than Republicans and Democrats in distinguishing between the parties, with only 17% seeing a big difference. Irritable nonvoter Melody Lewis says the terms *Republican* and *Democrat*, as well as *conservative* and *liberal*, are empty labels. "I'm this, I'm that, so what? When it boils down to the candidates, they're all fighting for the same issues."

Blacks were far more likely than whites to see a clear difference between the parties: 45% compared with 19%. Early in his life, Keith Roberts, an African American nonvoter profiled at length later, was a hard-core Democrat and saw clear distinctions between the parties. Now, he's skeptical that either party cares about improving race relations.

Paul Rains, a member of the Doers cluster and another profile subject, says there are no clear distinctions between the two major parties, including the fact that neither tells the truth. "I wish that they could make a point. Don't dance around the issues."

The Don't Knows' answers to questions about political parties reflected their nearly complete lack of interest in the political process. One of the group, George Perez, cannot define the difference between liberal and conservative, nor can he name any fact about either party. Only one member of the Don't Knows had a favorable opinion of the Republicans, which was one more than had a favorable view of the Democrats. More than 90% of the Don't Knows expressed no opinion—favorable or unfavorable—of either party.

THE ISSUES: GOD, MOTHERHOOD, AND THE ECONOMY

Nonvoters have low opinions of Congress and the political parties, but there appears to be one institution they like: In the Medill survey, 77% had a favorable view of the religion or religious institution with which they were most familiar. In fact, among the 10 institutions the survey reviewed with nonvoters, it was the most trusted.

Each cluster had favorable views, from a high of 83% among Doers to a low of 66% for Don't Knows.

Charlene Beighey, a 74-year-old member of the Christ Episcopal church in Columbus, Kansas, told Medill News Service reporter Jennifer Hamilton that many of her opinions are based on what she hears in church.

And JoAnn Arrowood of Weaverville, North Carolina, was quoted in another article in the Medill series as saying "I feel like our nation is getting away from religion, morals, just what it takes to make a good person."

Serena Slaton, an Unplugged nonvoter living in Atlanta who was interviewed for this book, attends her Baptist church three times a week. "If you read the Old Testament, you'll find out that the people asked God for a king, and they were just asking him for a leader. . . . So I believe we need a leader, but we need a godly leader, and it's hard to find today."

She believes that faith, not political leaders, will shape her destiny.

Terril Printy feels guilty when she doesn't vote. "We women fought long and hard for the vote," she said in a Medill News Service story, "and I suppose it's our duty to get out there and do it."

In general, women who don't vote are less likely than male nonvoters to believe in the power of their votes or to believe that the future of the United States is bright.

"It's a waste of time," was Dottie Turner's succinct analysis of the power of her vote.

Only 28% of female nonvoters believe the country is headed in the right direction, compared with 34% of the men we surveyed.

"I feel like [the country is] going to hell in a hand basket," Elizabeth Baxley told a Medill News Service reporter. Baxley, a Don't Know cluster member from Scranton, South Carolina, also is profiled later in this book. "I think the government is more male oriented. I just don't feel like our vote has much say anyway."

Very few women in our survey completely agreed that Americans always can find a way to solve their problems: 25% of men completely agreed with the statement, compared with 16% of female nonvoters.

However, men were more negative in their views of Congress, with 41% giving it an unfavorable rating compared with 30% of the women nonvoters.

That may jibe with women's stronger belief in an active role for the federal government in improving middle-income families' health care, housing, and education—a belief held by 61% of female nonvoters and only 52% of the men. Karen Pelling calls health care costs "outrageous" and laments the diminished quality of medical care, and Nancy Smith says medical coverage problems keep her husband from switching jobs.

Pelling worries about her future because, although her Winter Park, Florida, neighborhood is safe, "10-year-olds are taking guns and knives to school."

Smith also worries about crime, saying that the problem is creeping out from Washington to her suburb in Maryland, where more and more neighbors are installing home security systems.

In polls leading up to the 1996 election, Americans cited crime as the nation's biggest problem. That was true in the Medill poll of nonvoters too. However, among nonvoters who had been to college, the economy was their biggest concern.

They reflect the theme of Clinton's 1992 campaign, when a sign in his campaign headquarters admonished workers to remember "It's the Economy, Stupid," so that all of Clinton's campaign themes revolved around the basic idea that President George Bush was responsible for the bad economy.

Among those in the Medill poll who had attended college or obtained a degree, 21% cited the economy compared with 9% of those with high school educations or less.

Irritable Caren Freigenberg told us that Reaganomics forced up apartment prices in New York, leading her to move, unhappily, to New Jersey. President Ronald Reagan "destroyed the country . . . built everything on a false economy."

Gloria Johnson, a 25-year-old single mother in Greensboro, North Carolina, who has been in and out of community college for 7 years, told the Medill News Service, "I'm looking for a job, and it's hard to get a job. I need some money."

Another nonvoter interviewed for the Medill series of stories, Dr. J. H. Sleeper, of Lincoln, Maine, cited the economy as his biggest concern because "the government is running the country into debt."

Among those nonvoters we interviewed at length for the book, welfare reform also was mentioned frequently.

Pelling, for instance, says she received public assistance for her two children after divorcing her first husband and remembers many female welfare recipients who continued to have children to get bigger payments.

Another Unplugged we will hear from at greater length later in the book, Paula Ryan, says, "I disagree with welfare . . . because it lets them be lazy. I think the welfare system should be eliminated."

Doer Jason Caldwell joined in the criticism of welfare for encouraging recipients to stay on public assistance rather than forcing them into jobs. But as we explain in detail when we profile him, Caldwell believes time limits on benefits would hurt honestly needy people. Baxley also emphasized the need for compassion along with firmness toward slackers. She remembers a time when her mother needed help and the social workers ignored her.

OFTEN INVOLVED AND INFORMED, BUT NOT NECESSARILY IN POLITICS

Avoiding the voting booth has little to do with avoiding other aspects of community involvement and quasi-political activities, according to the results of the Medill poll. Sixty percent of the likely nonvoters reported having done volunteer work for a charity or other nonprofit group at some time; 52% of those who had volunteered indicated that they had done so within the 12 months prior to the survey.

Irritable Caren Freigenberg volunteered for a political campaign and marched in a pro-choice rally.

Keegan, another Irritable, wrote to Pennsylvania officials to criticize a proposed addition to a Veterans Administration hospital near him.

Forty-one percent of the nonvoters reported participating in at least one of five quasi-political activities surveyed in the Medill poll.

Nearly one quarter of the nonvoters said they had called or sent a letter, telegram, fax, or e-mail message to their U.S. representative or senator; 16% had communicated with a state official; 14% had contacted their local school board or a member of their city government; and 13% had expressed an opinion to their local newspaper. Eleven percent of the nonvoters interviewed had attended at least one political meeting or rally during the past 3 or 4 years.

As might be expected, the Doers were the most active, with 81% reporting that they had at some point been a volunteer, contacted a politician or government official, attended a political meeting or rally, or contacted their local newspaper.

Wolkow, the New York doctor who is a member of the Doers cluster, has written to his local newspaper, the *New York Times,* on several occasions; one of his letters was published. He also wrote the mayor and has called local officials to complain about garbage pickups. Caldwell wrote his congressman to protest the Brady Law.

Again following the established pattern, the Alienateds were the least likely to have been involved in any of these civic activities. However, even among the Alienateds, 56% indicated that they had somehow found time to volunteer, write letters to their elected representatives, attend political meetings or rallies, or contact their local newspaper to express an opinion.

Nonvoters are not necessarily oblivious to current events or news. Roughly half of nonvoters said they watch a TV news broadcast 6 or 7 nights a week, and 28% said they read a newspaper as often.

However, their overall interest in political or public policy news, at 57%, was much lower than among the population as a whole, according to an October 1995 poll by the Times Mirror Center for The People, The Press and Politics (now the Pew Research Center for the People and the Press). It found that 81% of the adults surveyed followed political news at least some of the time.

In the Medill survey, the differences in information consumption were dramatic among the five types of nonvoters, with 78% of Doers saying they read a paper at least four times a week, a level of news consumption virtually matched by the Irritables at 73%. Doers Rains and Nancy Smith are daily news consumers, as are Irritables Freigenberg and Wolkow, for instance.

Although only 57% of nonvoters were tuning in to news about government and public affairs, 73% of Doers were relatively plugged into political news. Thirty-four percent said they followed government and public affairs news most of the time, and 39% did so at least some of the time. Among Irritables, 62% followed such news at least some of the time, including 29% who responded "most of the time."

Roughly half of the Alienateds and the Unpluggeds said they followed what was going on in government and public affairs only occasionally at best, a statement echoed by 60% of the Don't Knows. Perez watches TV news every night but cannot name the governor of his state. Another Don't Know, Erica Smith, only found out about First Lady Hillary Rodham Clinton's campaign stop in her town because Clinton visited her son's school.

It may be that many nonvoters who regularly watch television news and read newspapers do so for reasons other than following the public policy debate.

They also may be tuning out political news because of their negative views toward the news media: 48% said the news media get in the way of society solving its problems. Although the Irritables were most likely to criticize the media, at least 41% of every cluster believed the media were getting in the way of solutions to the country's problems.

Even Clinton has chimed in. In March 11, 1997, remarks at the National Press Club in Washington, he noted that it's unclear whether there's a direct connection between television viewership and diminished voter turnout, but he suggested that it is worth considering.

To further explore nonvoters' distrust of the media, Medill News Service reporters in the fall of 1996 surveyed 225 of the original poll respondents. The most popular criticism of the media was that they exaggerate stories, were too sensational, or were driven by ratings. Two thirds said there were too many reports about candidates' personal lives.

Other criticisms included too much emphasis on stories about who's ahead in a political race, favoritism toward Democrats, and a liberal bias among journalists.

In the July Medill survey of 1,001 likely nonvoters, respondents gave more favorable marks to their local newspaper than to TV news. And TV news viewers were more likely than newspaper readers to think that the media were a hindrance to solutions for societal problems, 43% to 28%. However, among those who believed the media could help society, 8 of 10 approved of both media.

DOERS

The largest group of likely nonvoters, representing 29% of the total, looks a lot like voters. Although disproportionately young, even for nonvoters, Doers also are more affluent, better educated, and more involved in their communities or volunteer groups. They are avid news consumers and follow political news regularly. They are more likely than other nonvoters to have contacted a politician and, as a group, think better of politicians, the parties, and political institutions than other nonvoters. They believe they control their success in life. They believe that if they voted, their vote would count.

Shawn Curtis, a 24-year-old college student from Laguna Niguel, California, is typical of Doers in saying he would "probably vote" on Election Day 1996: 75% of Doers said they would definitely or probably vote, far more than any other nonvoter cluster. In the end, however, he didn't, according to the Medill News Service series, saying Clinton's victory already was assured. That, too, is typical of many of the Doers who view their vote as a negative tool to be used

TABLE 2.3 Attitudes of Doers

Question	%
Voted in 1992	17
Moderate	44
Independent	39
Volunteered	70
Daily newspaper reader	53
Daily TV news viewer	58
Elected officials care what people like me think	53
Success in life outside our control	28
Does make a difference who is elected	66
Issues in Washington affect me personally	79
Good opinion of Republicans	63
Good opinion of Democrats	63
Contacted member of Congress	30

to fix a political problem or change a bad situation rather than as a measure of civic responsibility.

Although a solid majority of Doers had good intentions to vote, 62% were not registered when we polled them in July 1996.

Dr. Robert Wolkow, New York City physician and researcher, has voted only twice in his life—each time to oppose a candidate more than to support one: He wanted to use his vote to try to keep President Richard Nixon out of office in 1972 and to block Senator Alfonse D'Amato 20 years later. But he also fully supported each man's opponent, Senator George McGovern and New York Attorney General Robert Abrams, respectively. Like many Doers, Wolkow believes his vote would count and won't give it to a candidate he only supports as the lesser of two evils.

Jason Caldwell, a roofer who lives outside of Kansas City, voted for Clinton in 1992 but refused to vote for him in 1996 because he signed the Brady Bill into law or for Republican Bob Dole because he seemed out of touch with real Americans and more in touch with Washington insiders. Caldwell also reflects what seems clear from our interviews: Doers are more likely than other non-voters to move in and out of the electoral process, occasionally finding a reason to opt into the system.

Often, however, Doers prefer direct interaction with a politician to voting. Caldwell wrote to his congressman to urge defeat of the Brady Bill, which set a 5-day waiting period for the sale of handguns. He also put up yard signs for a school board candidate when he was a teenager, saying he liked the candidate and wanted to help him. Claudine D'Orazio was at a mayoral campaign headquarters in Savannah, Georgia, on Election Night 1995 to help with catering, but she didn't vote; her candidate was narrowly defeated.

Doers are more likely to have contacted their congressional representative, state or local official, or newspaper; 30% had written, called, or faxed their U.S. senator or representative, and 22% had contacted a state official.

They are more likely than the other nonvoter groups to have volunteered for a charity or nonprofit group. Doers represent 34% of the nonvoters who had volunteered. Among Doers, 70% had volunteered—another indication of their belief that direct action is the best use of their time. Nancy Koscher, owner of a carpeting business in Elkhart, Indiana, raises money for the local Red Cross chapter, according to one of the Medill News Service stories, and follows the local school board actions because she cares about her three grandchildren's education. Although she chooses those activities, she chooses not to vote.

Sue Jablonsky, a homemaker, also keeps up with what is going on at her local schools in New Brighton, Pennsylvania, because she wants to be sure her sons are getting a good education. Yet she also decided against voting because she can find no connection between it and her life. However, the disconnect is not the result of a lack of information.

Doers generally are information consumers: 58% said they watched TV news 6 or 7 times a week, and 53% read newspapers that frequently.

They accounted for just more than half of all nonvoters who said they read the newspaper daily. Jablonsky watches television often to learn, but the knowledge she wants is on the Discovery Channel, not the local news. Paul Rains of Cheyenne, Wyoming, is more typical of Doers; he reads the newspaper and watches TV news most days and speaks knowledgeably about local politics.

Nancy Smith, a former postal service supervisor who now cares for her children in a suburb of Washington, D.C., has little free time because caring for her younger daughter, who has cerebral palsy and is almost blind, takes most of her time. However, like Rains, she makes sure she is informed, reading the newspaper daily and newsmagazines weekly. What she reads, however, doesn't make her want to spend her precious spare time on voting.

"[Politicians] are spending too much time on what I consider petty things rather than on problems. Like [Clinton and Vice President Al Gore] can't ask for money when they're in the White House. They should know that stuff. But it is a little petty, too. How is it affecting us?" she says.

Despite the debilitating illness of her daughter, Smith believes she and her husband are former voters who one day are likely to return to the voting booth, but only because they want to, not because "someone says you should. I'll do it if I can and if I want to."

Like Smith, Jablonsky believes in doing whatever it takes to take care of her family—and she has vowed never to get to a point where she would need government help. Rains, a successful subcontractor, also is an example of the 71% of Doers who disagreed with the statement, "Success in life is pretty much determined by forces outside our control."

Rains says he doesn't vote because, like many other Americans, he is content with the way things are going in his life and his country. "As long as people have convenience-filled homes and nobody is bothering them . . . then there is nothing to complain about."

Or to vote against. "It takes something like a Vietnam to get people involved," says Rains, a striking example of how many Doers view voting as an action only undertaken to correct problems.

Gene Tencza, a farmer and worker at a machine and tool firm in Orange, Massachusetts, is another. He is content with his life and is comfortable leaving politics to others. "I'm not interested enough in politics to participate in it. . . . My way of participating is to give back some of what I've learned during my life and to be a good neighbor."

He believes his vote would count because "it's been proven in a lot of cases where one vote did make a difference." In fact, the only circumstance that could impel him to vote would be an attempt to take away his right to vote.

"Voting is not a duty," Tencza says. "It is a privilege."

UNPLUGGEDS

Only slightly smaller than Doers is the group called the Unpluggeds—27% of the total nonvoters. The group is, in many ways, a mirror image of the Doers. Although its members also are quite young generally—81% had not reached age 45, including 46% who weren't yet 30—that is one of the few characteristics they share.

Unpluggeds are much less educated than Doers and less likely to read newspapers or watch TV news or to follow politics. Barbara Beth, a bartender in Lakehead, California, dropped out of school in the seventh grade to start working. At 51, she has never voted, saying she doesn't pay much attention to national or local politics and doesn't know enough about the candidates to vote. She stopped watching TV news because she didn't like what she saw. "It's all a bunch of garbage to me, you know. All you hear is murders, rapes, car accidents."

Like Beth, a Wisconsin machinist named Steve Gordon tuned out the news because the political updates often made him angry; other Unpluggeds just never tuned in.

No Unpluggeds said they read the newspaper every day; only one third watch TV news six or seven times a week. "The only time Kelly Smith watches TV news is when it doesn't interfere with the Mets, Lakers, and 49ers games,"

TABLE 2.4 Attitudes of Unpluggeds

Question	%
Voted in 1992	13
Moderate	44
Independent	39
Volunteered	59
Daily newspaper reader	0
Daily TV news viewer	35
Elected officials care what people like me think	24
Success in life outside our control	47
Does make a difference who is elected	36
Issues in Washington affect me personally	52
Good opinion of Republicans	49
Good opinion of Democrats	60
Contacted member of Congress	19

according to the Medill News Service series. A 39-year-old construction worker in Spokane, Washington, Smith says he makes little effort to watch the news or learn about politics. Iris Llamas of Austin, Texas, stopped paying attention to the news because it never involved what she and her twenty-something friends, mostly coworkers at a computer chip manufacturer, discussed.

That belief reflects Unpluggeds' lack of interest in discussing politics with family or friends; nearly three fourths said they rarely discussed politics with either family or friends.

"If I want to talk politics, I will, but I would rather talk about sports," Smith said in the Medill story.

Members of this cluster are fairly skeptical, more so than the Doers. Kris Hoffland, a 19-year-old college student in Madison, Wisconsin, reflects the 64% of Unpluggeds who completely or mostly agreed with the survey question, "It makes no real difference who is elected; things go on just as they did before."

In the Medill series, he said, "Part of the disenchantment we feel is just seeing someone going by in the car and waving. They say this candidate was in town today, and you see him in front of city hall shaking hands. That's the only connection there is. . . . Politics has gone from people making change to people just doing their jobs. I don't see a lot of politicians [who] are voicing their own opinions. I see a lot of politicking and politicians saying what they think should be said."

Hoffland is registered but already had decided in July 1996 that he would not vote that November. Forty-seven percent of Unpluggeds also had decided they definitely or probably would not vote in the 1996 presidential election; among all nonvoters, they were the most likely to have made that decision when we surveyed them 4 months before the election. Although 32% said they were registered, only 13% voted in 1992; 45% said they chose not to vote in 1992, and 38% said something prevented them from casting a ballot.

Jack Daniels, a former jazz musician who is recovering from a stroke in Chicago, has voted in local elections in the past. In those days, his Democratic precinct captain would pay him $5 to vote a straight party ticket.

President John Kennedy would have been the first president for whom he was old enough to vote, but Kennedy was assassinated a year before that 1964 election. Daniels couldn't bring himself to vote for Lyndon Johnson and hasn't found anyone who has met Kennedy's standard since. Beth also cited Kennedy as the last president she liked, a sentiment held by a number of the 30 nonvoters profiled later in this book.

This group got its name not only because its members are disconnected from news and voting but also because among all nonvoters, they were the most likely to completely or mostly agree that "most issues in Washington don't affect me personally."

Karen Pelling, a homemaker in Winter Park, Florida, is worried about health coverage and affordable child care, but the connection between her quality of life and public policy decisions in Washington is too remote. "Everything the government is trying to do . . . the rich get richer."

For Paula Ryan, who works at a mortgage company in Phoenix, the government is a more sinister presence deliberately set up to be outside her control. She believes a popular vote for president, rather than the electoral college system of winner take all in each state, would give Americans more voice in their government. But those in power won't allow it because "they don't want control taken out of their own hands. I am so convinced in my own mind that they already know who the next president's going to be." That belief—that events and decisions in Washington are beyond her control—is reflected in other Unpluggeds.

Unpluggeds comprise 60% of the nonvoters who completely or mostly agreed that "most elected officials don't care what people like me think," making them the most likely among nonvoters to believe their opinions are ignored. Within the Unpluggeds, 75% agreed with the statement.

As Tracy Rowley, an administrative assistant at a truck dealership outside of Portland, Oregon, notes, "Every time we vote on something and it gets passed, they find something else to turn it around. Here in Oregon, we voted on the lottery and it was supposed to go to the schools, and it's not going to the schools." More evidence, she believes, that elected officials will ignore ordinary citizens, even if they vote.

TABLE 2.5 Attitudes of Irritables

Question	%
Voted in 1992	22
Moderate	44
Independent	53
Volunteered	58
Daily newspaper reader	52
Daily TV news viewer	62
Elected officials care what people like me think	25
Success in life outside our control	43
Does make a difference who is elected	39
Issues in Washington affect me personally	57
Good opinion of Republicans	37
Good opinion of Democrats	52
Contacted member of Congress	28

IRRITABLES

The third largest group of nonvoters, the Irritables, knows what's going on in politics and public affairs and doesn't like it. The group is the second oldest of the five, with 33% of Irritables at least 45 years old. Its members are more affluent than all other nonvoters except the Doers; 48% earned at least $30,000 a year. And they are educated: 25% of all Irritables had a college diploma, the highest percentage among the five clusters. Irritables represent 18% of all nonvoters.

Medill News Service reporter Kelly McEvers interviewed a member of the Irritable cluster named Terril Printy, a 49-year-old homemaker and former waitress in Montrose, Iowa, who is informed and unhappy about politics. The results of her last vote before we surveyed her, in the 1988 presidential election, convinced her to become and remain a pessimist about government.

Printy got nervous as she stood in the booth on Election Day 1988, and she pulled the wrong lever. The lifelong Republican accidentally had voted for the losing candidate, Democrat Michael Dukakis.

"Experience has taught me a lesson: Even when we vote, we have no control over what's going on in government."

Sixty-two percent of Irritables said they follow current events in government and public affairs most or some of the time, a close second to the Doers. They are a newspaper publisher's or TV station manager's dream: 52% read newspapers six or seven times a week, and 21% read them at least four times a week; 82% watch TV news at least four times weekly.

But for many, their generally negative views of institutions carry over to the news media: 54% said in the Medill survey that they believe the news media "get in the way of society solving its problems" compared with 48% of all nonvoters. Robert McInnis of rural Morrisville, Missouri, is a 33-year-old father of four who distrusts most institutions, especially the media. "I think it's important to hear all different sides. I don't trust just one source," he told a Medill News Service reporter. According to Michael Keegan, a 35-year-old stonemason who lives outside of Philadelphia, journalists too often go after the sensational, the quick sound bite, and the information citizens need gets lost in the glitz.

Congress is a particular target for their anger, with 58% recording an unfavorable opinion compared with 35% of nonvoters overall. The political parties also fared badly: The Republican Party received an unfavorable rating from 59% of the Irritables, and the Democratic Party, although apparently held in somewhat higher regard, was given an unfavorable rating by 48% of the cluster.

But their real anger is saved for the elected officials themselves. A whopping 74% believed in term limits for members of Congress, including 53% who completely agreed with the idea—the largest percentage among those in all clusters who completely agreed with term limits.

"Everybody in politics has lost the reality that the public wants to hear the truth and not the bull," Keegan says. "I want an individual in there who will take responsibility for what they do."

Henry Montoya, mentioned earlier for his unique way of registering his dislike of politicians—voting for an empty ballot—says there's no one worth voting for on the ballots that he sees each Election Day.

Keegan registered to vote as a way of showing that his vote is available to be had, but politicians haven't earned it yet.

"Politicians say they make an effort, but they don't really listen. They say it's not their problem. 'Not my problem' is the problem," he says.

Melody Lewis, who recently moved to West Plains, Missouri, agrees. "You hear all these things they're gonna do, they're gonna promise. In the end, usually, it seems like all the things they promise don't get followed through on."

Printy says politicians don't talk directly with citizens, preferring polls to face time with constituents. "If these guys want to get to know people, they should go to the mall, go to the grocery store, go to Wal-Mart, go to Jack's and see that nobody smiles anymore, nobody talks to anybody anymore. They all look like they could eat nails. These politicians need to go to these places, look people in the eye, and ask, 'Why is that?' " Printy told the Medill News Service.

Caren Freigenberg, a fabric sales entrepreneur from northern New Jersey, says today's politicians "have a hidden agenda. And I don't trust them. I don't believe in them."

The Irritables don't see much difference between the two political parties, with 36% saying there's hardly any difference. Only the Unpluggeds believed that more strongly, but only by 1 percentage point. Lewis says the differences between the parties are minor and partisan battles are merely "nit-picking" that allows politicians to avoid real issues.

Almost half—47%—supported the idea of a third party, which is just about the same percentage as for nonvoters overall. Many appreciated Ross Perot's 1996 campaign as an effort to shake up the political system. Montoya says he would vote again if political maverick Lyndon LaRouche were on the ballot.

Irritables aren't shy about letting members of Congress know their views: 28% had contacted their representative or senator. Twenty-three percent had contacted a state official. Freigenberg has worked on the campaigns of two Democrats in New York City, and she has given money to and volunteered for Planned Parenthood and abortion rights groups.

Sixty-five percent of Irritables, the same percentage as among Alienateds, believed the country is headed in the wrong direction. That percentage is the highest among all five groups.

But although they dislike politicians and political parties in general and are pessimistic about the direction of government and the country, they have less trouble with some actual government programs. For instance, 82% supported an active role for the government in health care, housing, and education improvements for the middle class.

Their nonvoting status doesn't have to do with mobility, often cited as a major reason that Americans don't vote. Eighty-three percent had lived at their current residences for more than 1 year, and 72% had been in the same home for more than 2 years.

Of the four Irritable nonvoters we followed for the book, three are past voters. "It was just feeling like that was your obligation to vote and maybe that's part of the reason why I don't [vote] since I'm not that involved in it politically," says Lewis.

Freigenberg voted when she lived in New York City. Since moving to a New Jersey suburb from which she can see the City across the Hudson River, she hasn't registered because she feels no connection to her community.

Like Keegan and Montoya, 41% of Irritables were registered to vote, the highest percentage among the clusters. But when we surveyed nonvoters in July 1996, 5 months before the election, nearly half already had decided they probably or definitely would not vote.

DON'T KNOWS

The Medill students chose the name Don't Knows for this cluster because its members are more likely than members of any of the other four groups to

TABLE 2.6 Attitudes of Don't Knows

Question	%
Voted in 1992	13
Political philosophy—don't know	36
Independent	49
Volunteered	54
Daily newspaper reader	19
Daily TV news viewer	39
Elected officials care what people like me think	27
Success in life outside our control	41
Does make a difference who is elected	30
Issues in Washington affect me personally	48
Good opinion of Republicans	1
Good opinion of Democrats	0
Contacted member of Congress	15

respond "I don't know" when asked questions concerning politics, government, and public policy. Fourteen percent of likely nonvoters are Don't Knows.

Indifference to civic life and a preoccupation with family and work characterized Susan Godoy's reasons for not voting in the past. Then her son got into serious trouble, including being charged with attempted murder, and she no longer could remain uninvolved with government and public officials.

The Southern California mother and sales engineer started paying attention to the news but now realizes that she doesn't know enough to make an informed voting decision. "Voting is a very responsible thing to do," she says, and she's not prepared yet to cast a ballot.

Other Don't Knows also cite their lack of political knowledge as a reasonable impediment to voting. And they generally have no intention of remedying the situation.

Dottie Turner, a 50-year-old mother of two from Rio Linda, California, said she's not voting in 1996 because she doesn't have a grasp of the issues or politicians. "It's so confusing," she said. "They say one thing and do another," according to a Medill News Service profile.

She said voting is a "waste of time" because she cares nothing about politics.

George Perez, a 36-year-old resident of El Paso, says he doesn't know the duties of a senator or U.S. representative, although he can name one or two of his state's congressional delegation. He cannot distinguish between political parties. Among Don't Knows, 73% had no opinion on Congress, 43% could not make a definitive statement on the Supreme Court, and more than 90% didn't express any opinion on either the Republican or Democratic parties.

Perez never has voted, a common trait of the Don't Knows we interviewed and those interviewed by the Medill reporters. "I don't see how one vote's gonna make any difference."

Among nonvoters who said they had voted in 1992, the Don't Knows were the second least likely to have voted, at 12% of the total nonvoters who said they had voted. Only Alienateds were less likely to have voted in 1992, at 10% of all nonvoters who cast ballots that year. Among members of the Don't Know cluster, 83% said either they chose not to vote in 1992 or something prevented them from voting.

They also were the least likely to be registered to vote, with 72% saying they were not registered in July 1996. Admits Perez, "I don't know how the process works."

Sixty-three percent of Don't Knows have never gone to college; many didn't have high school diplomas. Fifty-two percent earned less than $30,000 a year. Only the Alienateds and Irritables were older: Among Don't Knows, 27% were at least 45 years old, including 12% who were older than age 65. The Don't Knows also were the most female dominated of the clusters.

Don't Knows do not have information on politics and government, either because they consciously avoid it or because they are oblivious to it.

Elizabeth Baxley is an extreme example. She deliberately leaves the television off on Inauguration Day because it falls on her birthday every 4 years, and she doesn't want politics poisoning her celebration. She assumes whichever candidate lied most effectively is the one who's taking the oath of office that day.

Sixty percent reported they followed what was happening in government and public affairs infrequently or rarely. About 44% read newspapers once a week or less, and 23% watched TV news programs no more than once a week.

Active participation in politics is rare among Don't Knows. Eighty-four percent never had corresponded with their congressmen, 91% had not contacted a state official, and 97% had never written or called their local school boards.

Baxley did sign a petition once to block a company near her home in Scranton, South Carolina, from dumping waste into Lynch's River, where she likes to fish. She'd go that far—signing a petition again—but only for a worthwhile issue and, with her skepticism toward anything political, only after reading the fine print.

Perez is much the same. He says he would vote if the benefit to him was obvious and direct. "I get Social Security and if [a candidate] said, 'We'd give these people a significant increase,' I'd probably be the first one" to vote. He has never voted.

Erica Smith isn't embarrassed to identify herself as a nonvoter. She thinks politicians should stop ignoring nonvoters. "If they're only going to cater to

TABLE 2.7 Attitudes of Alienateds

Question	%
Voted in 1992	14
Conservative	42
Independent	45
Volunteered	49
Daily newspaper reader	2
Daily TV news viewer	49
Elected officials care what people like me think	22
Success in life outside our control	51
Does make a difference who is elected	34
Issues in Washington affect me personally	51
Good opinion of Republicans	32
Good opinion of Democrats	34
Contacted member of Congress	16

those who vote, then they're going to cater only to those who give money," the Lynn, Massachusetts, resident says. "Maybe you didn't vote because you were misled because of all the lies that are being told on TV."

A 29-year-old mother who has been battered by her son's father, she is a single-issue nonvoter. Smith says she would vote if politicians cared about her issue—domestic violence. She remembers calling a few campaign offices several years ago to determine the candidates' positions on custody and visitation rights for men who abuse their mates. She left messages, but no one called back. She got the message: Her opinion doesn't matter.

ALIENATEDS

Only 12% of nonvoters fall under the description of Alienateds. They are the hardest core of nonvoters. In July 1996, nearly one third already had decided they would not be voting in November. Politically, they're the most pessimistic.

With 38% age 45 or older, the Alienateds were the oldest of our nonvoting clusters and the poorest, with less than 30% earning more than $30,000 per year. Only 11% were college graduates, the lowest of the five clusters again.

Among nonvoters who were registered, the Alienateds represented the second smallest cluster, beating out the Don't Knows' 11% of total nonvoters who were registered with their 13%. Within the Alienateds, however, 40% said they were registered.

Alma Romanowski is among the registered Alienateds; in fact, she has registered three times in her life. The Flint, Michigan, mother and volunteer says she intends to vote, but her list of reasons for not voting gets longer with each passing election.

"Maybe it's just the fear of going in that little booth and not knowing how [to vote]." Or maybe it's lack of knowledge: "I wouldn't feel comfortable voting for someone I don't know much about." Maybe it is the politicking that keeps her away: "You hear the person talk and they sound really good and then you hear their opponent talk and they put them down, twist things around, and you don't know what's true and what's not."

They may be registered, but only 14% of Alienateds voted in 1992; 52% said they chose not to vote that year, and another 29% said something prevented them from casting a ballot.

Thirty-one percent already had definitely decided in July 1996 against casting a ballot in that year's presidential election, and another 22% said they probably would not vote.

"I don't like anyone they've got up for it," says Maralynn McDonald, a retired craft-business owner in Oceanside, California. "I don't like anyone who fools around in their marriage. It seems like they're all doing that. It seems like a common thing today, and I think that's just disgusting. It's discouraging when you find out about how they actually live."

McDonald's opinion of politicians couldn't be lower, and it is typical of Alienateds' attitudes. In fact, their alienation shows itself most in their views concerning politicians, political institutions, and the impact of elections; they had the most negative views among all five clusters.

Sixty-three percent believed it makes no difference who is elected, and 65% were convinced the country has gotten "pretty seriously off-track."

Kathy Smith remembers watching election returns on television when she was a kid. The network anchor announced the winner of that year's presidential contest before the polls in her hometown of Tacoma, Washington, had closed. Her father, a lifelong Democrat, had voted, but his vote didn't really count, she decided.

Smith has saved up examples of how the system works for the privileged, how individual rights are giving way to the interests of the rich, and how money, not citizens, is the prime focus of politicians.

Her father had to hire a lawyer to get Social Security benefits after he became disabled. She and her husband tried to get welfare and food stamps, but "they denied us because we had no children." Politicians aren't trying to help struggling families, she says. "They care about their money and how they can make more. Little people don't count."

Romanowski says, "I just don't trust them, I don't trust what they're saying."

Forty-five percent of Alienateds believed elected officials don't care what they think, twice as large a percentage as the next closest group.

Says Smith, "Voting won't help."

Romanowski recalls a school board meeting at which the principal's decision to discontinue potato sack races was brought up. "The head honchos blew off the ideas people had. Their minds were already made up."

WORDS VERSUS DEEDS

Who nonvoters really are is more complicated than conventional wisdom would lead us to believe. Why they don't vote is even more complicated. But it is clear that who they are and why they don't vote are inextricably linked.

Our research shows that although some nonvoters have a clear idea of why they don't vote, many more cannot completely explain why they stay away from the polls. Their answers sometimes are contradictory, at other times so plentiful that they create confusion.

Doer Claudine D'Orazio said in the Medill survey that she was registered to vote and definitely would vote in 1996. In 1992, she responded in the survey that she was prevented from voting because she was working; it was the first presidential election in which she was eligible to vote. But when we talked to her, her reasons were more complicated.

She's embarrassed at her nonvoting status, believing educated people ought to vote. She says public policy doesn't affect her but then can cite examples of federal laws that have had an impact on her work. She says she would vote if she could do so by mail to make the process easier but then admits no one would mind if she took time off to cast a ballot on Election Day. She feels she doesn't know enough to cast a meaningful ballot, yet believes voting is an important duty that all Americans should perform.

Unplugged Barbara Beth is 51 years old and never has voted. She says she doesn't know enough about the candidates, a lack of knowledge she has no intention of remedying. She can't think of an issue being debated in Washington that would affect her and doesn't care much for politicians. But in the survey she said she definitely intended to vote in the 1996 presidential election. She chose not to vote in 1992, she told the Medill questioner. In reality, she says making ends meet is her top priority, and voting isn't something that makes it anywhere on her priority list.

Irritable Caren Freigenberg sounds like she knows exactly why she's not voting. Her survey responses said she was not registered because she had moved recently, but she had voted in 1992 and definitely would do so again in 1996. In fact, she didn't vote that year.

And although it is true that she had moved from New York City to the suburbs of New Jersey, it wasn't the move itself that turned her into a nonvoter. She admitted it would have been easy to register, but she feels no connection to her new community, remaining a Manhattanite at heart. Her complaint is not the difficulty of registering after a move but the difficulty of voting in a place whose issues mean nothing to her.

George Perez, one of the Don't Knows, responded in the Medill poll that he chose not to vote in 1992 and was not registered in 1996. But his voting choice really is more basic. He has chosen to keep himself unaware of what's going on in politics and government. He doesn't know what members of Congress do, nor does he have more than a vague idea of what the parties stand for. His political choice is to opt out.

Although Alma Romanowski, an Alienated nonvoter, responded in the Medill survey that she also chose not to vote in 1992 and that she probably wouldn't vote in 1996, her failure to vote appears to be more indecision than conviction.

She has been registered to vote three times in her life. Each time, she says, she came close to going into the voting booth, but her good intentions never crystallized into action.

In trying to figure out for herself why she never takes the final step, Romanowski makes a long list of reasons: lack of information about the candidates, no connection to public affairs, and distrust of elected officials.

Yet more fundamentally, something that was ingrained in her parents, political involvement, failed to take root in her.

3

Doers

Nancy Smith used to vote. So did Robert Wolkow and Jason Caldwell. It's possible they will again—for Smith, when her family circumstances become less time-consuming; for Caldwell, when a candidate or issue excites him enough; and for Wolkow, when a candidate so offends him that he has to take action. They believe their votes have value.

They are members of the Doers cluster and are among the eight Doers profiled in this chapter. We chose the number of profiles in this and other chapters to roughly match the percentages each cluster represents of all nonvoters.

It offends Wolkow, a 46-year-old pharmaceutical research physician from New York City, that people blithely vote for the lesser of two evils. When you deal with life-and-death issues, as he has in his family practice, the idea of endorsing unimpressive candidates election after election seems demeaning.

Smith left a career as a post office supervisor after her second child contracted cerebral palsy. The 38-year-old resident of Silver Spring, Maryland, used to vote but now thinks her free time is too fleeting to give it over to voting because elected officials are more interested in creating controversy than solving problems.

Caldwell, of the Kansas City suburb of Belton, Missouri, has handed out bumper stickers for school board candidates and written his congressman to oppose the Brady Bill. He voted in 1992 but didn't like the candidates in 1996. Only 24 years old, Caldwell thinks he might vote again one day but can't name an issue that would draw him to the polls, not even gun control.

The cluster of nonvoters we dubbed Doers is one of the most intriguing because many of its members either have voted in the past and say they intend to do so again or feel strongly that although they haven't voted yet, they will be counted among the electorate one day. Savannah, Georgia, resident Claudine

D'Orazio, for instance, is embarrassed that she doesn't vote but believes she needs to learn more about politics so she can be an informed voter one day. Ironically, the 27-year-old was helping the caterers at a mayoral campaign headquarters on Election Night 1996.

Ryan Gerali, a college student in Itasca, Illinois, turned 20 the week before the November 1996 election. He was well aware of the campaign to rock him to vote; he was seeing campaign ads on TV "every 5 minutes," but he put off registering until he had missed the deadline. "I'm not as interested as I should be," he regrets, but figures he will be more involved when he's older and paying taxes.

Paul Rains and Gene Tencza are baby boomers of about the same age and, in some ways, share the same political philosophy: Let others make decisions because things are going fine as they are. Like Smith, Wolkow, and Caldwell, they believe their votes have worth. Rains, who lives in Cheyenne, Wyoming, will take on his voting responsibility if things start going wrong, and Tencza says voting is a privilege, not a duty. The Orange, Massachusetts, resident likes to show off his farm and relishes his hobbies—music, photography, and collecting antique tractors. He's content to let those interested in politics carry the load.

Our last Doer, Sue Jablonsky, believes in taking care of herself and her family and keeping the government out of her life. The 35-year-old mother and outdoorswoman who lives in New Brighton, Pennsylvania, seldom listens to the politicians she sees on television because they can't improve her life. She would rather cast her fishing line than cast a ballot.

As we introduce you to Jablonsky and the other Doers we interviewed after the 1996 presidential election, it's important to understand that no one of them will match all the attributes of the Doer group, which will be true of those we interviewed in each cluster. The clusters were created using survey questions in four basic subject areas: demographics, news and information consumption, past voting behavior, and political-social alienation or engagement. No single answer or set of answers caused a nonvoter to be assigned to a particular group. Rather, the cluster process looks at the range of answers to decide which cluster is the best fit for the person. Therefore, among each cluster's members, there will be at least some young people and some older people, even if the cluster's age characteristic is generally 18 to 29 years old. Jablonsky is a good example of a cluster member with some characteristics that don't follow the general Doer profile; for instance, she is poorer and angrier at political institutions than the Doer profile.

Gerali, with his youth, civic awareness, and family history of voting, fits the profile better, as does Smith, who's informed, believes her vote counts, and is involved in her community.

Dr. Robert Wolkow

Advocate Against Lazy Voting

Dr. Robert Wolkow will know one when he sees one. He can't recall the last time he has seen one, so he cannot describe to his own satisfaction what a political candidate worth voting for will look like. The candidate's position on issues will be vital. So will his or her character. The person will have to be honest and have the best interests of the public at heart. And if the person comes off phony, Wolkow feels he will see right through it.

A native New Yorker, Wolkow is fiercely discriminating. He reads *The New York Times* every day when he gets home from work. He engages with family and friends about their political choices. He has taken on an advocacy role against lazy voting. "When you deal with life-and-death decisions," as he has in his family practice, Wolkow explains, the idea of endorsing unimpressive candidates election after election seems demeaning.

At 46, Wolkow has voted only twice in his life. In 1972, he voted for George McGovern for president over Richard Nixon. It was a "no-brainer," he says. He identified with what McGovern had to say, but he voted with purpose because he considered Nixon dishonest, vicious, a crook, and a disgrace. He voted again in 1992 in the election for the U.S. Senate in New York. He voted for Robert Abrams, the Democrat, in his unsuccessful bid to defeat Republican incumbent Alfonse D'Amato, again because one candidate offended him so viscerally he felt compelled to cast a ballot. He regarded D'Amato as dishonest and of "questionable ethics regarding patronage," putting people in jobs regardless of their qualifications. "Just listening to him," Wolkow says, "he's obnoxious, has no class, and on every level he's a turnoff." If Wolkow had felt less passionate, he would not have voted. That's why he didn't vote for George Bush, Bill Clinton, or Ross Perot for president in that 1992 election. He skipped the line for president, voted for the U.S. Senate, skipped all the other races, and left the polling place. He does not believe in voting for the lesser of two evils.

"When you're born and grow up in New York," Wolkow says, as if he's establishing pedigree, "you're different. It shapes people's attitudes." Wolkow attended public grade and high school in the west Bronx. He skipped two grades and went to college at age 16, yet maintained "an irresponsible attitude toward school." If he wasn't interested in something being taught, he says, he wouldn't pay attention.

He approaches his role as citizen in much the same way. Wolkow's varied life experiences have exposed him to an expansive array of subjects to which he pays attention. But his patience is short with people he feels exploit opportunities for their own political or commercial ends.

Wolkow has worked as a private school teacher and as a physician in a rich tableau of settings. He's been a doctor in family practice and at a community health center and a doctor to college students, union laborers, and cruise ship passengers. "The traditional role of seeing patients all day every day didn't have the kind of challenge I was looking for," he says.

For almost a decade, he's been in the research division of Pfizer, Inc., one of the nation's largest pharmaceutical companies. As senior associate medical director, he designs research protocols and works with, among others, an elite corps of psychiatrists to study Zoloft, a drug used to treat depression and panic disorder. He still sees patients a half day a week at the college health service at Barnard College. As a student, he studied geography, environmental science, and journalism, in addition to medicine. Every other week, he volunteers as a tour guide at the Museum of Natural History, about a mile from where he lives on New York City's Upper West Side, two blocks west of Central Park.

Wolkow lives with his parents on the 14th floor of a 27-story building, in the same room where he lived when he was a teenager. He moved back in with them after he broke up with his girlfriend in 1995. He maintains collections of minerals, dinosaur models, and antique marbles that he has built up over 30 years. Neither he nor his parents cook much. He eats takeout or goes out to eat with friends or his parents in the restaurants near the apartment.

"The most important issues facing the country are local, not national," Wolkow says. "Not foreign policy, but poverty, crime, and the environment." Even though poverty, crime, and the environment may have obvious national implications, he says, the problems manifest themselves differently in different places. He has never voted in a local election, even when he has felt okay about a candidate. "It has never meant enough to me to cause me to vote for them," he says. He follows public affairs most of the time, he says, but readily admits that he's not interested in them.

He is neither angry at government nor invested in it. He sees government as having the natural waste that all large organizations have. More important to Wolkow, "Success in life is outside the control of government. People have choices and free will and there's some serendipity."

He recounts an incident from 1970, the first year of the selective service lottery. The draft had ended but the Vietnam War had not. He had a low lottery number, but when he went for a physical, he was given a temporary 1Y exemption because he had high blood pressure. He was to return in 3 months. At the time, he knew nothing about blood pressure numbers. He learned. On the day he returned for a physical, he drank five cups of coffee spiked with salt. He took the subway into Manhattan, got off at the stop before Whitehall Street (where the selective service office was located), ran the rest of the way, and took the stairs up. His blood pressure read 160/120. He had beaten the system. The cause for him was just, the peril real.

He regards the Vietnam War as the essence of politics gone wrong. He thought then and he believes even more firmly now that the United States got involved to prop up a government and to stop a perceived Communist expansion, neither of which was in America's best interest. "There's nothing special about Americans that gives us a unique perspective." Politicians of all stripes tend to oversimplify and pander, he says, by making it "always us against them."

He might vote, Wolkow says, if he thought that a candidate or a political party would make a difference. "To get ahead in politics," Wolkow believes, "the types of people [who get involved] are not great thinkers or the most ethical people. There's too much glad-handing and compromises that cause them to lose sight of the principles they may have had."

He has seen it with his own eyes. "I've actually gone to Washington and watched [Congress in action]," Wolkow says. He took a break from a conference he was attending in the early 1990s to visit the Senate chambers. "It was like a production, watching a show. They were like actors more than politicians, everyone trying to be in the limelight." He's inclined, instead, to put more faith in a body such as the U.S. Supreme Court. "It is part of the system that works," he says. Because the justices are appointed for life and they don't campaign, he says, "they don't have to pander."

Wolkow is less trusting than he once was of the news media. He tends not to watch television news and never watches CNN or the TV newsmagazines. He doesn't read the national news magazines or listen to news much on the radio. When he's working on his computer, he says, he pulls news from the Internet "as a distraction." He catches headlines off the Yahoo ticker. But mostly his information comes from *The New York Times,* delivered to his apartment, and scientific journals.

He reads the *Times'* financial pages first, then reads the rest of the paper. But, he says, he skips past many stories. "What doesn't interest me, I don't read," he says. He doesn't read the political stories, or stories on the Whitewater probe, or on First Lady Hillary Rodham Clinton, or about state government unless there's legislation that interests him.

He's interested in features, in science, in other countries, and in conflicts and environmental matters. He doesn't read the crime stories or the sensational stories, but he checks out "About New York," a column in the paper's Metro section about the city's issues and people.

Wolkow no longer believes everything he reads, even in *The New York Times.* "Recently, I went to a 2-day symposium on extinction at the museum," he recounts. The headline in the *Times* about the event read, "Disease Is New Suspect in Ancient Extinctions." "Even the one scientist who advocated that position said it was 'out there,' " Wolkow says. "The story was unfounded and the public was misled." He recalls another incident a few years back in which a strike by interns and residents at a New York hospital ultimately broke the union. He says he was shocked that the newspaper editorials were so "uninformed and biased against the union." He assumes other newspapers are much worse.

Wolkow has tried to set the record straight a few times by writing letters to the editor. One was published in 1990. It was in response to travel section stories about the safety of cruise ships. He wrote, "As a former ship's physician with years of experience on several noteworthy vessels, it became apparent to me that a ship's safety is not only related to the knowledge and experience of the crew in handling the physical hazards that may occur but also to the size and competence of the ship's medical staff." He advocated a greater investment by the cruise lines in medical personnel. The *Times* ran a reply to the letter from a spokeswoman for one of the cruise lines. It noted that doctors are aboard but conceded that nurses do not assist them.

Wolkow also has gone out of his way to do something about the early morning noise in New York City. He wrote Mayor Rudolph Guiliani to complain about the garbage trucks. He says he chose the mayor because he had built a reputation as a "quality of life" official. Wolkow wrote that "quality of life begins with a good night's sleep." He didn't get an answer so he wrote again. He received a reply from the commissioner of sanitation, who referred him to the area superintendent. He called and was told that the superintendent's staff would see what they could do to have the trucks come later than 6:30 a.m. Nothing happened. "I called several times, maybe 4 or 5 times, until they didn't want to hear from me any more, then the trucks began coming later," Wolkow recalls. He says all it took was for the city to make the effort to change the truck schedules. "I guess because I bugged them, they chose to expend that effort."

Wolkow is passionate about his interests and views, including his decision election-by-election to not vote. "I have very strong ideas about when people should vote and when people shouldn't vote," Wolkow says. His beliefs predate when he became a physician but have been reinforced by a life of intense dedication and exposure to the pain and suffering of others. "To some people, maybe politics and voting seems like a very important thing; to other people . . . maybe it's not a very important aspect of living," he says. He has learned to respect an individual's priorities, he says, and finds ludicrous the act of voting just to vote.

He breaks down his views into two parallel philosophies. The first he uses when he talks to people "whose standard mantra is 'If you don't vote, you have no right to complain.' I say that if you're going to vote for somebody simply because they're running and you don't really like them, but you like the other guy less, to me, you're contributing to perpetuating the system where you're not given a good choice. As long as people will vote for people they don't really want, they can't complain about the choice."

He would vote, he maintains, if the ballot had a place where he could vote for none of the above. "If on the ballot, you could say, 'I don't want any of these candidates,' " he explains, "and 'no' could win, that would mitigate a serious weakness in the system. Then it would force candidates to be truly a choice that people would want." He says he has believed this for a long time and cannot quite understand why the idea hasn't gotten greater acceptance.

Until such an option exists, Wolkow expects he will continue to choose not to vote and to argue his position to family and friends. His sister is apolitical and doesn't vote. He says he may have convinced his former girlfriend, who is an environmental activist, "to back away from voting if she doesn't like who's running." His parents are converts. They were once regular, enthusiastic voters and registered Democrats. His father is middle-of-the-road, his mother more liberal. In 1992, they voted for Bill Clinton over George Bush and Ross Perot. "Through the years," Wolkow says with pride, "I've discouraged them and they're following my example." " 'Maybe he's right, the hell with them [politicians],' " Wolkow reports of his parents' evolution. In 1996, they also didn't vote.

——— ◄o► ———

Nancy Smith

No Time Left for Voting

Nancy Smith used to vote. So did her husband, Chet. Then life became a series of ambulance rides to the hospital with their daughter, and her days became consumed with changing feeding tubes, hooking up oxygen, and helping her young daughter communicate. Voting was relegated to the list of nonessential duties, to the "not part of my reality" pile.

She still reads the newspaper and watches TV news every day and finds time for *Newsweek* magazine most weeks. She has strong opinions about what is important in public policy—education and crime—and what's not—politicians' private lives and "petty" issues such as whether President Bill Clinton and Vice President Al Gore made campaign solicitation calls from the White House.

But her life now centers on the care of 3-year-old Lyndsey, who has been severely brain damaged and has had cerebral palsy since she was 6 months old. Smith's other daughter, 4-year-old Sarah, also has had numerous medical problems, including a hernia and a condition that required the removal of part of her intestine. Sarah's hands and parts of her body are needle-scarred from all the injections she's been given.

Smith, a petite 38-year-old with shoulder-length blonde hair, matter-of-factly recounts the horrors of ambulance rides and priests meeting her at the emergency room prepared to administer the last rites, sometimes injecting a joke about how experienced she has become in dealing with the unexpected. And how the unthinkable has become her daily life.

Nancy and Chet Smith's life together started as a typical suburban tale.

They met in grade school in their native Albany, New York, and started dating in seventh grade. They drifted apart in high school and went off to different colleges—she to study sociology at the State University of New York–Cortland near Ithaca, New York, and he to Siena College outside Albany. They rekindled their relationship when they returned home after college and married on June 1, 1985.

Chet started working for a wine company in sales, and she began a career in the U.S. postal service after working briefly in the carpet business.

In New York, she was a registered voter. The last presidential election in which she cast a ballot was in 1984; she remembers it was Ronald Reagan's bid for a second term, but the name of his Democratic opponent, Walter Mondale, escapes her. In 1988, she missed Election Day because she and her husband were vacationing in Mexico with friends.

In 1990, when they moved to the comfortable Washington, D.C., suburb of Silver Spring, Maryland, it was for Chet's promotion to a sales management position with an international liquor distributor and a pay increase to about

$100,000 a year. She had moved into a supervisory position at the Albany post office and found a similar job, supervisor of delivery and mails, at the main post office in Silver Spring, about 7 miles from their colonial-style split-level home on a quiet, well-maintained cul-de-sac in an area where subdivisions and shopping plazas are sprinkled among farms.

Her first child died at birth due to a kidney disease that runs in her family. The second pregnancy was a miscarriage. Then came Sarah in September 1992, about 13 weeks early. The infant was in the hospital through December, and Smith visited her every day. The November 1992 presidential election was not as important to her as being with her daughter throughout the day. After Sarah came home, Smith took another 3 months off work to care for her before placing her with a friend who provided day care and returning to the post office.

A year later, Lyndsey was born while Smith and Sarah were visiting her parents in Albany. Also premature by about 15 weeks and weighing less than 2 pounds, Lyndsey had to stay in the hospital there for 13 weeks. While she was in the hospital, Smith noticed that Lyndsey was vomiting a lot, but the staff assured her that the baby was keeping enough nourishment down.

"In the hospital, she was ventilated at birth and was on it for 2½ months. They thought that her stomach just wasn't primed and she was getting sick from that. I said, 'No she's got reflux,' " a condition that causes continued severe, projectile vomiting.

Smith needed to remain with Lyndsey but had used up her leave time so she quit her job. "The doctor wrote that Lyndsey needed me in the hospital with her. And they [her employer, the U.S. postal service] wrote back that it was my daughter in the hospital, not me. 'You're expected back at work.'

"President Clinton had just signed the Family and Medical Leave Act into law, but I didn't qualify," she says, noting she had taken the law's allotted time off after Sarah's birth.

When they returned home to Silver Spring, Lyndsey was on apnea monitors to make sure her breathing or heartbeat did not drop or stop, but the vomiting continued, and often the vomit would get into her lungs so that she had trouble breathing. Smith administered cardiopulmonary resuscitation twice.

Three times Lyndsey went to the hospital with asphyxiated pneumonia, a result of the vomit in her lungs.

Then came the day Smith will never forget.

"Lyndsey and I had just woken up. We had been up during the night a lot. Sarah kissed her. Lyndsey's eyes rolled back. Her alarms [on her monitors] went off. And we checked her pulse, managed to roll her on her side. It was cardiac arrest. We called 911 and they got here quickly.

"The guy just came in and saw what was going on and he grabbed her and ran."

The ambulance raced Lyndsey to Holy Cross Hospital in Silver Spring; the Smiths followed in their car.

"They met me with a priest. They still didn't have her [revived] by the time we got to the hospital. She was still out, and they didn't know if they were going to revive her. I started talking to her pediatrician and said, 'I don't know if she's coming back,' and he said, 'No, they got her.' "

Lyndsey had stopped breathing for nearly 45 minutes, causing severe brain damage. The cause was diagnosed as severe reflux. Once she was stabilized, she was moved to the intensive care unit at Children's Hospital in Washington. The doctors said the lack of oxygen had caused blindness and cerebral palsy.

Five weeks later, she came home, and Smith became her constant companion and caregiver.

"She couldn't walk, she couldn't talk, she couldn't sit up, she couldn't roll over. She was basically a vegetable."

Then, a little more than a year later, on April 13, 1995, she got so sick that Smith took her back to Children's Hospital, where she was given high concentrations of oxygen continuously for several days.

When they brought her home, they put her in bed, and "she just looked up at me and smiled. She just smiled. She had smiled once before—in October.

"The only thing we could think of is that all the oxygen getting pumped into her woke her brain up a bit. And now she's a smiling fool."

Smith talks proudly of the progress Lyndsey is making in learning to eat, although most of her food must be ground up, and learning to communicate by looking at objects and by using an augmentative communication device that involves pressing on keys to make decisions.

She has some limited sight. "The doctors know she can see but don't know what her brain is processing. And she can't tell us. But she's the happiest little thing in the world."

There continue to be regular trips to the hospital for pneumonia and other ailments.

"She coughed this morning so she'll be back on the oxygen tonight because something is starting. I keep tanks of oxygen and a steroid to open her lungs up. I can get unlimited refills of amoxycillin. We have a few backup systems. We keep a stethoscope handy."

Sarah is in preschool, and Lyndsey recently started going to a special education nursery school three mornings a week, which allows Smith time to do grocery shopping and household chores.

There had been discussions by the school board about closing the school. She was upset that the news media never wrote about the issue. "I don't know what I would have done. I would have gone crazy."

Her role as nurse to Lyndsey was a blow to the family income because they had counted on her $45,000 annual salary from the post office when they bought their home.

"That makes it tough. It's also hard that sometimes I'm stuck in here for days. Especially before they went to school. Lyndsey's mine, attached to me the entire time she's around because she can't walk, she can't sit up."

Although her husband sells liquor, she had never enjoyed alcohol much. Now, she says with a laugh, she's learned to like having an occasional drink.

But Smith, her blue eyes brightening as she smiles, also talks about the joy she's found in her changed path.

"The good part is I'm home with them. And I can do things with Lyndsey and keep on top of her so I know that things are okay. I can do things that I've learned from the therapists. . . . I can make different toys and adapt them for her to help her.

"I'm here for Sarah to help her not get bored. I can take the time to help her write."

Their home is filled with the hallmarks of small children: Large stuffed animals sit in the living room, a puzzle covers the dining room table, and the kitchen appliances have labels with their names to help Sarah learn to read.

But Smith always keeps the house tidy and has chosen colonial-style furniture and coordinated curtains and wallpaper to give a warm, elegant appearance.

The family spends a lot of time on the grassy circle in the center of the cul-de-sac with the neighbors and their kids. On the Fourth of July, the kids decorate their bikes and parade around the neighborhood.

The neighbors watch out for each other. A lot of them have installed alarm systems in their homes. The Smiths haven't, although someone tried to break in one night while Smith's husband was out of town. A house down the street was burglarized recently. And an armed robbery at the nearby shopping plaza really worried her.

"In Albany, we had the drive-by shootings and all that. I thought this place was safe from that. I don't know where to go, probably the moon. It's everywhere."

She is angry that crime is moving into the suburbs from Washington.

"You go out to the suburbs and they just come out farther and farther, whoever is robbing and stealing."

Distressed as she is about crime, she's even more vocal in her criticism of the health care industry—and with all the medical care Lyndsey has needed, she's become quite an expert on the subject.

She has spent days on the phone trying to get the drugs, therapists, and other help that Lyndsey needs.

Managed care has made it much more difficult for complicated cases, she believes. She also says health care legislation should be passed to allow people to switch into new plans without limits on coverage for preexisting conditions. Because most plans have such clauses, she says, Chet cannot switch jobs if he gets a better offer.

In 1996, Clinton signed into law a bill authored by Senators Edward Kennedy, a Massachusetts Democrat, and Nancy Kassebaum, a Kansas Republican, that was intended to provide so-called portability in health insurance. It shortened the period for preexisting conditions: If a person hadn't been treated for the condition in the year prior to switching insurers, the person could be covered for that condition immediately. Not much help for the Smiths, however, because Lyndsey hasn't gone 12 months without some type of treatment.

Smith ticks off a list of other issues that concern her: children being killed in Bosnia, the need for gun control, drugs, and better education for American children.

"I think we have a lot of problems we need to clean up."

And she believes the right elected officials can change things.

"We definitely need to vote to get people in there to represent you and who have a proven track record. If all of us don't vote, what happens?"

She says she and her husband don't vote because, between his frequent business trips and her responsibilities caring for Lyndsey and Sarah, there's too little spare time in their lives. She doesn't want to use her precious few hours alone to get registered or to vote.

"My priorities have changed. Before, you thought you have to vote. It's your right. You've got to vote. But I guess I've learned to say no and learned to question things and also realize that I don't have to do something because someone says you should. I'll do it if I can and if I want to."

She says she would be inclined to register if she could do it by mail, and she believes a lot of other nonvoters also would be willing to mail in their registrations. Her state, Maryland, does allow mail-in registrations.

But registering is one thing, voting another.

Her opinion of the political system couldn't be lower.

"They're spending too much time on what I consider petty things rather than on problems. Like [Clinton and Gore] can't ask for money when they're in the White House. They should know that stuff. But it is a little petty, too. How is it affecting us?

"It's over and done with, and who got harmed by it? And the Republicans bring it up because they lost. In the long run, what is the issue here? Get to the point.

"There's something out there more worthwhile, more newsworthy. If they're talking about that on the news, I'm going to flip the channel. My time is very valuable to me."

Too much of what passes for political debate is simply mudslinging, she says. Politicians should give their positions on important issues, and the news media should stop reporting on the candidates' private lives.

"I don't care what he does behind closed doors. Is he fair? That's the bottom line. Is he rational? That's when I knew I would never vote for Ross Perot," whom she didn't consider to have views that could be taken seriously.

If she had more time, she might vote again. She knows she would only vote for someone who doesn't compromise on issues of principle. But it's hard for her to think in real terms about becoming a voter again. It's not as important as keeping Lyndsey safe.

"Lyndsey is my reality."

———— ◄◦► ————

Jason Caldwell

A Step Away From Voting

Jason Caldwell likes riding in his blue pickup truck out from the Kansas City suburb where he lives to the small town of Concordia, Missouri, where he grew up, heading for the country he loves. The dashboard of his truck is littered with more than a dozen rifle shells.

He enjoys hunting and fishing and uncrowded spaces. "The more you know how to survive on your own, the better person you'll be. My dad taught me how to hunt and fish."

In the first presidential election after he turned 18, Caldwell says he voted for Bill Clinton. In the next presidential election, in 1996, Caldwell chose not to vote.

"I'm not going to vote for someone I do not believe in," he explains.

Caldwell says he had followed Clinton's policies during his first 4 years in office and had too many disagreements, particularly over the president's support for the Brady law, which Clinton signed in 1993 to create a 5-day waiting period before people can buy handguns to allow background checks of the purchasers.

He's a fierce believer in the Second Amendment to the Constitution, calling it the last defense against government control of the right to own guns. Like many of those opposed to gun control, he believes crimes that involve shooting should be linked to the criminals, not the guns the criminals use.

"The way Clinton's going about it, I think it's really wrong. You could ban every gun in the world, but there's still going to be people out there committing crimes with guns. Guns are just pieces of metal, pieces of wood that fire a projectile. The man that's behind the gun is the problem.

"Honestly, he can ban all the guns in the world, and I probably won't be in the United States anymore. I'd probably move to another country. I think he's trying to move into more of a political position instead of doing what the forefathers said. And he's not listening to what the common citizen has to say."

Caldwell is registered to vote, he can talk knowledgeably and passionately about public policy issues, and he says he definitely intends to vote again—when the time is right.

"It will depend on what the issues are. If there's something I really need to vote on or something I feel strongly about, I'll get off work and vote."

Issues and candidates clearly can spur him to action, but he likes his political actions to be direct and immediate and within his control. The act of voting doesn't pass the test. The act of putting up yard signs for a school board candidate, which Caldwell did right after graduating from high school, does.

He was exercised enough about the Brady Bill that he and his stepfather wrote to Representative Ike Skelton, a Democrat who represents Missouri's

Fourth Congressional District that includes Caldwell's home of Belton, to oppose congressional approval of the legislation.

His stepfather is a member of the National Rifle Association (NRA), and Caldwell intends to join.

"The NRA is a very good, supportive group. We want the freedom to still possess and own our own gun."

With such strong feelings, a vote against Clinton in 1996 would have seemed worth his effort, particularly because the NRA opposed Clinton vigorously in that election. But Bob Dole didn't resonate with him, even though the Republican candidate opposed gun control. "For me, Dole was a career congressman and he thought that because he had spent so many years as a congressman, he should be president. I don't think he was quite ready for it. If he ran again, I might vote for him."

Although he's adamant in not voting for someone he doesn't believe in, he's not waiting for the perfect politician either because he knows there is no such thing as a candidate without flaws.

"If I was waiting for the perfect one, then I'd never vote. And I do intend to vote. If it's presidents or congressmen, I listen to what they have to say and I choose which one I like the most. Some people are hard-core Democrats or Republicans. Me, I just pick the one that will do the best job. Listen to what they have to say and see what their past efforts have been because your past is going to tell a lot about you as a person."

However, he does not want to learn about personal peccadilloes of politicians and castigates the news media for focusing too heavily on officials' private lives.

"Some of the media needs to stop digging for dirt and dig for true facts. If he cheats on his wife, I don't care. I don't care who the president sleeps with. I want to know if he's going to do something for me. What's he done in office? His public life is all I want to know about."

Caldwell, who was 24 when he passed up voting in the 1996 presidential election, cares deeply about the need for strong family values, partly because of the turbulence in his family after his parents' divorce 13 years earlier. Because of his feelings about family, he believes politicians have a right to keep their family lives, even if they are imperfect, out of the public eye. He knows how wrong turns in family life can happen to good people.

But he also thinks politicians—and Americans generally—don't support family values and the need for a strong family as much as they should.

"People think money makes the world go 'round. I think money just makes greed go 'round. People put too much emphasis on money. They're trying so hard to get that money, they let their families slip by their fingers."

He plans to have a house far out in the country, in a place like Concordia, where he grew up until his mother remarried and the family moved to Belton, a suburb of Kansas City. He also plans to have children because he believes they are what turn a husband and wife into a family.

Concordia, a dot on the map with a population of 2,160, remains a focal point of Caldwell's life. He returns regularly to visit his father and to get his truck fixed.

"I lived there for my first 13 years. It was a lot of fun. Everybody knew everybody. We'd all go to parties in the middle of someone's farm."

His parents divorced when he was 11 and his brother, Edward, was 4.

"I had to be the man of the house because we had to move in with my grandma, and we had to deal with the usual big divorce fight. There was a lot of animosity."

He and his mother became close during that time and remain so today.

"I can tell her anything. I can tell her what happened on a date or if I was out partying and was too tired to come home. She doesn't get offended or look down on me for it. It's something I hope to pass on to my kids when I have them, this camaraderie I have with my mom."

He helped his mother care for his brother but also watched out for his mother, who took a job as a waitress in a bar.

"The divorce was hard on her. I was the only stable thing in her life. You grow up real quick when you got your mother crying on your shoulder because you're the only stable thing in her life."

It was an adjustment when his mother remarried. "I went from mom's only support to being second in her life. There was a power struggle. For the first 2 years, it was real tough because there was someone new in the household, but as the years went on, it became very acceptable, and it became a lot of fun." He still lives with his mother, stepfather, and brother in their three-bedroom home in a quiet middle-class neighborhood of single-story houses.

Moving to Belton from Concordia was another adjustment: Caldwell went from a seventh-grade class of 75 students to an eighth-grade class in Belton of 200 students.

"It made me more reliant on myself. In Concordia, you can trust everybody. Here, you've got to know your friends. You've got to know them deep in your heart. There were only two or three people that I ended up really trusting.

"Every chance I get, I go back to Concordia. The people I trust are in Concordia." That includes his father as well as his paternal grandfather, who owns an auto shop where Caldwell takes his pickup truck for repairs. "In Concordia, I could go and leave my keys in my truck and it'd be fine. Now here [in Belton and Kansas City], you've got gangs and local criminals."

Caldwell is looking around to buy a house, and he's only looking in small towns.

"If I had anywhere in the world to live—if I could look out my front door and I could see the light pole on my neighbor's house, I'd be too close. I like my space."

His love of the outdoors is one of the reasons he decided on a career in roofing after working in the mailrooms of a few companies.

"When you're in an office, you're trapped by what's around you. When you're outside working every day, you don't have the walls that bind you."

He's learning the roofing trade in his job at a residential roofing company with offices in Kansas City and nearby Butler. He joined the firm in 1995 and hopes to start his own company in a year or two.

The long hours he's putting in at his job are among his excuses for not voting.

"The reason I didn't vote was because I worked late and I couldn't get to it at that point. I'm up on the roof at six in the morning. The polls open at seven and close at five. I don't get out of work until five." In fact, the state's polling hours are 7 a.m. to 7 p.m.

His long hours also are the reason he's not helping out in campaigns any more, he says. "I helped with the campaign for the school board after I graduated from high school. Now I don't because I'm too damned tired." He says he knew the candidate for the school board, so putting up signs was worth the effort.

He's also more inclined to follow national news than local news now and calls himself a political moderate because he's a conservative on some issues, such as gun control, and more moderate to liberal on others, such as education and abortion.

"I very strongly believe in abortion unless it becomes a form of birth control. I think that if a woman wants an abortion because she's not ready for children, she's not going to be able to take care of the child, or it was incest or rape, she should be able to have one." In high school, he remembers, some girls didn't use birth control and had several abortions, a practice he says should be outlawed.

He also believes that education is a local issue, best settled locally. However, some changes made in school hours and classes in the Belton area, particularly lengthening class periods, were done mainly for the benefit of the teachers, he thinks.

He supports welfare reform. "They'd been giving checks to people who were lying when they said they were looking for a job. I don't think they follow up on stuff like that."

However, he doesn't like the idea of a set time limit on welfare benefits.

"I would sit down and review each case. When I was in high school, this guy would come in to the grocery store and would have to pay with food stamps. He was driving a ratty car, but he'd work his butt off. I'd seen him working two jobs before. He had one daughter and they were barely making it. In a case like that, I would continue governmental assistance."

His family never needed government help, despite his mother's divorce. His grandmother worked on the assembly line at a Banquet Food plant for 45 years; she was widowed in 1974.

"I thoroughly respect someone who has the gumption to make it more than 20 years by themselves."

Although he admires his grandmother's long stint at the same job, he thinks such longevity has no place in a place like Congress. He points to Skelton, who was elected to his eleventh 2-year term in Congress in 1996.

"Since I was little, he was in the House of Representatives. Nobody knew the new guy [who was running against Skelton—Republican Bill Phelps]. They only knew Ike. So nobody voted for the other guy. I think a lot of congressmen are that way. They get so attached to one district for so many years that people say, 'Who's this other guy running?' "

When congressmen stay too long in Washington and make a career out of representing their district, Caldwell says, they stop listening to their constituents. Elected officials don't care enough about his views, he believes, in part because they've been spending too much time with lobbyists and other Washington insiders rather than with their constituents.

"They've really got to listen to their people for four or five terms. But after so many terms, they say, 'Everybody knows me so I'll get reelected. I'll just drive through my district once.' "

He knows the issues discussed in Washington affect his life, such as gun control or health care reform.

As he thinks about the future—he's talking marriage and kids with his current girlfriend—the need for health insurance looms large. Neither he nor his girlfriend receives coverage from their employers.

"If something happened to me, I'd be of no use to her. I have nightmares about it," he says. "My boss and I talked about it, but the occupational hazards of the roofing business make the insurance cost more than he could afford."

Caldwell says elected officials should find a way to give all Americans quality health care that's affordable for employers, particularly small businessmen like the one he works for. He also puts a lot of the blame for the lack of affordable health care on insurance companies.

But he chastises politicians, presidents, and congressmen alike for forgetting their campaign promises about health care reform.

Caldwell admits that he also has failed to follow through on his best intentions. Months before the 1996 presidential election, he had said he probably would vote in 1996. But when the time came, he didn't, even though he was registered.

Just as he criticizes politicians, he's ready to take criticism for not voting. "You have a right to your own speech. Say what you want about anyone in the country. You can try to look down on me because of my choice to not vote, but you're just trying to say you're better than me."

With great sincerity, he says he will be in the election booth one day, when the right issue moves him to take the final step.

"It would have to do with protecting the Second Amendment," he says. "But that's not enough. I'd have to feel like this candidate would uphold his end of the bargain. No president in my time has done that."

———— ◄○► ————

Claudine D'Orazio

Dedicated to the Hospitality Industry

Claudine D'Orazio cares about her town. She revels in the tourism and convention boom that Savannah is experiencing, in part due to its role as the charming coastal setting for John Berendt's best-selling book, *Midnight in the Garden of Good and Evil.* She was disappointed when one-term Savannah Mayor Susan Weiner was narrowly defeated in a runoff election in November 1995 that "got nasty." She was at campaign headquarters election night to help with the catering. She is embarrassed for Savannah because she feels that the new mayor, Floyd Adams, speaks poorly, is extremely overweight, and doesn't project a polished image for the town. She was embarrassed for neighboring Buford County, South Carolina, when she heard on television news that voter turnout was so low for one of its city council elections that only 300 people voted.

Yet D'Orazio doesn't vote, and at 27 years old, she never has, either when she lived in Atlanta or since she moved across Georgia to Savannah in November 1994 to accept a $22,000 a year job offer as an individual travel sales manager for the Hyatt Regency Savannah.

D'Orazio works hard and cannot recall a time when she hasn't. Her office, a reconfigured photocopier room, is small, as is she, at 5 feet, 3 inches tall. On one wall is a poster of the canals in Ghent, courtesy of the Belgian consulate where her mother works. On another wall is a poster of *Les Miserables,* courtesy of the company touring the musical through Savannah. Two photos are propped on the bookshelf adjacent to her desk, one of the sales team she works with, the other of her mother, brother, and herself in a frame with the Serenity Prayer. She recites it often to herself and has since she was a child. "God grant me the serenity to accept the things I cannot change, to change the things I can and the wisdom to know the difference." She can make a difference at work and with her family. With politics, she feels she cannot.

D'Orazio's reasons for not voting would confound the most scrupulous of pollsters because her answers validate almost every reason traditionally given by nonvoters, until she refutes them one after the other.

She says initially that she doesn't vote because she doesn't recognize the effect of public policy on her. Yet she offers examples that, she concedes, belie that. She says that she knows firsthand of someone's son who is attending college because he received a Hope Scholarship that she credits Georgia Governor Zell Miller for securing out of state lottery money.

D'Orazio also brings up affirmative action that, she says, affects her and her hotel directly. She observes that the hotel has hired minorities who, she believes, are not appropriate for the job, whether to fulfill a quota or to promote diversity in the workplace.

She revises her reason for not voting, opting instead for the gut feeling that her vote would not change affirmative action or much else around her. "What can they [elected officials] do about it?" D'Orazio ponders. "What I say doesn't really matter. That's probably more my feeling."

She feels she should vote, and she's embarrassed that she doesn't; after all, she's "an educated person."

"But I feel naive sometimes," D'Orazio counters, "and not able to actively participate in conversations that I should be able to." She is bothered by her own indifference. To D'Orazio, who dresses conservatively in navy or black suits, appearances matter, and the appearance of being uninformed about voting is worse than not voting. "I have the right to do it [vote], and I'm realizing that for years, people fought for this right for us and I should be exercising that right."

She registered to vote for the first time in 1995 at a Wal-Mart because it was convenient. She complains that voting is inconvenient, that the polls should be open earlier so she could vote before work. She says she would have voted if she could have done it by mail. She reconsiders and notes that no one at work would have cared if she took off time during Election Day to vote. One colleague told the election authorities he wasn't going to be in town just so he could get an absentee ballot. "I thought that was such a clever idea," D'Orazio says.

Her mother doesn't vote. Neither does her brother, but her father did. Her best friend, who lives in Birmingham, Alabama, votes and is involved politically. D'Orazio knew the campaign manager for Susan Weiner when she ran unsuccessfully for reelection. And when she was a college student at Georgia State University, she would see Governor Zell Miller eat regularly in the university cafeteria across the street from the state capitol. "I thought that was pretty cool," she recalls, "that he'd come in the cafeteria and eat with the students."

Yet she never voted for him. "I think I just always had an excuse," D'Orazio catalogs. "I was busy, I was studying, I was working and I guess I never really cared enough to get up and do anything about it."

D'Orazio can readily identify some of Georgia's political players—House Speaker Newt Gingrich, former U.S. Senator Sam Nunn, Savannah alderman Gary Gephardt, and Spencer Lawton, Jr., the local district attorney who was featured in Berendt's book—and knows who she likes and doesn't like. She was pleased when the county commission chairman was voted out of office after criticizing emergency management officials during Hurricane Bertha in July 1996 because they called for a voluntary evacuation of all homes. Even though she favored Weiner in the Savannah mayoral runoff election over a candidate she didn't respect, she came away from the campaign disappointed that her candidate acted like a sore loser.

D'Orazio has only the faintest memory of anything political when she was growing up. She recalls her father, a clinical psychologist, being a Republican and voting. He would show her his "Voted Today" sticker. Beyond that, nothing. Her mother is Belgian and became a U.S. citizen in 1976, but D'Orazio has never known her to vote in either an American or Belgian election. D'Orazio retains dual nationality because it will make it easier for her to work overseas, a big asset in the hospitality industry. Politics wasn't discussed in her home or in the Catholic schools she attended for 12 years before college.

"I don't ever remember it being stressed to me, not at home, not at school," D'Orazio says. "It might have been and it might not have filtered in, but I really don't remember it ever being an issue."

She remembers fulfilling a social science requirement in junior high school with history and in her senior year with economics. She surmises that maybe in public school there might have been a civics requirement, and that possibly in Catholic school religion took up the time. "I don't even remember having exposure to real-world types of things," she offers. "I did have a drama class every day, I did have religion every day. My free period where I could have chosen what I wanted to, I had to work."

D'Orazio grew up quickly—too quickly, she thinks. Her parents divorced when she was 13, after which her mother returned to Belgium and she stayed in Philadelphia with her father. When her mother came back to the United States 2 years later and D'Orazio chose to join her in Atlanta, the contentiousness of the divorce intensified. Her father refused to pay for her schooling. D'Orazio worked her way through school—Catholic high school, DeKalb College, and Georgia State University.

"Once I was 13, I lost being an adolescent," she adds later, as she recalls her deteriorating relationship with her father, who died 5 years after the divorce. "I was more concerned about getting the bills paid and that type of thing."

She describes the college campuses as urban and transient. "Eighty-two percent of the students were working [while attending college]," she says, as if citing travel and tourism demographics she has researched. "People came and went. There were no community connections or activism or young frats or sororities or young Republicans, and I wouldn't have had time to join them if they were there because I worked."

During her sophomore year in college, D'Orazio took an unanticipated turn that she now considers the most formative in her life. She was majoring in public relations and working as a desk clerk at a Budgetel Inn. She took an elective course in fairs and expositions, loved it, and switched to a major in hospitality management, a small department that allowed her to develop close relationships with faculty. She worked at Budgetel and Hyatt and took courses in marketing, meeting planning, menu preparation, and design. "I can't even think of a course that would be close to something in current events or political science," she notes.

Her goals at 27 years old are to become a director of sales or a national account sales manager and to go back to school. "My long-term goal is one day to be able to teach college," she says. "I had some very influential professors and I'd like to be able to influence people."

She supposes that something had to give in the process of working, taking classes, studying, staying up late, paying tuition, and then working from 7 a.m. until 8 p.m. after college. "Perhaps the emphasis on responsibility kept me from paying attention to politics, issues, and candidates," D'Orazio suggests. "I had more immediate concerns that directly affected me, that I could see."

D'Orazio feels she may now be stepping into a more participatory phase. Her commitment to the hospitality industry and the vitality of Savannah are providing the gravitational pull. "It's very political here," she says of the town of 140,000. "It's been the first exposure I've had to watching city council meetings and the politics of a small city."

She volunteers at a food bank, as a representative of the hotel, and tutors at work some afternoons. Periodically, a grade school student shadows her on the job. "I'm always the first to volunteer when they need something extra at work," she says. "I'm very vocal within the hotel and very participative in any kind of hotel activity." She prides herself on talking to everyone in the hotel from custodian to manager. "When I was at Budgetel, I did the laundry, the house-keeping, and I was front desk clerk," she says. "I realize how hard it is to clean 20 rooms in a day."

She is paying more attention to news and public affairs. She gets most of her political news from television. She watches the local news every morning, the 11 p.m. local news a few times a week, and knows the names of the anchors. The O. J. Simpson and JonBenet Ramsey murder cases intrigue her. Someone D'Orazio works with had met the 6-year-old victim, and because of the Ramseys' ties to Atlanta, where the family lived before moving to Colorado, D'Orazio knew all the places the TV news was depicting there. She empathized with the children and the families in both cases because her family also had imploded. She sees herself changing. In the past, she says, she paid more attention to commercials than to news stories.

She reads the *Morning News,* Savannah's daily newspaper, mostly on week-ends when she has more time. She reads the business section first because she wants to keep up with news that might affect her hotel or the local companies she deals with. Then she reads about the local community, the letters to the editor, and the "Vox Populi" column in which people sound off. She reads more local than national or international news and usually skips over the whole first section of the paper. If she picks up a *USA Today* at the hotel, she'll read mostly the Life section. "I like that paper because it gives you just the quick highlights on the front page on the left-hand side," D'Orazio says.

As for political news, she thinks she gets the basic gist of the issues but then doesn't read on. She reads hospitality trade magazines, not news magazines. On the weekends, she may check in on CNN's Headline News. She gets her news "in quick spurts" and in conversations with colleagues in the sales office and with visitors and convention people who talk politics.

For D'Orazio, the first national political figure of note is Ronald Reagan, although she considers him before her time. "He is the first person I remember or cared about enough to watch on TV," she says. "He was probably already in office, so I wasn't able to vote for him."

She considers herself neither a Republican nor a Democrat. "I know I have to distinguish that eventually," she says, "because most people do." She assumes she's more in line with the Democratic Party because they are more for working-class people.

She feels strongly about health insurance and personalizes it. She says it's ridiculous for a person like herself who went to college and earns more than $25,000 a year to feel strapped by the cost of health insurance. She doesn't know who supports what nationally, but recalls that First Lady Hillary Rodham Clinton led a task force and whatever it came up with didn't happen.

She feels cheated that Uncle Sam gets 40% of her wages. She would have better tax advantages, she notes, if she were not single. She favors a more socialistic European way that her mother has told her about—6 weeks of holiday, better overtime pay, and better insurance. "In Europe, in Belgium, when you resign and you give, I think it is, 3 months' notice, you are given 2 afternoons off a week to look for another job," D'Orazio says.

She feels strongly about the accessibility of a college education. "I would say that I really would like to see somebody get in office who would make education available to everybody," she says, noting that she is still paying off her student loans and her younger brother is not going to college because he cannot afford it.

Mostly her interests are local. Savannah does not have enough parking around its waterfront and historic district. Police are ticketing too much. It discourages tourism. She is aware of the issues over management and budgeting for a new international trade center and of the need for more airlines serving the Savannah airport. "Now I'm having more time to think about these things and I'm getting older," D'Orazio says of her expanding political horizon.

She would like to be more active, but something is holding her back. She finds that when she looks into issues, she doesn't know enough. "As I'm getting older and starting to care a little bit more," she says, "I wish I was more knowledgeable." She says she doesn't like to feel incompetent and dreads having to ask the first time she enters a polling place, "How does this little booth thing work?" With a sigh, D'Orazio sums up her continuing status as nonvoter. "I think that I care about issues and, up until this point, have been pretty inactive," she says. " I *will* get out there and vote, eventually."

———— ◄◦► ————

Ryan Gerali

Put It Off and Missed His First Election

During the 1996 election campaign when he turned 20, Ryan Gerali often would walk past registration tables and get-out-the-vote posters in the bustling halls of the College of DuPage, the community college he attends not far from his suburban Chicago home. He was always in too much of a hurry to register. He arrived at the community college for an 8 a.m. class and would go from class to class until about noon, when he would return home so he would have enough time to catch his breath before going to work at the Itasca Bank and Trust.

"I don't like having huge gaps. I like to go there, get done, and leave. I don't like to stay around," says Gerali, who is working toward a degree in business administration or finance.

He noticed other entreaties to register and vote. His church, St. Luke's Lutheran, where he went to school from kindergarten through eighth grade, had a voter registration drive. He recalls voter registration signs at the Nordic Hills Resort and Golf Course, just up the street from the home he has lived in since he was born. He isn't sure, but he thinks he could have registered and voted at any of those places.

Then there was television and radio. "TV was like constantly. I don't know, the radio stations I listen to would have 'rock the vote' and 'your vote counts.' They'd be saying, 'Don't be like everyone else and not vote. Vote,' " Gerali recalls. One campaign advertisement, in particular, sticks with him, he says with a broad smile. He passed it whenever he drove on the expressway near his home in Itasca, a middle-class suburb west of Chicago.

"There was a huge billboard. It was the Dole campaign. It was huge. It was right over [Interstate] 294 going north towards Schaumburg. It was over the expressway. It said, 'Screw the media. Elect Dole.' I remember this. This was good. And then it says, 'Screw the country. Elect Clinton.' Big letters, too. It was probably up for a month, right before the elections."

Yet Gerali didn't know when the registration deadline was and never quite got around to registering. "I planned on voting. This was my first election, I'm gonna vote. But then I was just like, I don't know, I didn't see the big deal about it. I do plan on voting in the next election. I don't know, I just put it off and put it off and put it off, and finally, it was like too late to vote. The deadline came . . . and I just kept putting it off. School and work and all that."

Gerali was raised in DuPage County, often described as one of the most Republican counties in the United States. His dad, a career postal worker, died of emphysema when Gerali was 16, a high school sophomore. His mom works as a paralegal for his uncle in a nearby suburb. They didn't talk politics much. Typical dinner conversation would be about his or his sister's school day. Now that his dad is gone and he and his sister are buzzing through school and work, the family seldom shares a dinner hour. Gerali and his dad used to talk sports, playfully picking opposing teams to root for, and play video games together on the television.

Gerali's mother and sister are voters. His dad was, too. "I wasn't brought up any particular way," Gerali says. "My parents weren't Republicans or Democrats. They were pretty much for who they thought was the better guy." He isn't sure, but he thinks his mother voted for Ross Perot in the 1996 presidential election. His sister voted for George Bush, and both times she has voted, she has opted for the straight Republican ticket.

The schools Gerali attended chipped in with periodic curricular contributions to the political process. Gerali recalls favorably going on a field trip that took his grade school class at St. Luke's Lutheran to the museum in Itasca, the town's oldest house, and then on to the home of the mayor. When he was in eighth grade, the school tried to imbue its students with an appreciation for voting. "Whoever was running for the election at that time, we had a mock vote to see who won. That's right," Gerali recollects, "it was Bush and Dukakis."

In public high school in Illinois, students are required to take an American government course and to pass an exam on "American patriotism and principles of representative government." Gerali's class would break off into groups, and, one group at a time, about five students each would engage in a discussion. "We all had chairs in front of his desk, and we would talk about an issue and [the teacher] would grade us on our performance," Gerali recounts. One topic, he recalls, was guns in America. They were told the Democratic and Republican positions and asked what they believed. For another class assignment, he had to send a letter to a government official, lobbying on the right to bear arms. Gerali can't recall what position he staked out or to whom he wrote, but he liked the class, found it "pretty interesting," and got a B. He could have taken political science courses as electives, but he chose psychology, sociology, and accounting instead.

He sensed even then that he was headed for a future in business or finance. Although he's completed 86 of the 96 credits he needs to obtain an associate's degree in liberal arts at the College of DuPage, he has yet to take a political science or government course. None is required. For a required speech course, he wrote a letter to the mayor of Itasca, complaining that there were no stop signs in the residential area around his house. "I really couldn't think of anything," recalls Gerali. "I think I was almost hit by a car that day, so maybe I should write about that." Within a few months, stop signs were installed.

By most indicators, Gerali appears to be a model citizen, a "down-to-earth guy," as he thinks of himself, and an active, engaged member of the community in which he may live the rest of his life. His part-time job at the Itasca Bank and Trust is key to his vision of success in the business world. He hopes to work there as he completes his community college degree, return for a summer stint after he goes away to college, and eventually move up the ladder.

"They don't like hiring from the outside. They like to keep the people who work there, there, so hopefully, if you stay there long enough. . . . The executive VP there started as a teller," says Gerali as he notes that he was recently promoted to teller, a position in which he deals with customers regularly and must be entrusted with money.

His mother and family are key to his life. He thinks often of the last game that his father saw him play before he died. As point guard on his church league basketball team, he scored 40 points as his team lost by 15. For male role models since his father died, he looks to friends and their dads. One of them serves on the local school board and works with him at the bank. Yet he has never talked politics with him, hasn't voted for him, and hasn't been asked to. Another man who is an executive at the bank is a former judge and former mayor of a neighboring suburb. Gerali is aware of the man's political involvement only in the vaguest way, through the photos and plaques on the banker's office walls. They've never talked politics together, and Gerali wasn't aware that the man had recently lost by one vote an election for trustee of the neighboring village board.

Gerali wanted to go away to college, but his mom convinced him to enroll in the nearby community college. "Moneywise, maybe, going to a junior college is, of course, a lot cheaper than going away right away, it's like $1,500 a year. She just didn't think maybe I was ready, that I would go out and have a good time and waste my education away. I was only 17 or 18. Now that I'm 20 years old, she thinks that maybe I'm more responsible," Gerali says, and adds, "If it was up to me, I'd have gone away right away. I'm kinda glad I didn't, in a way."

Gerali values his lifelong connection to his church, where his mother still teaches Sunday school. In the family room where he often watches television, a card placed over a family photo says, "Jesus loves you and so do I." He attends church less than he used to, though he tries to get there at least once a month on Sunday mornings. He sells tickets at the church booth at the annual Itascafest. He also volunteers at a local nursing home.

Gerali sees himself as typical of his friends and of the young people with whom he goes to school.

He reads a newspaper every day, more often than he watches television news, but he reads the paper mostly for sports and business. "I check to see how the stocks are doing," Gerali says. He doesn't own any stocks, but he's interested because "I plan on doing a lot with it in the future." He also consults the *Daily Herald* to see what is going on in the neighborhood and what movies are out. Sometimes he will read the front page if there is a story that catches his attention. He almost never watches a half-hour TV news program in its entirety. He picked up a habit of reading *U.S. News & World Report* because he was able to get a cheap subscription through one of the business classes he was taking. He's favorably disposed to the news media and trusts them to keep the public informed. "Who else is gonna show you exactly what's going on?" he asks. "I mean someone has to do it, and they're the ones who are there."

Had he voted in the 1996 presidential election, Gerali would have voted for Ross Perot, like his mother, over Democrat Bill Clinton or Republican Bob Dole. But he knew Perot "didn't stand a chance of winning" and "his vote wouldn't mean anything." Why Perot? Gerali thought Perot was straightfor- ward, told the public just what the country needed and what he was going to do, and he paid for his campaign with his own money. Gerali recalls Perot saying on television after his first campaign effort in 1992 that if people had voted for who they believed in "deep down inside," 60% of the people would have voted for him. Two of his friends voted for Perot in 1996, including one friend who is a staunch Republican. "I think Perot had this thing for the younger gen- eration."

That's not to say that Gerali was turned off by the other candidates. He discounted Dole's age, which some of his peers objected to, and preferred Dole to Clinton. He felt Clinton had done a decent job in his first 4 years, though "nothing to brag about," and he believed Clinton was "crooked, what with all the scandals going on. But I mean he's a good president though. The economy's doing good, can't complain about that, the job market's really good right now actually."

Gerali concedes he hasn't paid enough attention to politics or government to "fully understand." He's confused about party politics. He tends to favor the Republican Party over the Democratic Party, though he regards himself as a liberal, and he bases his notions of party differences on an American govern- ment class he took in his senior year in high school. From what he can recall, Republicans believe in a woman's right to choose, and Democrats believe "a woman shouldn't have a right." He lines up with a woman's right to choose, not knowing that he has the party positions reversed.

Taxes also come to mind. "The Republicans were more for the middle-class and lower-class people. The Democrats were more for raising taxes on the wealthy." On that issue, he favors raising taxes on the wealthy because they can afford more, so as he thought about it, he realized he lined up with the Democrats. He had thought the opposite.

Gerali would confound the best intentions of pollsters. His opinions are under construction, and the foundations shift. He catches snatches of political issues but doesn't plug into them. He seizes almost every explanation to rationalize to himself why he didn't vote, and none fully convinces him. He was too busy, but then again, it wouldn't have taken long. He preferred Perot, but the alternatives weren't offensive to him. The election results were predictable, so it wouldn't have mattered anyway. He hasn't paid enough attention. He believes that politicians care about what the public thinks only during elections and "don't do anything about it." As he thinks about it, no matter who is elected, he would live his life the same anyway. "It doesn't affect me yet," Gerali figures, "because I don't pay taxes and all that, but I'm sure it will."

"It's really the whole political scene," Gerali says. "For some reason, I'm kinda like uninterested, I don't know. Actually I don't know why, just maybe because of how I was brought up. We never really talked about it, as a family, so I was never really interested in it. And then when I did learn about it, I didn't really care about it. I took a class because I had to, but other than that, you know."

Then, looking ahead, he adds, "I'll do my voting and all that, but other than that, I won't get too much involved."

——— ◄o► ———

Paul Rains

A Member of the Silent Majority, Content to Follow

Life is good for Paul Rains. As he goes about laying carpet in a nearly finished new house in a subdivision of split-level homes north of Cheyenne, he and his longtime business partner, Joe, joke about friends, squabble about a lost hammer, and talk about what's going on in their town, which sits high on the plains of southeast Wyoming.

Rains has lived in Cheyenne, the capital city of Wyoming with a population of about 50,000, most of his life and has no desire to leave, although he couldn't wait to leave when he was a kid.

"I was going to get out and move to a big city and live the fast life," he says, smiling at the memory of the headstrong teenager with a rebellious streak that he used to be.

Now, at 42, he's mellowed and found what he considers the good life, working in his subcontracting business—a job he says gives him flexibility and independence—and seeing his college-aged daughter on weekends and his 10-year-old son nearly every day and going golfing when he can.

"This is home. I will always be here."

He lives about 3 or 4 miles south of town on an acre of land in a home set off from neighbors. Although he lays carpet for many of the new subdivision homes, he wouldn't want to live there because the homes are a little too close together for his comfort.

"I like living in Cheyenne, I guess, because it is calm and peaceful. Everybody is not rushing to get anywhere. It is not a fast-paced kind of world. You go your own speed. Look at our paper. Not a whole heck of a lot goes on."

He reads the local newspaper every day and watches national news most nights, usually on CNN, but rarely watches the local TV news because he says it's not serious enough. If big news happens in Cheyenne, it often makes national news just because sensational events are a rarity, he says.

"Anything that has to do with us that's national [news], people really get into it. Because we don't get anything sensational around here. It doesn't happen very often. It is a big thing to have a murder around here. It really is an experience, and the town is not really that small. But the biggest thing around as far as crime goes is that there have been a lot of robberies lately . . . convenience stores being robbed."

The lack of sensational goings-on is the way he likes it. But it may be one of the reasons he feels no real connection to local or national politics.

"As long as people have convenience-filled homes and nobody is bothering them, and as long as everything looks like it's going their way, then there is nothing to complain about."

And nothing to vote about, as far as Rains is concerned. "It takes something like a Vietnam to get people involved."

He was in Turkey with his family during the late 1960s because his father was in the military and they moved a lot, with previous stints in England and Germany. Then, when Rains was 13, his father was sent to Warren Air Force Base in Cheyenne.

"We missed a lot of the political upheaval and the violence. Everything was calming down, kind of."

He hung out with friends in high school but couldn't wait to graduate. "The last 3 years of school were dumb. I didn't think they had anything else to teach me. I just wanted to graduate and get out." When he did graduate, the draft was waiting, and the Vietnam War was continuing. He had a high lottery number and expected to be drafted into the Army quickly, so instead he volunteered for the Air Force. Within a year, in January 1973, the end of the draft was announced.

The Air Force sent him to Williams Air Force Base outside of Phoenix, where he spent the next 4 years as an aircraft mechanic.

He had hoped to be a pilot, and when his first 4 years of service ended, he requested pilot training but was rejected. "They were trying to tell me, 'Well, your career field is too critical and, therefore, we don't think that we'll let you get into something else.' And I said, 'Well, if you can't let me . . . then I am out.' I couldn't see doing that for 25 years."

In 1974, while he was in the service, he got married at age 20; a divorce followed 3 years later, but first he and his wife had a baby girl, Summer, named after Miss USA 1975, Summer Bartholomew.

After the divorce, he joined his old high school buddy, Joe, in the carpet-laying subcontracting business in Cheyenne. His ex-wife moved to Colorado—first Greeley, then Longmont—but Rains had joint custody of his daughter and saw her regularly. She spent most summers with him, and when she was in second and third grades, she lived with Rains.

He sent her to St. Mary's, a Catholic elementary school.

Those were the years when he was most connected to community affairs. It was about that time that he started voting in local elections. "I was more idealistic when I was younger," he says to explain why he has since stopped voting.

"When my daughter was in school, I used to do things with the school. With my nephew [who's about the same age as his daughter], I used to help his coach run a baseball team. It was a little league team."

His nephew, Mike, who is the son of one of Rains's two sisters, is nearly 20 and living with Rains now because Mike doesn't get along with his new stepfather. His daughter is majoring in computer science at Colorado State University in Fort Collins, where she went on an academic scholarship. His

10-year-old son, Steve, lives with his mother, Rains's ex-girlfriend, down the road from Rains. The two get together several times a week and go on camping trips during the summer.

He keeps up with what's going on at his son's public school and is happy with the small class sizes and quality of the education Steve is receiving, but he doesn't volunteer much for school activities.

And he doesn't vote anymore.

"The process is too hard—I mean registering to vote. I like the idea they had in California. Did they work that out? Where when you get your driver's license you register to vote. Did they do that? I would like to see something like that."

The National Voter Registration Act, called the motor voter law because it requires states to provide voter registration information along with driver's license applications or renewals, became law in 1993. Wyoming was exempted from the law because it had passed a state law allowing voters to register on Election Day. In fact, U.S. Senator Alan Simpson of Wyoming, was the author of the amendment exempting states that had same-day registration and voting, citing the cost to smaller states of implementing the motor voter law.

Rains also says he doesn't want to register because he fears it will put him on the list for jury duty. "Isn't that how they get jurors—registered voters?" In fact, jury lists in Wyoming are created from driver's license lists as well as voter lists.

But deeper than his fear of jury duty or his unwillingness to make the effort to register is his willingness to let others decide the future leadership of the country. "I guess that I am just like mainstream America. We all want to be led. We just don't want to be bothered. [The politicians should] do their job right, or otherwise we will [vote]. As long as they are within the guidelines . . . you don't need to get involved."

Although he still dresses in torn jeans and wears his long gray-streaked blond hair pulled back in a ponytail like the '60s radicals he remembers as the icons of his youth, he never really joined in the '60s rebellion. And to Rains, many of those baby boomers who were part of the anti-establishment movements— antiwar, feminist, or Black Power—have lost their edge in the '90s.

"Even the political radicals of the '60s are all pretty much establishment now," he says.

He calls himself a member of the silent majority.

"The only difference between nonvoters and voters is just that: They [voters] are pretty much mainstream also, but we're the silent majority. They're the leaders, and we're the followers."

He may stop following and start voting one day, when change is needed. "Change is always going to be a part of history. I imagine sooner or later in our history, it will be the same way." And when that change goes against his views of what is right, he will participate.

"My life is comfortable and nobody is trying to take anything away from me. The government doesn't intrude in my life too much."

A few of his friends vote, but not many. He's not embarrassed to tell them he sits out Election Day. "It is still my right not to vote. I guess that's why they call it a free country. But if you don't vote and you don't like the issues, then you have nothing to complain about if you didn't vote."

One of the problems in motivating people to vote is the lack of distinctions between the two major political parties, he believes. Another is the candidates' focus on name-calling and political bickering instead of straight talk about the many issues that ought to be discussed.

"As far as I can tell, the Democrats want to control your life for you and the Republicans want you to control it. As far as the issues go, neither one of them will tell you the truth, that's what I've found. There's a whole lot of double-talk. I'm not saying that I don't trust them.

"I wish that they could make a point. Don't dance around the issues. It's the old saying: You can please some of the people some of the time, but you can't please all of the people all of the time. That's how politicians present themselves—trying to please all of the people all of the time. That's when they're not trying to backstab each other or retain their jobs indefinitely."

Two issues animate Rains: universal health care and tax reform, both issues that were on President Bill Clinton's campaign agendas in 1992 and 1996.

Because he's an independent subcontractor, Rains has to buy his own health insurance, which costs him $310 a month for family coverage.

"Most countries in the world have a national health plan, and I don't think it's hurt their medical care any. I don't understand [critics] who call it socialism. What they don't realize is that Social Security is socialism any way that you look at it. Or they say the medical field will be hurt if we have a national health plan. I don't understand that. That's a joke."

He cites England as an example of a country where socialized medicine has worked. His mother, who was born in England and lived there until she married his father, and his grandmother, who still lives there, swear by it.

Clinton proposed universal health care coverage in 1993, but the Republican-controlled Congress sank it. Despite his passion for the issue, Rains says, "I wasn't so annoyed that they didn't do it" that he would vote to try to punish the Republicans in the 1994 congressional elections or the 1996 presidential and congressional elections. "I wasn't annoyed to the point where I wanted to get out there and bitch about it. I wasn't annoyed to that point. I imagine as long as things go the way they are going as far as health insurance goes, eventually there will be some kind of national coverage. The middle- and low-income families: Look at how many aren't covered now. Eventually, we won't have to do anything about it. The federal government will have to do something about it because it is a drain on them" to provide Medicaid.

He also quotes his English grandmother's advice on taxes: She told him the English system of taxation hits everyone, particularly the rich. It has made him a proponent of a flat-tax structure that would levy taxes on everyone at the same rate because he thinks the current system places an unfair burden on the middle class and upper middle class and hits those with low incomes particularly unfairly.

With his annual income at more than $30,000, he doesn't feel that he's the hardest hit on taxes but believes multibillion-dollar companies are getting off too easy.

But he didn't feel strongly enough to vote for Steve Forbes, an independent candidate for president in 1996 who ran on a flat-tax campaign. "There's just something about him that wasn't right," says Rains, adding he didn't think Forbes was prepared enough to be president.

His absence from the electoral process, however, is not a symptom of disaffection for the system, he says—it's more a sign of apathy.

"By the end [of the political campaigns], it gets to the point where it is, 'Please be over, be done.' "

It's a feeling he remembers from his days at Laramie County Community College, where he took 2 years of business management courses after he left the Air Force. "I took one political science course, and I hated it. It was so boring, so dry. It had nothing to do with me."

Politics still has nothing to do with him, he says. And he figures most Americans, even if they vote, feel the same way.

"I bet even voters didn't know what the issues were," he says, because there had been so much negative campaigning in the 1996 presidential election and so much media attention focused in the wrong direction. Like Clinton and whether he smoked marijuana in college.

"It has nothing to do with my life. What matters is, is he competent to do the job? What can he do for me? People were glad when the election was over.

"We don't care who's elected as long as they leave us alone."

———— ◄o► ————

Gene Tencza

The Pursuit of Ordinary Happiness

Gene Tencza likes to show off his farm. It might look ramshackle to the occasional passerby who drives up the hill from town, itself a depressed crossroads. He lives there, tucked away in Orange, Massachusetts, because it's rural, not too busy, and without much traffic.

But the 8 acres hold just about everything Tencza needs for a fulfilled life as he approaches 50 years old: a home for him and his hobbies—music, photography, carpentry, and antique tractor collection. He bought the vacant rundown farmhouse from his aunt in 1972. "It's a place to stand, a little place of history that I can call my own," Tencza says. He expects he will live there until he dies.

His continuing regret is that he doesn't have time for everything. Too many interests and not nearly enough time to pursue them fully: to play the accordion, electric keyboard, harmonica, guitar, and violin; to take photos that document his life and the before-and-after appearance of his farm; to do repairs around the house; and to dip into his collection of wind-up Victrola phonographs and the 78 rpm records that he plays on them. He would like to add to his 10 tractors, all John Deeres, all from the 15 years between 1937 and 1952. On the barn fronting the road are Deere signs and a deer crossing street sign, letting the uninitiated know that here lives a farm equipment lover with a sense of humor.

Tencza is comfortable leaving politics and voting to others. "I'm not interested enough in politics to participate in it. You can't participate in everything even if you are interested in it," he says.

"I just figure to let those who are interested in it do it. I'm happy with what they've done so far. I mean, not perfectly happy. Nobody is."

But content. With the political status quo, with the nation, and with his role in it.

Tencza has never voted, never registered to vote. He's thought about it. When he was 21 and working his way through school at Central Connecticut State College, he didn't consider it because he was too busy to participate. "I wasn't informed enough to even think about voting. I just wouldn't consider going to vote on something I didn't know anything about." That was his excuse the first time.

By the 1972 election, he was married and had recently moved with his wife and infant daughter from Connecticut to the farm in western Massachusetts. He had abandoned a career as a teacher of industrial education to buy the 110-year-old farmhouse from his aunt for $8,000 and work as a foreman in a cabinet kit plant. He was too busy "settling in, fixing up an old house, and living in a strange town." He recalls someone who welcomed them into the community mentioning the voter registration deadline and he missed it. After that, he stopped making excuses and became comfortable as a nonvoter.

Tencza has worked for more than 15 years for a machine and tool company in South Ashburnham, a 35-minute drive from his farmhouse. A picture of Tencza, bearded and mustachioed, and six coworkers is displayed prominently in the company brochure, which prides itself on making back knives and other cutting tools for the woodworking industry and having made engine parts for the amphibious tanks used in World War II. "Every job is different every day," Tencza says. "We never know what's going to come in the door, what kind of an item we're going to make a tool for." Tencza is proud that he has never been out of work for more than 2 days but expects that because he earns a modest salary of $40,000, with health benefits but no pension plan, he will never be able to retire.

As he thinks about the phenomenon of nonvoting, Tencza becomes more animated. He had viewed his nonvoting behavior as idiosyncratic, his own personal choice, nothing to be proud of or ashamed of, and nothing to discuss. "I'm not *not* voting in protest. I'm just not voting," he says matter-of-factly. "I never decided not to vote. I just never decided *to* vote.

"It turns out that we're a majority now. Even though we're a majority and there's more of us than you, we don't vote so we can't take over anything. I thought if we could organize all of the nonvoters, we could take over the government. But we don't vote."

Tencza pinpoints his own personal strain of nonvoter as somewhere at the convergence of avowed libertarian sensibilities and societal apathy. "There has to be some organization. There has to be government," he says. "They've gotten along for a lot of years without me and did a fine job, and they'll get along for hopefully a lot of years when I'm gone.

"It's not that I feel that one vote doesn't make a difference because it's been proven in a lot of cases where one vote did make a difference, but I feel that it ought to be left to the people who are interested in participating to make all those decisions rather than me who's pretty much happy with the way it is."

He was one of six nonvoters showcased in the television documentary *None of the Above* that aired on stations across the country in the fall of 1997. The show, produced by Chicago's public television station, WTTW, and hosted by John Callaway, gave him a chance to meet and mix it up with former U.S. Senator Paul Simon. It was the first time in his life he had ever met a politician, and he considered it a privilege to be in the same room with a man he recognized as having once run for president of the United States.

In a discussion that often became contentious, with the nonvoters at odds with Simon and his former congressional colleague Michael Flanagan, who served a single term in the U.S. House of Representatives, Tencza came to their defense. "There's a lot of stuff wrong with this country," he says in the dialogue, "and that's because it's run by human beings, and there's a lot of stuff wrong with human beings."

Tencza feels adamantly that the national debt, his "pet peeve," must be addressed and found himself comforted that Simon felt the same way. "If I ran my life the way the country is run, I'd be bankrupt. It's not right," he says in the documentary, and Simon concurs. Tencza says later that he always pays his credit card bills on time and has never even taken out a loan on his car. His farmhouse is the only large debt he has ever had. "We are mortgaging off our kids' futures," he says. "How dare the government do that?"

But in response to the pleas of Simon and Flanagan to get involved, to vote, and to make a difference if he's offended at how the government does its business, Tencza sees it differently. "Everybody's got jobs to do," he replies. "Let's let the people who are interested in doing those jobs—guys who like television can make things like this [the documentary], guys who like to run governments can run governments, and guys who are interested in supporting guys who run governments—let them do that." It's just not him.

Both of Tencza's parents voted. His mother still votes. His father doesn't get out anymore, but until his disability limited his mobility, he voted. However, they didn't talk politics at home when Tencza was growing up, and he rejected any attempts in school to imbue him with an appreciation for the democratic process.

"I didn't like history in school because it was the history of politics. It wasn't about people, it was about politicians," Tencza says. He recalls getting poor grades in history and having a hard time remembering names and dates. He appreciated the subject more in grade school than in high school because in the earlier years the subjects were about explorers—Columbus and Ponce de Leon. In high school, the topics turned to politics—Teapot Dome, Boss Tweed, scandals. "Silly names from the past that stick in my head," he muses.

Something else stuck from the 1956 presidential election. "I remember the kids in school being adamant about voting for Ike or voting for Stevenson. I didn't care. I liked Ike because that was a neat saying—'I like Ike, I like Ike.' I can remember one kid going home and suddenly discovering that his parents were Democrats, and all of a sudden he didn't like Ike anymore. And I thought that was silly," Tencza recalls.

He hasn't altered his political point of view much in the 40 years since. "I'm interested in who the president is, but I don't believe that either one of them [in most election campaigns] is going to do any harm because there are so many checks and balances against them that they can't even do what they promise."

Tencza knows the names of national political figures, including the higher-profile members of Congress, but no local or state politicians. He's aware that a board of selectmen runs his town, but he isn't aware of any of their names and is content to let them do what they do without his interest or involvement. He doesn't read any local papers, watch local television news, or talk with neighbors about community affairs. He stopped receiving the local daily newspaper, the *Athol Daily News,* a number of years ago.

But he knows generally what's going on. He reads one newspaper or another every weekday at work. The *Boston Herald, USA Today*—whatever is lying around—but he usually sticks to the national news sections. Neither would have much news about western Massachusetts anyway. He's an avid magazine reader, but not of news: He reads *Popular Photography, Men's Health, National Geographic, Model Railroader, Playboy, Tractor Hobby,* and *Antique Power.* He watches television news mostly when the weather is bad, when, instead of jogging, he hops on his "pedal machine" at about the time the 5 or 6 p.m. news is on. Summers he's outside, tending to his farm until it's dark, and he's asleep by the time the 11 p.m. news comes on.

Tencza sees himself as neither reclusive nor connected. Divorced since 1985, Tencza lives alone and talks to his neighbors periodically when he's jogging or when someone needs help, but they don't visit, and he doesn't visit them. At work, he and his coworkers talk plenty but seldom about politics. Mostly day-to-day things. If that includes a new sewer system in Ashburnham, then Tencza will absorb a dose of local affairs.

It's not that he believes political decisions aren't relevant to him. He recognizes that politics, national and local, affect his life. "I'd rather it didn't, and the less it affects me, the better." So long as politics don't bother with him, he won't bother with it. "The most important things in my life right now," Tencza says, "are to make a comfortable living and pursue my hobbies without being interfered with by anyone else."

Tencza once thought that he could avoid the imposition of jury duty if he didn't register to vote. But that isn't the case in Massachusetts, where employers are required to pay for up to 3 days of jury duty, and the court is required to pay $50 a day after that. Tencza has been called for jury duty a couple of times. He served once. He felt cheated when, after sitting through the trial in which there were hints of police selectively going after a man for driving without a license, it turned out he was an alternate juror and excluded from deliberating on the verdict.

"I am a citizen and I live in the greatest country in the world," Tencza says. He has come to appreciate that all the more since he returned from a visit with his mother and brother to their ancestral home in Poland in 1979. "I was told not to take pictures of bridges and locomotives and the police. So I went out of my way to take pictures of bridges and locomotives," he recounts. "But I shied away from taking pictures of the police because I kept noticing how the army and the police were the same thing. I saw how they lived. It gave me an uneasy feeling about not being free.

"People died to make us free to make our own decisions," Tencza recognizes. "I'm free to participate in the way that I feel I should participate. My way of participating is to give back some of what I've learned during my life and to be a good neighbor to the people who live around me, and I don't feel that I need to do any more than that."

Tencza can imagine only one circumstance that would prompt him to vote or to register to vote. That is if someone attempted to take away his right to vote. Until then, he is a confirmed nonvoter. "Voting is not a duty. It is a privilege," Tencza says as if he is staking out an inalienable truth. "And I am pursuing happiness my way."

For Tencza, his farm is his refuge and his portal to happiness. And a metaphor for his political worldview. "I can dig up anything I want to dig. I can plant anything I want to plant and I don't have to do any of it," he says. "I'm just an ordinary person working a pretty ordinary job, living a pretty ordinary life, and I'm pretty happy with it."

——— ◄o► ———

Sue Jablonsky

Gone Fishing

At the end of Main Street in New Brighton, Pennsylvania, a small town about 30 miles north of Pittsburgh in a valley ringed by the Allegheny Mountains, Sue Jablonsky lives with her fiancé and her three school-age sons in one of two narrow brick duplexes squeezed between the 5th Street Lounge and Fox's Pizza Den.

Main Street is populated by a couple of banks, a barber shop, the antique and used furniture store, and a True Value Hardware. An old stone police station stands guard near the entrance to Big Rock Park. At the edge of downtown, a sign welcomes visitors: "Our town is your town."

The windows of Jablonsky's house are inviting, too—lined with little twinkle lights and decorations appropriate to the season, hearts in February, pumpkins in October. The garden behind is a cornucopia of fruits, vegetables, and flowers.

The house, with its neatly arranged knick-knacks and tidy appearance, is a reflection of Jablonsky's outlook on life—which focuses on the importance of home, family, and enjoying the outdoors. It is the antithesis of how she perceives what happens in Washington—messy and dirty.

"Politics are a mess," she says, and it's her fundamental belief that the "mess" in Washington has little to do with her life.

Her primary concerns are that her children get a good education and that her family is secure enough financially to never need government help. And that she has time for her cooking and crafts, her garden, and fishing.

"I don't want all of the greatest things in the world, and I don't want to be at the bottom of the list, either. Hey, as long as I'm comfortable, my kids are comfortable, I think that would be about it. I don't ask for much. As long as I got my fishing in the summertime."

In fact, on Election Day 1996, she and fiancé Paul Porter had plans to spend the day fishing for bass in the Beaver River. But an overnight rain kept them home that Tuesday, watching television talk shows in the morning and the Discovery Channel in the evening, avoiding any election news.

That day they were interviewed by Medill News Service reporter Rod Hicks, who reported in a story published in about 20 newspapers the following:

> The discussion over a lunch of homemade hamburgers and fried potatoes . . . included a bit of talk about politics. Porter was much more talkative than Jablonsky. Both were sure President Clinton would be reelected. Neither seemed thrilled with their accurate prediction. But Porter spoke harshly about defeated Republican presidential candidate Bob Dole.
>
> "He's the biggest farce there ever was," Porter said without elaborating. "At least with Clinton I haven't seen anything rapidly deteriorate around here."

They briefly mentioned two state races that featured negative television and radio commercials. They were not quite sure of the names, but knew one candidate was accused of not paying income taxes for four years and the other of being a resident of another state.

They spoke of politicians as if they all are inherently corrupt. Porter suggested that a woman needs to be elected president. Jablonsky said that might prompt her to vote.

Jablonsky, age 35, followed the political news that fall a bit, "but we already knew who was going to win. It already was tied up and done. That's one of the reasons I don't vote."

She has never registered to vote and doesn't expect to in the future; Porter registered a while back because it was required to attend a gun show but didn't vote. She can't remember her parents voting, but Porter's mother works at a polling place in nearby Jackson Township. Jablonsky's reason for not registering in 1996 was that the registration office was inconveniently located.

More important, she sees no connection between her life and the electoral process.

Even as she talked about her middle son's need for tutoring through a special education program, she saw no connection between that and proposals being argued in Congress at that very time over education funding cutbacks. And even as she worried that her oldest boy's school troubles were, at least in part, because the high school isn't as quick at alerting parents to problems as the grade school and middle school, the presidential candidates were debating whether federal money should be given to parents for vouchers to pay for private schools. And the governor of Pennsylvania was trying to push a voucher plan through the state legislature.

But she doesn't think politicians care what she or people like her think. Although she says the federal government often does a better job than it's given credit for, she also thinks the system will continue to ignore average people no matter who's elected.

The disconnect is complete.

Her lack of connection to the body politic doesn't have to do with lack of information, however. She was well aware of the Clinton administration's proposal to set national standards for teachers as well as students and called it a much-needed step. She criticizes politicians for the fact that U.S. students are not leading the world in math, science, and reading scores.

"We should be working hard at education today," she says. "Kids are going to need much more education in 20 years." The need for a good education is a bedrock belief with her. She regrets still that she dropped out of high school at age 17 around the time she moved in with the man she later married and who is the father of her sons. She has been separated from him a few years and plans to get a divorce soon.

"If I had the chance to do it all over again, I'd have stayed in school. I'd have never gotten married that early. I used to say I'd have gone to college. I keep telling my kids, 'Do you want to be like your Ma?'

"I think they pretty much have their heads glued on right. I'm not sure what they want to be, but they're on the right track. I know they'll graduate. The only thing I really wanted to change in my life was that part."

The statement isn't made with self-pity. That's not her style. She relies on herself and believes you have to face life honestly. She wryly remembers countless hours spent on makeup and long, manicured fingernails. Now, she dresses simply in jeans and sweatshirts to be comfortable as she gardens, cooks, and works on her many craft projects.

She follows her kids' progress in school closely—middle son Matthew, a 12-year-old sixth grader, has a speech impairment and gets speech therapy through the schools; 9-year-old David, her youngest, made the third-grade honor roll; and her oldest, 14-year-old Michael, worries her because he's having trouble completing eighth grade.

The school district is doing a good job overall, she says, because the teachers work hard to keep parents informed. And Jablonsky works hard to be an informed parent. She's alert to any problems with her kids' schoolwork. She noticed when Michael hadn't brought home a report card and when he was clowning around too much. "That's why I'm always talking to the principal. If he's not calling me, I'm calling him."

"Student of the Week" medals decorate her refrigerator door.

And she's at the library every other week with the boys, getting *Goosebumps* books for David and Matthew and stamp or coin collecting books for Michael, who has collections of both. She also stocks up on cookbooks and craft guides for herself and books on trains or cars for Porter.

All of the boys play sports—football for Michael, baseball for Matthew, and basketball for David. In fact, Matthew went to the Pennsylvania Special Olympics in 1996. Their pictures are on a bookshelf in the tiny living room. Jablonsky makes sure they're active and involved; she volunteers at various local events from time to time.

Jablonsky's sports are fishing and, to a lesser degree, hunting. Her freezer, filled with venison and about 50 trout, shows she's good at them.

"Sometimes we just jump in the truck and grab the fishing rods and go."

She and Porter like to spend the weekends when the boys are with their father camping and fishing.

"I used to fish when I was a kid. We always had to fix our own rods, and when we needed sinkers, we'd use nuts and bolts and stuff like that. . . . These days, we mainly go for bass, unless we hit a pond or lake that's just been stocked with trout.

"I like it just for being outside. For the thrill of catching that fish and wondering how long he can stay on that hook until you get him in. Or is he going to fall off. That's about all we do, as soon as summer comes along."

She says she won't keep trout caught in the Beaver River because the water is polluted. A year earlier, pollution laws were debated in Washington, but she missed the stories detailing an attempt by House Republicans to overhaul the federal clean water act to ease or revoke a number of antipollution requirements.

In addition to the fish and venison, her freezer holds the spaghetti sauce she makes when the mood strikes her; the wine she and Porter made from their garden's grapes still is fermenting in the basement.

"I always knew what to do in the kitchen. My grandmother owned a restaurant. I was over there all the time when I was little. I really enjoy it. There are days when I can be in the kitchen from the time I get up 'till after everybody's done eating and gone to bed."

The kitchen also is where she makes her many craft items, such as the decorated wreaths that adorn the walls. The living room is given over to her broom collection.

"We're going to stay here as long as we can," she says, easing back to smoke a Basic cigarette in the doily-covered overstuffed chair that, along with a long couch, crowds the small living room. The next-door neighbors are nice, mainly minding their own business except for front-step exchanges of greetings, and she and Porter have found friends in New Brighton.

When she left her husband, she moved from their home in the Pittsburgh suburbs to Butler County and worked days as a cook and evenings at a grocery store.

"They didn't have benefits [at the restaurant], but it paid my bills, paid the rent," she says. She still has no health benefits and suffers from bronchitis, not helped by her smoking. But she's grateful that Porter has insurance through his job, and the boys are covered under their father's plan. Jablonsky doesn't know how she would pay for a major medical emergency of her own.

When money got tight after the separation from her husband, she started selling her popular nut rolls and apricot rolls to help pay the bills.

The three boys would help.

"The places I lived at before, the people always knew I was making them. I already had built up my reputation. Now, since I've moved here, the kids have got to help me start building up my business again. They have to go out and sell them. And they do good. This year was the first time I tried them for Halloween. I made $400 in a week, and I didn't even put out much money to make them. I make anywhere from 40 to 60 a day. It's an old Russian recipe; my stepfather had the recipe and gave it to my mother."

She asserts that she won't accept public assistance. At times she has worked two jobs and sold the nut rolls and homemade candies rather than turn to the government for help.

Jablonsky estimates she makes about $5,000 a year selling her nut rolls and homemade candies around Beaver County, where New Brighton is located. But Porter's income maintaining the equipment at a paper plant—about $26,000 a year—is the family's primary source of support.

During the 1995-1996 school year, shortly after she and Porter moved into the duplex, she went back to work as a cook at a restaurant about 2 miles down the road to bring in some extra income but quit in the summer because she wanted to be home to watch her kids. That summer, both political parties held their national conventions, with the Democrats pushing children's health care and the Republicans, particularly keynoter and new mom Susan Molinari, stressing family values.

Jablonsky says politicians talk about helping single moms but they don't crack down on delinquent dads who don't keep up with child support payments, which she claims has been a problem for her at times. It's more proof to Jablonsky that what's said in Washington doesn't make a difference in her life in western Pennsylvania.

"It's not that I'm cynical," she says with the wry humor that's a trademark. "I'm just not going to believe everything that's told to me."

When her children grow up, they'll have it harder than she does, she fears, because they will be saddled with the burden of paying for baby boomers' Social Security. "They're going to be paying double, and they still won't be caught up."

One of the problems with the Social Security system and other entitlement programs is the large number of people collecting payments who don't deserve them, she says with passion. Her list, which she says she gleaned from listening to radio news shows, includes alcoholics receiving federal payments, people claiming they're hurt or disabled when they could be working, and drug addicts. She believes it as fact.

"They're making it worse for everyone else. I think they should have more people put out there to catch them doing it."

Again, an election issue—who's entitled to Social Security and how to keep it solvent—that passed her by.

But the issues aren't off her radar screen—or her television screen. The large console television in the living room is on much the day, often tuned to country western music shows or other cable TV programs, but she and Porter do watch news most nights. They watch the parts of the news that interest them—area crimes, sports, but not political news. It's a choice.

"The mayor and council are always putting each other down. They go too far. If they want to say the truth, I'd listen. Just say it."

That's one of the reasons why Ross Perot appeals to her. If she had voted in the 1996 presidential race, it would have been for Perot, she says, because the country needs someone new and different as president. Besides, she believes Perot is a good businessman who feels for people more than Clinton or Dole.

But her honesty makes her admit that she's still unlikely ever to be a regular in the election booth. She chooses activities she believes offer some reward.

All in all, she'd rather be fishing.

———— ◄◦► ————

4

Unpluggeds

President John Kennedy's assassination is a recurring theme among a number of the Unplugged nonvoters we interviewed, as well as among several members of other cluster groups. He's seen as a symbol: The last president who could be trusted to act like a president and care about citizens' issues. It may be simply that his death in 1963 coincided with the rise of cynicism or anger toward political institutions that was a hallmark of the 1960s. Or it may be that the end of Kennedy's tenure marked the beginning of the rise of television in political campaigns, the escalating rhetoric needed for a good sound bite, and the increasingly negative TV ads as well as the explosion of lobbyists, consultants, and other Washington insiders that made the access to federal policymaking appear remote from most citizens.

Jazz musician John Danyo of Chicago, who goes by his professional name of Jack Daniels, came from a family of solid Democrats who voted in most elections. But Daniels's civic bond snapped when Kennedy died; he had intended to vote for Kennedy in 1964, the first presidential election in which he was eligible to vote. Ever since, he has watched the Democratic nominees but found none who measured up. The only place politics has had in his life is as heightened drama—Kennedy's assassination and Watergate.

Barbara Beth was a teenager when Kennedy was shot, but she also cannot name a presidential candidate since who has earned her trust. However, like many of the Unpluggeds, she admits that she doesn't try to learn much about the candidates, avoiding political news on television. "To be honest, I don't know what they say." The 51-year-old bartender in Lakehead, California, has had a life of low-paying jobs with occasional trips to the welfare office when jobs were scarce. Now she only learns of news beyond her town through customers and friends.

Janet Shepherd of Brunswick, Georgia, voted for Kennedy. Since 1960, the only other presidential candidate for whom she voted was Ronald Reagan. She thought they were trustworthy. Now 62 years old, she can't see well and doesn't stray far from her rundown mobile home. She drinks a 12-pack of beer a few days a week and catches political news so sporadically that she no longer trusts her own opinions.

Karen Pelling has no interest in politics, and cannot identify her elected officials by name, although she's lived in the same neighborhood in Winter Park, Florida, since she was 2. If her dream is realized, the 30-year-old will win the lottery and retire. If not, playing her favorite game of darts will do.

To Tracy Rowley of Troutdale, Oregon, politics is a game of bait and switch. Her family was Republican, and when she turned 18, she voted for Reagan. Now 30, she doesn't trust that politicians will come through on their promises, and her husband, who votes, can't budge her to go to the polls. She believes big government is of no help to ordinary citizens.

Government has gotten so big that the electoral process and citizens' opinions no longer can cause change, asserts Paula Ryan, who has voted once, for President Richard Nixon. The people whose opinions she values are close to her in her Phoenix, Arizona, neighborhood, and she counts on them, not the government, for help.

Steve Gordon, like Ryan, sees little hope that his vote will change things, particularly a welfare system he and many among those we interviewed criticized as too lenient. He gets angry when he watches TV news about Washington—at the way the news media highlight sensation over substance and the way lawmakers favor pat answers over solutions. To this 33-year-old machinist in Sparta, Wisconsin, elected officials are wasting time and taxpayer money on irrelevant scandals from the past instead of concentrating on what really matters to working Americans: making the laws more fair to the middle class.

The news bears no resemblance to her daily life, Iris Llamas believes. What she sees in her neighborhood in Austin, Texas, is never reflected. The youngest Unplugged we interviewed at age 23, Llamas says she and her friends never discuss politics and rarely read the newspaper. Why get involved when politicians are out of touch with her life?

Another twenty-something Unplugged, Serena Slaton goes to church three times a week at the Mount Gilead Missionary Baptist Church in a rundown neighborhood in the shadow of Atlanta's Georgia Dome. She trusts in the word of God and notes that the Bible tells us we need leaders. But at 24, Slaton doesn't expect to vote any time soon. She thinks even honest candidates will be changed for the worse by politics.

Jack Daniels

Missing in Action Since Kennedy

He had finally made it. Jack Daniels, the stage name John Danyo had been using since he was 31 years old, was a marquee lounge act. With his afternoon gig at the Four Seasons Hotel on Michigan Avenue in Chicago and his evening act at the Ritz Carlton just down the city's Magnificent Mile, Daniels was taking in $1,183 a week as a jazz pianist with a soft spot for Gershwin.

It was 1990, and his new life was beginning to make the hard life that preceded it worth the trouble. At 17, Daniels dropped out of his high school, the Detroit Conservatory of Music, to play jazz. At 19, he passed up a chance to go on the road with Glenn Miller's band because he wasn't ready. He was too scared to leave home. He played clubs in the downriver area of Detroit until the race riots of 1967 convinced him and his wife to give Chicago a try. For a few years in the 1970s, he would shuttle between St. Louis, where he played the Chase Park Plaza and Colony Hotels, and Chicago, where his wife lived with her mother and sister. He would take the 2 a.m. Saturday flight from St. Louis and fly back Sunday night.

He spent his days watching the Watergate hearings, every day, morning to night, for weeks during the summer of 1973. He regards Sam Ervin, the North Carolina senator who chaired the hearings, as a great man. "He used to say, 'I'm just a small-town country lawyer,' " Daniels recalls and adds, "Howard Baker, who was a Republican, used to cut him off, as if to say, 'We know you're a smart man.' " For Daniels, the images are embedded. He sees Richard Nixon on television, resigning. He cites the resignation date: August 9, 1974. He fixes on the farewell speech Nixon delivered to his cabinet and staff, telling them he came from a poor family, saying his "old man" was a "common man" and his mother was "a saint."

Daniels's life then was his music and what came with it: a piano, hotel lounges, a cash economy, J&B Scotch straight, marijuana, junk food, late nights tumbling into early mornings, and detachment from family and community. He inherited from his father his devotion to music and his place as a Roosevelt Democrat whose fanfare was the common man. He measured politics by two benchmarks, the Watergate hearings and John Kennedy's assassination. Once Kennedy and Nixon were gone, one by bullet, the other by blind ambition, Daniels's civic bond was snapped. He had long since stopped voting by the end of 1990, when the bottom fell out of his world.

He had just quit the Four Seasons because he was working too much when new management at the Ritz let him go. He was out of work, except for a token club date here and there when, on April 2, 1991, he suffered a massive stroke that "hit like a bomb," ended his music career, and left him debilitated and depressed.

To encounter Jack Daniels in 1996, using a cane to get around and favoring his left side, it would be understandable to assume he doesn't vote or to write him off as a nonvoter because of the stroke. He didn't vote in the 1996 presidential election, he says, because it was hard for him to get around. He didn't have transportation to get to the polling place at his son's grade school two blocks away. He didn't vote absentee because he "didn't think of it."

As he talks more of his life since his stroke and his life before, he comes to see his falling out with the political process as complete long before he had his stroke. By 53 years old, when Bill Clinton was reelected president in 1996, Jack Daniels had not voted in a single presidential election. The only elections in which Daniels recalls voting were Chicago's local elections in the late 1960s and early 1970s, when his Democratic precinct captain would pay him, his wife, and mother-in-law $5 each to vote a straight party ticket.

Daniels remembers his youth, as John Danyo, fondly. His family moved from Passaic, New Jersey, to Detroit before he was 5 so his dad could play his music, "bass and piano, with bands, trios, whatever was called for." The family lived on the southwest side in an ethnic neighborhood. "I loved it," Daniels says, "the stores, everything you wanted in a two-block radius." His father, and later he and his brother, played the neighborhood clubs.

His dad and mom talked politics at home. Franklin Delano Roosevelt, who died 2 years after Daniels was born, could do no wrong. "He's the one who pushed through Congress welfare, medical care, and public assistance for poor people," Daniels recalls his mom passing along. "She thought Roosevelt was for the average man," like their middle-class family. Daniels's dad played supper clubs at night and worked in the post office during the day. Civil service provided the family with security Daniels failed to have when he ventured off on his own. "The biggest mistake of my life," Daniels says, "is I didn't take the civil service test."

For the Danyo family, there was a direct line from FDR to JFK. "All the kids in my era liked Kennedy," Daniels recounts. "They would talk politics over lunch." It was as if the 1950s of Eisenhower and postwar prosperity rubbed Detroit's downriver area the wrong way. "We disliked Eisenhower. Everyone I know did. My grandparents, dad and mom, and the neighborhood. He was for the rich people," Daniels recalls. "That's not saying he wasn't a good man. [But] Kennedy was a great man who could do something for the country. He was trying to."

Daniels was torn by Kennedy's assassination, and he hasn't shaken it. He was 20 years old when Kennedy was killed and intent on voting for him in the 1964 election, the first presidential election in which he could cast a ballot. By the time the election rolled around a year after the assassination, Daniels had become dispirited. His dad voted for Lyndon Johnson, Kennedy's successor, whom Daniels says "was under pressure to follow through on Kennedy's ideas." Daniels, who had turned 21 two months before Election Day, took a pass. He's not sure why, but he's taken a pass ever since.

"I consider myself a fanatic about [Kennedy's assassination]," Daniels admits. He says he's read book after book about the assassination, as well as many of the volumes of the official Warren Commission Report, and doesn't know which conspiracy theory to believe. "Before I die," Daniels says with uncharacteristic resolve, "I'd like to know who was behind it. It'll eventually come out."

No politician has measured up to Kennedy. Even though Daniels detested Nixon, he did not convert the disdain to electoral participation either time Nixon ran for and was elected president. In 1972, he didn't like Democratic candidate George McGovern's style. "He wasn't sincere when he spoke," Daniels says. Four years earlier, it was Democratic nominee Hubert Humphrey who didn't impress him enough. "I would have voted for him if asked" by the Democratic precinct captain in Chicago, he says. But in 1968, after the tumultuous and divisive Democratic National Convention in Chicago, some of the city's ward heelers weren't in the mood to heal.

Daniels had grown up in the age-old tradition memorialized by Democratic House Speaker Tip O' Neill, who said, "All politics is local." "My dad knew the local pols [in Detroit]," Daniels recounts. When he moved to Chicago, Daniels liked what he saw in Mayor Richard J. Daley. He never met Daley but respected him and his patronage-enforced power. He respected Daley even more after reading the book *Boss,* the hard-edged portrayal of the legendary mayor written by newspaper columnist Mike Royko. "The precinct captain would come to the house to make sure we voted. Every election," Daniels recounts. "If there was any trouble, if you had parking tickets and didn't have money, he'd take care of it. Then on Election Day, the precinct captain would say, 'You gotta vote today.' " Daniels's mother-in-law would ask, "What are we gettin' for this?" Daniels recalls. After they came home from the polling place, they would receive $5 apiece. Daniels estimates he voted straight party ticket in three local elections under that nominal incentive system until the precinct captain died. After that, with the incentive gone, Daniels's registration lapsed and he never reinstated it or voted again.

He didn't need to. Other people could fix parking tickets. For a few years in the early 1970s, Daniels worked days in a downtown Chicago restaurant. "My boss knew everybody," Daniels says. "Steve had political influence and made one phone call. He told me to go to traffic court and ask for Mrs. Miller." He recalls giving her $15, and the tickets were "taken care of." "In fact," Daniels reinforces, "Steve gave me the $15 the first time."

The experience reminds Daniels of earlier lessons learned from his father. "My dad knew a lot of important people downtown [in Detroit]," he says. When Daniels was drafted in 1965, his father didn't want to risk that his son might be assigned to Vietnam at a time when President Johnson had publicly announced massive bombings. By the end of the year, more than 180,000 U.S. soldiers were engaged in the conflict. Daniels thought he was taken care of when he arrived at the Selective Service office with a statement from a doctor that he was mentally unfit for the military. After being separated from other draftees, he was told he was being classified 1Y and was not eligible for service. "What does that mean?" Daniels asked. "Are you getting married?" the draft board officer asked him, then said, "Then we can't take you. So go get married."

Though Daniels's political disaffection hasn't altered since his stroke, his daily habits have. He doesn't read the newspaper anymore. Instead, he watches television news and reads the *National Enquirer* and *Star* "as much as [he] can" for gossip. Where he once got his news and views from the *Chicago Sun-Times* and its editorials, he now gets them from *60 Minutes, CNN, Inside Edition, Good Morning America,* and *Larry King.* He regards TV news as "straight-forward." "They don't try to lie," he says, "though they put in their 2 cents too much and make stories when there isn't a story."

He spends 4 hours a day with a physical therapist who helps him with exercises and massages his left arm and leg, which were paralyzed by the stroke. He walks a half-mile every day. When it snows, he walks in the street. The walk takes an hour. He and his family are on public assistance. He has no pension and has let his driver's license lapse. He has been approved for federal housing assistance but is far down on a waiting list because he lost his place a few years back when he failed to inform authorities that his family had moved.

He pays attention to a narrow range of public affairs, like scandals such as Paula Jones and Bill Clinton. And now, health-related information, particularly news about new drugs. "I've seen too many sick people in 5 years," Daniels explains. "Before my stroke, if I saw people like me I'd laugh."

"A cure for cancer is out in Russia. I saw it on a special. The cure is made out of rocket fuel," Daniels says, with an enthusiasm he reserves for such affairs as the Kennedy assassination. "If it doesn't involve money, the bureaucracy will eat it up and it will never happen."

Daniels regards politicians mostly as "crooks." Nixon, despite his protestations, was a crook, as are local politicians, Republicans and Democrats, and members of Congress. Chicago city council members do "nothing for nobody but themselves." Congress is "a joke" whose members will "do anything for money."

What would make a person such as Daniels, who regards politicians as crooks who "say a lot of things they're gonna do but never do" and who hasn't voted since Kennedy, register and vote? He met Adlai Stevenson, Jr. once and considered him an honest, intelligent candidate. He likes President Clinton and thinks Clinton might get more things done if Congress would let him. Yet he didn't vote for either one. He would vote for Retired Gen. Colin Powell, "even as a Republican," he says, because "he doesn't beat around the bush and has a great mind." He might vote in the year 2000, Daniels says, if the candidate's ideas are like Kennedy's.

As he looks back on his life, on his political disaffection before his stroke, and on his bitterness and despair thereafter, Daniels says in frustration, "Everything is political." Yet for Daniels, who hasn't played the piano since his stroke and who wouldn't allow himself to listen to any music for more than 6 years since the stroke, the words to his favorite Gershwin tune, "Love Is Here to Stay," apply: The more he reads the papers, the less he comprehends, the world and all its capers and how it all will end. For little in the world and all its capers has been his affair.

———— ◄o► ————

Barbara Beth

A Hard-Scrabble Life Focused on
Raising Her Kids and Getting By

Barbara Beth has raised four kids and divorced five husbands. She never finished seventh grade and started working when she was 15. Now 51, she's tending bar in the resort area where she spent much of her life—wooded, mountainous lake country at the foot of Northern California's Mt. Shasta.

Although she's moved to New Mexico, California, and Alaska, she always returned to the area near Lake Shasta where she grew up. She's lived in Redding (the largest town in the area), Dunsmuir, Mt. Shasta, and Lakehead, earning a living mainly by waitressing and bartending.

The tiny town of Lakehead, where she now lives with her English springer spaniel, Babe, in a small house off Interstate 5, is a vacation spot for summer tourists who enjoy boating and fishing on the enormous Lake Shasta or hiking through the foothills studded with pine trees and mansanita bushes—which appear to shine in the right light.

The Basshole, the bar and bait shop where she now expertly pours drinks, serves as an unofficial meeting place for the people of Lakehead, population 2,500.

They take up collections for newlyweds, celebrate birthdays, plan group trips to Las Vegas or Reno, and talk about the weather, their neighbors, and local news. Although not as important to them as what's going on in their community, politics comes up regularly. The politics, like the gossip, is mostly local.

Beth says the bar patrons, mostly construction workers, retirees, and other local residents when the tourists aren't around, keep her informed about what's going on in her community and beyond.

"This is the information center," Beth says of the wood-paneled bar with two pool tables, fish mounted on the walls, and a long bar where customers mainly drink beer, shots of whiskey, or mixed drinks.

She can't get the newspaper delivered to her home, so she relies on the Basshole to be her information source. She watches a lot of television, mainly movies and San Francisco 49ers games.

But she has given up on TV news as a method of keeping informed.

"I don't even listen to it any more because it's all a bunch of garbage to me, you know. All you hear is murders, rapes, car accidents. So if anything goes on, I hear it down at the bar—word of mouth, you know."

The big talk in the summer of 1996 was a decision by U.S. Forest Service officials to require access permits to use the lake. There was a public meeting, which she didn't attend, and the residents overwhelmingly disapproved of the plan.

But the U.S. Forest Service adopted the plan anyway.

"They had a town meeting and everybody up here voted no, but they'd already passed it. It was a done deal."

Although Beth didn't get involved in the effort to stop the access fees, she says she would have if someone had asked her.

She isn't active in community affairs but knows most of her neighbors. During Easter weekend in 1996, she dressed as the Easter Bunny for the town's big parade and was featured on the local news that night in her bunny suit.

She follows national politics generally but doesn't listen too closely because the issues don't engage her. But local politicians don't grab her attention either.

The last president she liked was John Kennedy; she was a teenager then. She didn't vote in 1996 because she thought she was registered in Redding but had moved to Lakehead. On second thought, she says, she probably was registered in Lakehead and didn't care enough to check.

If she had voted, it would have been the first presidential election in which she had cast a ballot.

"I save my input when I hear people talking about politics. They ask, 'Did you vote?' I say no, I don't vote. They say, 'Then you don't have anything to say.' I say, 'Fine, then. Talk to yourself.' But that's their attitude, just because I don't vote."

Beth says she doesn't vote because she generally doesn't learn enough about those running for office to make a decision.

"To be honest, I don't know what they say."

But the 1996 race between President Clinton and Bob Dole was an exception: "That time I wouldn't have picked either," she says. "I did know enough that I didn't like."

She particularly didn't like First Lady Hillary Rodham Clinton. She says Mrs. Clinton's ideas have too much influence in the White House; she knows about Mrs. Clinton mainly from her neighbors and discussions at the bar.

She also says she doesn't vote because she has less at stake in elections now than when her children were in school, although she didn't vote then either.

She can't think of many public issues that she has followed or that would affect her, although she is eligible for disability pay and has been on welfare in the past. There are two exceptions to her disinterest: bans on smoking and welfare.

Laws prohibiting smoking in the workplace are discriminatory, in her opinion. But she feels powerless to do anything about her opposition to the new bans.

"So I smoke down at one end of the bar while everybody else sits there with their big old cigars and stuff. And they want to write a ticket on me. . . . My boss said, 'We've had complaints about your smoking behind the bar.' "

She says she would like to protest to her boss, but she's afraid he might fire her.

"And I know I'm right . . . but I can't even stand up for myself and feel right by doing it," she says. "So I just eat crow, and that's not a good way to live."

Like the smoking bans, welfare laws also are discriminatory—against the working poor, she believes.

When she was between marriages, she received welfare payments to help provide food and shelter for her kids, but she says she only used the federal money as a temporary crutch until she could get settled again and get a job.

Today's welfare recipients, she says, are able to get payments for food stamps and their children while still earning some money, sometimes putting them financially ahead of people like her.

She mentions a woman she knows who works and receives welfare payments for her five kids. The woman's annual income, in Beth's estimate, is about $10,000.

"It doesn't make sense to me. They're taking all my taxes, and I made less than what she did. So there she was sitting in the bar trying to say, 'Wonder where to take my kids on vacation.' I haven't been on a vacation in I don't know how many years so that upsets me." Beth's annual income is about $7,000; if the Basshole didn't rely so heavily on tourists, she could make more, she says, but the seasonal nature of the business means her hours are cut back when the tourists are gone.

Beth hadn't heard much about the welfare reform law enacted in 1996 that sets limits on how long recipients are eligible for welfare payments but liked the idea. Welfare should not be a permanent means of support, she says.

"See, I've been on it, but I needed it. Because if you're having a baby, or I had a hysterectomy, otherwise I was out there working supporting my kids."

Working hard and raising her kids are the two constants in Beth's life.

In her current job, she works 5 nights a week. It's hard work, but she enjoys talking to people and knows she is good at mixing drinks. She stopped waitressing several years ago because carrying dishes was too painful due to her arthritis.

"Now it's getting hard and harder to work behind the bar every year, especially when we're busy. I'm older, and it's hard on me.

"I go home sometimes at night and just cry because I hurt so bad, because I do have arthritis real bad and . . . I've got chronic bronchitis. Even if I got disabled, I still wouldn't be able to afford to live."

She doesn't feel secure in her job either.

"It's like, gee, they don't want to hire no 51-year-old bartenders, you know. They want the young ones, and all I know is this business."

She says she is less secure than when she was younger, even though she was raising four kids.

"I feel that I'm worse off now than what I was when I was raising my kids because I'm not physically and mentally like I used to be."

What has kept her going, she says, are her kids—three girls and a boy, now grown. All but one live in the area.

She had her first daughter, Cheryl, in 1961 when she was 15. Her parents had divorced, and she was living with her mother in Farmington, New Mexico. After she had the baby, she moved to San Diego to live with her mother. She met her first husband, a Marine, there and got pregnant again.

"He deserted the Marines and me."

She joined her mother, who was in Englewood, California, by then and delivered her second daughter, Michele, in 1964.

She returned to Mt. Shasta to work later that year and subsequently married her second husband, with whom she had her third daughter, Deborah, in 1966.

She got her second divorce 4 years later. "I had terrible luck in men. But he was the only one that ever paid child support."

She moved to Alaska with her boyfriend and had a son with him, Shawn, but moved back to Mt. Shasta after the boyfriend had an affair with another woman.

"I got on welfare and picked up the pieces, lived over a little grocery store in an empty apartment. I sold a pair of my wedding rings to get me a car for 150 bucks. I just managed."

She returned to Alaska and married her third husband but says he was bad for her daughters so she left him. She returned to Mt. Shasta.

About that time, she was put on disability because of her arthritis and an old knee injury that were making waitressing too difficult. During that period, she learned how to groom poodles in a trade school paid for by the government but didn't get her license because her son became seriously ill and she had to quit.

Then she met her fourth husband. That marriage also was short-lived, she says matter-of-factly.

In 1985, she married her final husband and divorced him in 1990.

In her five marriages, she says, she experienced everything from living with an alcoholic to worrying about her daughters' safety.

"My kids were the only thing that kept me going" through all the marriages, she says.

She says her daughters are regular voters and remembers her mother also voted sometimes. But the electoral process passed Beth by.

The daughters all are settled in their communities, and the oldest is particularly active in her children's schools. "Their lifestyles are a whole lot different than mine was," she says as an explanation for why they became voters.

Beth's not sure whether her son votes but thinks he may be an occasional voter. "He's more like me. We don't talk about it much."

She is proud that her daughters all graduated from high school, remembering her disappointment that she had to quit school.

And she carries with her, like any doting grandmother, photos of her six grandchildren. She had hoped her children would remain close to her, she says, and they have.

Her dream now is to travel, but she quickly adds that it won't happen. If she could, she would buy a trailer and roam around the country, exploring.

"If I had the chance to go anywhere, I would."

But her more realistic goal is to keep working and keep her health. Her biggest fear is not being able to take care of herself.

So she keeps working nights at the Basshole, making Manhattans and pouring shots. And listening to the talk.

"After 35 years in the business, I've heard it all."

But nothing she has heard will move her to the polls come Election Day.

"I try to make a difference every day. When I wait on people, I try to help them enjoy themselves. Life's too hard as it is."

———— ◄o► ————

Janet Shepherd

Runaway Mother Who's Seen All She's Gonna See

Janet Shepherd's life is not a pretty picture. Nor is the view of Billy D's bar and the Speedy car wash and laundry from her trailer home set back from Highway 303 in Brunswick, Georgia. No matter. For her, the view is blurry anyway. The cataract surgery she had in 1990, thanks to full veteran's benefits she receives for serving in the Air Force during the Korean War, has left her with frequent floaters. The other eye is worse, needing surgery she is afraid to undergo. She and Jim, the man she lives with, drink at the bar two or three times a week, a 12-pack each, a habit that doubles as their meal on those days. Shepherd, who is 62 years old, has been drinking regularly since 1970, just after walking out on her four children and moving from Massachusetts to Southern California.

Shepherd recalls the day vividly. It was noon when she left Sudbury, Massachusetts, for Long Beach, California, to move in with a male friend. "My husband had beaten me once, and I didn't want it to happen again," she says. She said good-bye to her children and told them to wait until the next day to tell their father. She left behind two daughters, ages 17 and 16, and two sons, ages 14 and 11, and didn't look back, except to talk with 16-year-old Maria when the girl would call her collect once a month. At 36 years old, Shepherd already had been married three times, helped raise 11 foster children, adopted one of them, and had been told she would die of cervical cancer. She calls herself "a runaway mother" with the same matter-of-fact detachment as she reports an IQ of 140.

Shepherd enlisted in the U.S. Air Force at the age of 18. American troops were fighting in Korea. She wanted out of her small town of Shelburne Falls, located in the Berkshire Mountains in the northwest corner of Massachusetts, near where she was born and raised. She and her mother didn't get along—never had since birth, when she was supposed to have been a boy. Her father committed suicide on July 4, 1936, when she was 2 years old. "Every day when it rained, my mom would get in a bad mood and talk about him," she recalls.

Shepherd dropped out of high school after her sophomore year. When she entered the military, Shepherd was told she had to have a high school diploma or the equivalent. She took an equivalency test and was told that her score was the highest in the state. "So I'm not stupid, and back then, I could learn a lot, but no one ever encouraged me to learn," Shepherd says. "I have nothing against teachers. I think teachers should know children. If you're gonna teach those children, you should know them."

As with other enlistees, Shepherd moved around in the military. She served in Texas, Colorado, and New York during the Korean War. When she became pregnant, she was told she would have to give up the baby for adoption or leave the service. She chose to leave the service. She had served exactly 9 months and 26 days. She married an airman and went back to Massachusetts when her husband was transferred to a base in Westover.

By 1956, Shepherd had two children, whom she was raising herself while her husband was stationed in England. The Korean War was over. She was 22 years old and duty-bound, she felt, to vote. She voted for Dwight Eisenhower. "He was military and, coming out of the Korean War, I thought we needed someone military," recalls Shepherd.

She voted in the next presidential election, this time for Kennedy. Since 1960, she has voted for only one other presidential candidate: Ronald Reagan. Instinctively, she says that "they have nothing in common really." When she voted, she muses, she thought the candidates would do some good. "It was worth voting for them," she says as she postulates that things have changed.

"Kennedy, he was young and I thought he was gonna move the country, which I think he did. There wasn't a thing Kennedy said that I didn't believe. I don't remember Kennedy saying anything bad about his opponent."

She voted for Ronald Reagan in 1980 because she thought he had been a good governor of California, where she had lived. She felt he would be good for the country but doesn't know if he was.

"Lately it seems like all you hear is this mudslinging. Every year it seems to get worse," she says. "Almost everything I've seen on television, their political ads, are always what somebody did wrong."

She cites the 1996 campaign. She recalls ads in which President Clinton was portraying Bob Dole, the Republican challenger, as voting against education. Then Shepherd recalls Dole's ads in which he countered that he supported education, that he merely wanted to get big government out of education. She concludes that Clinton was being dishonest, attempting to portray Dole as a liar.

Shepherd wouldn't have voted for Clinton. She wouldn't have voted for Dole either. She preferred Ross Perot. But she doesn't vote and isn't registered to vote.

"To me now, it's just not worth voting. I don't feel that my vote's gonna do much good. I don't even know where to go to register to vote," Shepherd says, despite having lived in the same area of Brunswick since 1989.

Shepherd spends most of her time in her trailer home. She was fired from the last job she had at Goodwill, she says, because she knew more than her boss. The job before that, at Woolworth, ended when the store closed. The most money she has made in her life was $9,000 a year, back in 1974, when she assembled and tested parts for an electronics company. In the 1960s, when she was out of work and raising foster children, two at a time, to help get by, she received $16 a week for each child. Now she gets out during the day mostly "to mess with my garden and rabbits." She and Jim breed rabbits to supplement their Social Security checks. They butcher the rabbits at home and get $7 for each of them. The $150 a year the rabbits bring in helps pay for food. She has a credit card that carries an ongoing balance of about $8,000, on which she pays interest of more than $100 a month.

Most of the day she reads, does crossword puzzles, watches television, and smokes Private Stock menthols. She favors novels by Stephen King and Dean Koontz, though she doesn't have the money to buy them and doesn't get out enough to find them in the resale bins. She spends about 4 hours a day working the crossword puzzles. She subscribes to Dell and gets four different puzzle books. The ones in the newspapers are too easy for Shepherd, except for the ones in *The New York Times.* She and Jim don't subscribe to newspapers or read them. The only newspapers around the house are for the animals, rabbits, and one guinea pig. She reads the *Reader's Digest* as well as *Modern Maturity* magazine and the *AARP Bulletin,* both of which she gets as a member of the American Association of Retired Persons. On television, they'll watch police shows, soap operas, and an occasional comedy. She watches news programs only during the day when Jim is out doing handyman work. Jim doesn't like the news, and they don't talk much about the news of the day. They talk about hunting, fishing, and working.

Shepherd knows she has lost touch with the world around her. She also has lost track of three of her four children, all except for Mark, the second oldest. She sees herself as opinionated and as likely to be off-base as accurate. Her self-esteem fluctuates. "I'm an all-around, know-pretty-much-of-everything, move-about, and unsure-of-herself" person, Shepherd says.

She picks up information in image clusters that make her believe that politics have gotten negative and ugly. She recalls political ads from the 1996 U.S. Senate race in Georgia. One candidate was criticizing the other for letting a murderer go free. The target of the negative ads was the secretary of state, she remembers, who "had had his legs and arms blown off in Korea or Vietnam." She was pulling for the secretary of state to win. Max Cleland, the Democratic secretary of state who lost both legs and an arm in Vietnam, narrowly defeated Republican businessman Guy Millner in that election, though Shepherd cannot remember either of their names, which political parties they represented, who had won, or who either of her senators is.

She recognizes Newt Gingrich's name, though she can't pinpoint what post he holds. "Gingrich, isn't he Georgia? Yeah, I know about him," she recollects. "All he's done is make mistakes so far, I guess. I know he got his hands slapped. I don't know what it is he had done; I didn't get that part. Probably saw it on an ad for the news." She favored Perot in the 1996 presidential election because of an article by him that she read in the *AARP Bulletin.*

She is not as trusting of the news as she once was. Her confidence was shaken when she found out that the man mentioned on news reports as connected to the bombing at the 1996 Olympics in Atlanta was never arrested. What network anchor Tom Brokaw had said on the nightly news proved not to be true, according to an article Shepherd read in the *Reader's Digest.*

Beyond what she reads and views on television, there is not much in Shepherd's world. Social interaction starts and stops with the patrons at the bar across the road. She frequents the bar with Jim two or three times a week. They walk over in the middle of the afternoon and stay until 7 or 8 p.m., two six-packs later. On those days, they drink dinner, sometimes have an ice cream to go with it, and are in bed and asleep within minutes of leaving the bar.

Shepherd sits at the bar for hours smoking, along with the others who have joined her. Sometimes she plays the Cherry Master slot machine, sometimes pool, but mostly she sits. The television runs continually. The talk is of fishing, hunting, and women. "They're all poor people in the bar," James, the bartender, says with fraternal pride. He jokes that "politics is not allowed in here."

Politics seep into the occasional conversation, nonetheless. There's talk of Medicare being put in the hands of private insurance companies. Talk of people cheating the government and of the government doing nothing. Shepherd mentions a story she read in the *Reader's Digest* about a dentist who submitted $80,000 in fake bills.

Shepherd's indifference to politics mixes well with the bartender's disdain for it. He's 39 years old, never voted, and never met a politician. None has ever walked into the bar. "I ain't never met a candidate that I thought was worth voting for. I think they're all shysters and crooks," he says as Shepherd nods. "They're full of promises they don't keep. Ninety-five percent of them are born with a silver spoon in their mouth. They don't know what it's like to work for a living. They pass laws according to their way of life, not according to my way of life."

Shepherd knows a half-dozen neighbors in her trailer park but only in passing. One from whom she borrowed tools, another family whom she met when she sold Avon products a few years back. She has lived in the trailer home since 1991 when she had a falling out over money with Maria, the daughter with whom she kept in touch after walking out on her children in 1970.

Shepherd has kept her distance from the people she has worked with at the dozens of jobs she has had in her life. "I've never tried to associate with people at work. I don't know," Shepherd says, "I think it's because I didn't want people that I work with close to me."

It is ironic, she notes, that for someone who gets around so little now, she marks her life as one in which she has moved about, during her stint in the military and then after, from Massachusetts to California to Arizona to Georgia. She has no prized possessions, she says, because nothing has made it through her many moves. "In a lot of ways, it seems like I've seen and heard just about everything there is to see and hear. But I know I've missed a lot in life. I've missed out on close relationships," Shepherd says.

She has only a few photographs of herself, her family, or the men to whom she's been married. She doesn't like to look at them. They are a reminder not only of her dispirited life but of the legacy she has passed on to her children. One, to whom she has hasn't talked since he was 15, was in and out of jail by then. She heard he went on to a logging job in Oregon.

Mark is Shepherd's only child who wasn't a high school dropout. He's the only one Shepherd can imagine ever voting or participating in political affairs. He actively campaigned for a candidate when he lived in Massachusetts, and she recalls him telling her he wants to get into politics. She wants him to be careful. She believes her past will be held against him. "So many times, when you hear about politics, they always dig into what your parents have done," Shepherd says. "I don't have the clothes or anything to be at his rallies. If he ever runs for president, I'd be something he'd want to hide."

———— ◄o► ————

Karen Pelling

Distracted by Darts

Karen Pelling recalls that she cringed when her 8-year-old daughter brought up the subject of voting in a mock election at the girl's grade school before the 1996 presidential elections. Pelling re-creates their conversation:

"Mommy, who are you gonna vote for?"

"Neither. I don't like any of 'em. All politicians are the same. They tell you what you wanna hear, then do their own thing."

Pelling cringed because she wasn't planning to vote, she wasn't registered, and, at 30 years old, she had never voted or registered to vote. Moreover, she didn't know much about the candidates who were running. She knew President Bill Clinton was running. She didn't know what political party he was in. And she couldn't remember that Clinton was running against George Bush and Ross Perot.

"Now what am I gonna tell her?" she thought as the conversation lagged.

Pelling told her daughter to ask her grandmother the question.

Pelling has lived in Winter Park, a suburb of Orlando, Florida, most of her life. She now lives with her husband and three children a few blocks from where her parents still live. She doesn't know the names of the governor of Florida, of its senators or other representatives, or of the mayor of Winter Park or Orlando, though she's sure Orlando's mayor is a woman, which Glenda Hood is.

Pelling's mother and father vote and did when Pelling was a child. Pelling and her husband don't and never have. She thinks her parents don't have a political affiliation and vote "for the person." Much has changed, Pelling observes, since she was a child, growing up in the same Winter Park community where she now raises her children.

"When I was growing up, everybody knew each other. We would play ball at a big park called Rock Springs," Pelling says. "The whole street would get together and do things together, with the kids. Now we don't even know our neighbors." The Pellings live in a subdivision off Horatio, one of the main streets cutting through Winter Park. A security system sign is prominently displayed next to a small palm tree in front of the house. They have an inflatable swimming pool in the backyard next to an orange tree and an abandoned, rusted-out playground set.

Pelling says hello to the people who live on one side of her house, but she doesn't know their names. She doesn't interact at all with the people on the other side. "Both sides are rentals, so we don't know them," she says. "People come and go. Sometimes we don't get a chance to meet them before they move out." She likes where she lives because it is near both her parents and her husband's mother. It is also just around the corner from the Red Lion Pub, where she met her husband and where they play darts three nights a week.

The pub is Pelling's village. "Everyone knows everyone," she says. She and the owners are friends. When she was off work after giving birth to her third child, she worked there for tips only. "There are enough people in the bar to build a house," she says, as she looks around the pub at all the familiar faces. The pub is filled with laborers and construction workers. One man is a plumber, another an electrician, a third a carpenter. One patron does tile work, another does masonry. Pelling's husband, Tom, does glasswork. She calls the Red Lion "a family pub," even though people seldom bring their children there. She is there every Tuesday night from 8 p.m. until almost midnight; her husband is there for Thursday night league play. They go there together most Friday and Saturday nights while their parents baby-sit the kids. She also practices darts at home and plays for fun, with friends and her children, in the rec room they have furnished with a dartboard, sports paraphernalia, and a bar.

Pelling is no longer on the circuit. For 2 years, she and Tom played on the same league team, representing the pub and touring once a week on Monday or Wednesday nights. But it became more time-consuming than she could manage. Pelling began throwing darts when she and Tom started dating and had only been playing for 3 months when she joined the team. She throws left-handed.

When she plays at the Red Lion, she has to shut out the visual distractions all around her. The furnishings, the posters, and the dart paraphernalia are all advertisements. The pub is an equal opportunity promoter. The overhead light showcases Bud Light. Framed on the wall are ads for Coors Light, Foster's Lager, O'Doul's, Elephant Red, Michelob PGA Tour, and Busch Great Talks of NASCAR Daytona. Hovering over the pool table is a horizontal Bud bottle. Two dartboards are set on a red backdrop promoting Budweiser; the other two are set on a blue backdrop promoting Bud Light. The chalkboards next to them that record the scores are sponsored by Miller. Pelling's best game ever is a "ton-44." A ton is 100 points. To get 144 points in three throws, Pelling threw two triple 20s and a double 12, only 26 points less than a perfect score.

Most of Pelling's childhood friends have moved away. She keeps in touch with only one, the one who stayed in Winter Park. Pelling moved away once herself. She lived in Plattsburgh, New York, while her first husband was in the Air Force. She met him when he vacationed in Winter Park to scuba dive. She followed him to New York, and within 2 weeks they married, in part because they had to be married to live together on the base. When they divorced, Pelling returned to Winter Park to be near her parents.

Pelling holds some strong views on issues but not about government. She describes herself as "not very well informed" and thinks she should read the newspapers or watch television news more than she does. When asked to choose, she says she's more of a political liberal than a conservative but doesn't know why.

The first policy issue that comes to her mind is welfare. "People are on it too long and have kids to stay on it," Pelling observes. "I've seen people walk into the welfare office, loaded down in gold, yet can't afford to feed their kids." She recalls that scene from 1992 when she was on public assistance, with her first two children, after divorcing her first husband. She assumes that little has been done about welfare since then because she remembers from the 1996 presidential election campaign that candidates were still promising to do something about the welfare problem, though she is unaware that Clinton signed the welfare reform law 3 months before the election.

The problems Pelling considers most important are crime and violence. She worries about it as a parent, although she considers her neighborhood safe. Winter Park has had a few break-ins and a few murders, she notes. "Ten-year-olds are taking guns and knives to school," she says, though not yet at her children's school. "We had a problem a few months ago. A guy was trying to get kids into his car," she recounts. She was informed about it by a warning to parents that was sent home from school with her children.

She says she doesn't have time, now that she works again full-time, to read the daily newspaper or watch television news much. The family subscribes to the *Orlando Sentinel*. Her husband complains that it's a bad paper, but he reads it for the sports. Pelling leafs through it mostly for coupons but also for sales, Ann Landers, medical advice columns, pet columns, and mortgage rates to see if it is worth refinancing their home. She will catch the headlines—for instance, a story that stuck with her about an alligator that was discovered in Ashby Lake, not too far from their home. The headline read, "Alligators seldom prey on humans; There have been 225 attacks in Florida since 1948, making them rarer than lightning strikes or shark attacks."

Pelling says her concerns and her dreams are mostly financial. She dreams of winning the lottery and retiring. She and her husband buy 2 dollars' worth of lottery tickets every week. They won $5.50 one time. She regrets not having gone to college directly after high school. In high school, she just hung out, she recalls, at the roller skating rink, at football games, at the movie theater. She was bored, so she took a year off before considering college. Then she put it off and kept putting it off until 8 years later. After having two children and getting divorced, she enrolled at Orlando College. She made the dean's list her first two semesters, then got bored again, and, after 2 years, dropped out. She doesn't know if she will go back to complete her degree, although she thinks it may be the only way to get much beyond her current job as a service coordinator for a vehicle fleet company.

With Pelling and her husband both working, they are "doing okay." Her husband earns $11 an hour, and she earns $7 an hour, with opportunities to pull in overtime pay. She wants to "not have it as rough financially," Pelling says, and "to not have to worry about what to do in an emergency." She and her husband have tried to consolidate their bills: home mortgage, credit cards, and student loans. She works overtime to help pay off their obligations. Health coverage worries her. She regards health care costs as "outrageous." As it is, they have a $2,000 outstanding hospital bill from the delivery of her third child, and they cannot get to the bottom of why their insurance hasn't covered it. She says it's hard to find an English-speaking doctor and often cannot understand the doctors her family has seen.

Pelling knows there is a connection between her quality of life and the political system, but it is too remote for her. "Everything the government is trying to do," she observes, "the rich get richer." She cites taxes. "The rich don't have to pay as much. They have tax breaks here and there." Something should be done about mothers with children, she says, to make it easier for them to work and still afford child care. Of the Pellings' $720 gross income each week, $105 goes to pay for day care.

Elected officials don't care about people like her, she says. "We don't have the money, so why should they care about what we think?" she asks. None of the presidential candidates she remembers since she has been able to vote in 1984 have cared. Not Jimmy Carter, not Ronald Reagan, not Perot, not Clinton. And no names of any Florida or local politicians come to mind. "They all promise you stuff for the election, then when elected, don't seem to do any-thing," Pelling says. For instance, she says Clinton has that look about him— the look of someone who admits he smoked marijuana but claims he didn't inhale—that you can't trust. "Perot didn't have that look," Pelling continues, "but he wasn't presidential material. He didn't know enough about politics."

Pelling erects a series of barriers between herself and the polling place. She hasn't liked any of the candidates. They don't care about people like her. She hasn't been sufficiently interested in public affairs to be informed. "If I was going to vote, I'd register," Pelling says, "but if I'm registered, all I'd get is jury duty." If she found a candidate who is honest, that might get her to vote, she thinks.

She is at her most committed to vote when she thinks about the future and about her children. "I don't want the future to get worse for my kids," she says, as she recalls the 1993 Sylvester Stallone film, *Demolition Man,* which depicts a world in the year 2036 in which "half the people are underground because they don't like government." Pelling doesn't discuss public affairs much with her children yet: She says they still are too young to understand. Whenever politics comes up in family discussions, she says, she takes the kids outside to play.

She wants to change. "I will have to follow more if I want to talk to them about it," Pelling realizes. "I won't be able to do that overnight, but I will be able to do it."

——— ◄○► ———

Tracy Rowley

Baited, Switched, and Out

The word that comes to Tracy Rowley's mind when she thinks about voting is *nonsense*. She tells that to her husband, Robert, who is a committed voter and who tries to convince her that she also should be one. He appeals to her interest in education and in school matters that affect their children. He tells her that she does make a difference. But Rowley is fed up and equally committed to her position. "Things have changed, and I've decided not to vote ever again," she says.

She voted once. In 1984, when she turned 18, she and a girlfriend registered to vote while they were shopping in a mall in Clackamas, Oregon, near Portland. Rowley followed through and voted, she says, "out of curiosity about what to do." She voted to reelect Ronald Reagan for president. She voted because her parents voted. She voted for Reagan because Reagan was a Republican, and she voted Republican because her parents voted Republican. She didn't know then what being a Republican entailed. Today, she feels that there's no difference between the parties and that politics has become a game of bait and switch.

"Times were different," Rowley says. "Things did happen, but as time has gone by, and our government has gotten much, much bigger, it just seems totally different to me."

"When they [her parents] voted, the laws stayed in effect. Now, as times are different, we vote for something, and someone else does something to counter-act it," says Rowley, prepared to cite examples.

"Every time we vote on something and it gets passed, they find something else to turn it around. Here in Oregon, we voted on the lottery and it was supposed to go to the [public] schools, and it's not going to the schools." Rowley's convictions were reinforced by news reports shortly after the November 1996 elections of attempts to use $250 million in Oregon state lottery funding to pay tuition, fees, and books for college students. She sees it as a cynical way to cheat elementary and secondary school children who need education most. She has two sons, 7-year-old A. J., who is in public school, and 5-year-old Matthew, who is about to transfer into public school from a church-based program that stops after kindergarten. She is worried enough that gang problems at the school will compromise her children's education, she says, without having to worry that politicians will make matters worse by going back on their word and diverting needed funds.

Rowley cites another example. "They just passed a law about a cigarette tax. The cigarette tax went up . . . and that money is supposed to go to our Oregon health plan," Rowley says. "I just heard the other day on the news that they're going to try to get another bill to put it somewhere else, and that upset me." The cigarette tax hike of 30 cents a pack was approved by voters as Measure 44 in a referendum folded into the November 1996 election. Three months later, leadership in the Oregon legislature was proposing that the state budget reduce funding for the health plan to offset much of the money the plan would be getting from the cigarette tax. Rowley hadn't voted in the 1996 election and felt that her most dire suspicions were confirmed. She can't trust government, and voting means nothing.

"Our government's too big. Congress and the legislature, it's way overdone," Rowley says. "I don't think we need that many people to run our country."

Rowley grew up in Portland and has lived her entire life in Oregon. She and her husband moved to Troutdale, a farming community outside Portland, to get away from the traffic of the city when they had their first child. Her parents are only a 15-minute drive away.

"Society is in a worse place than when I grew up," Rowley laments. She remembers as a child playing hide-and-seek, even after dark. "I became a mother to have children, to bring them up in a society that I grew up in. When I grew up, things were different. They weren't as rough. We didn't have the gang violence. We didn't have the drugs. It was a much safer place to be. I'm scared for my children. I'm even scared for them to go to school every day."

She holds the political system responsible. "Nothing seems to happen," Rowley says. Rowley's sister wrote a letter to the PTA to complain that students are excused from their public school classes at noon on Wednesdays so that the teachers can attend workshops. Nothing happened. The teachers went on strike in Sandy, a nearby community, but were ordered to return to work because the strike was ruled to be illegal. "Our teachers are very unhappy. They do not get what they need to educate," Rowley says. "Politically-wise, our government needs to change a little to have more emphasis on education."

Rowley senses that public officials are attending more to education, slowly, but it's not enough. "[President Bill] Clinton said, 'Every kid should go to college,'" she recalls. "That's just wonderful, but we need to get them through grade school and high school first before we can send them to college." She respects Clinton. "He set out to change our country, but I think a lot of people don't understand he's got these goals—the deficit, education," she says, "but our government doesn't work that way." She has come to believe strongly that the system, the politics of it, keeps things from improving. She would talk with a candidate who made education a priority, she says, but she wouldn't vote. She's protesting the stalemate that keeps things from getting better.

Rowley doesn't have much use for the politicians who represent her. She doesn't know much about Oregon's two freshmen senators, Republican Gordon Smith and Democrat Ron Wyden, but she mentions Oregon Governor John Kitzhaber, Portland Mayor Vera Katz, and former U.S. Senators Mark Hatfield, who retired in 1996 after 30 years, and Bob Packwood, who resigned in 1995 amid allegations that he made unwanted sexual advances to more than a dozen women and altered his personal diaries to obstruct an ethics investigation. Rowley had a chance to express her opinion of Packwood on KTVZ-TV's news program in Portland.

"I was in downtown Portland and they asked me what I thought about the letters that he kept, and I said I don't care what he does in his private life, but I said it was very disgraceful of him that he wrote down this in his memoirs about what he did," Rowley recounts. "I think it's very shameful to our state to have someone like that—that we would elect someone who was like that—who is very chauvinistic and has no respect for women." Rowley watched the television news that night, as she often does, and discovered that the station had fouled up. "They put the wrong name up there. They put my girlfriend's name up and my picture."

Rowley recognizes that she could be more informed about public affairs than she is, but it is important to her to at least "know the status of our country." In addition to local television news at 11 p.m., she watches CNN and a number of the network newsmagazine programs. She says she gets most of her news from the magazine shows. As she drives to and from work, she will catch some news on the soft rock station she listens to. But she has stopped reading the newspaper. "I used to read it every day," she says, but she stopped when she and her husband discontinued their home subscription a few months back.

She picks up news from people at work. They talk politics at Ditch Witch of Oregon, the highway equipment dealership where she is an administrative assistant. She participates in discussions about property taxes and Ballot Measure 5, a people's initiative to limit property taxes that Oregon voters approved in 1990 but that forced officials to look for alternative ways of funding education and other programs. It is another example to Rowley of the government baiting and switching. The measure was "supposed to lower people's property taxes and *keep* them lowered," she says, "but then the state decided they would reassess everybody's homes, so the property taxes went up and made people very unhappy."

Rowley considers herself ambitious. She plans to go back to school in accounting. "That will happen," she pledges. She hopes to become a certified public accountant. "Maybe that'll happen," she says, less sure that she can control events so completely. She and her husband are working toward owning a home and are preparing to take in a teenage foster daughter whom Rowley befriended when the girl lived in their apartment complex. Rowley considers King's Garden, the lower-income housing development where her family rents an apartment, unsafe, dirty, and "a depressing place to live" that has gone downhill since they moved there during a period when her husband was unemployed. He has been steadily employed for a number of years, and their combined income of $40,000, she resolves, will make it possible for them to move into a nicer, safer place, even if not yet a home they own. She is putting off hip replacement surgery that would alleviate the arthritic pain she suffers on her left side until her children are both in public school.

Rowley cares intensely about her children's education, in part because she is critical of the education she got in public school in Portland and during the one year she attended community college. She remembers favorably, though, a course she took in her sophomore year in high school on how the government works. She liked it and thought she learned something, but she believes that the government she learned about in high school is not the government of today.

"Times have changed so much that we have a Republican and a Democrat for senators," she says, while admitting that she doesn't know what either party stands for. Oregon got its first Democratic senator in 34 years when Ron Wyden won a special election in January 1996 to fill the seat vacated when Republican Bob Packwood resigned. Republicans Packwood and Mark Hatfield had represented Oregon in the Senate since 1968, 1 year after Rowley was born. "There's no need for that. I don't see why there's a Republican and a Democrat so we can butt heads on different things that we're trying to make equal no matter what," Rowley says, unaware that after the 1996 election, 19 of the nation's 50 states had split Senate delegations of one Democrat and one Republican. "Our main goal is we're one country and we should strive for the same things, and we're not."

Rowley expects that she and her husband will continue to butt heads on whether to vote. Her husband pushes Rowley's education agenda. They joke about it and argue. "My husband says, 'You don't have to vote on anything else. Just vote on the education stuff.' And I probably should," Rowley says. But she won't give. She has no trouble explaining her position to their children. "I would say that was my point of view. 'You need to make your own decisions in life. This is your own choice. I will not force you to [not vote],' " Rowley says she will tell her children when they ask. "Hopefully, they'd respect my point of view, and I'd respect them if they decided to vote."

———— ◄◦► ————

Paula Ryan

She Counts on Herself and Her Neighbors,
Not Washington

On Election Day 1996, Paula Ryan went to her job at dawn as a loan closer for a mortgage company in Phoenix and returned home in late afternoon to spend the evening talking to neighbors and a reporter who was interviewing her for a story on nonvoters.

After the story by Medill News Service reporter John Shea was published in about 20 papers across the country, Ryan took a copy to her office to show coworkers.

"There were 10 people I let go ahead and read it. Nine did not vote. One did."

It was unusual for Ryan to talk about politics with coworkers. She doesn't normally discuss politics much with people other than family members because she doesn't think what happens in Washington has much to do with helping her or her family in Phoenix.

As Ryan, a slim woman with flowing brown hair pulled up into a ponytail and dressed casually in shorts and a sleeveless shirt to suit the Arizona heat, sits on her patio and sips coffee, she talks with unabashed motherly pride about her daughters, Chasidy and Karine, with teasing affection about her husband, Jim, and with satisfaction about her home and neighborhood.

It's only when the talk turns to politics and the role of the federal government that Ryan's tone becomes harsh and critical.

She believes that elected officials don't care what she thinks and that they do what they want regardless of what citizens, even voters, tell them.

"If I was ever invited to go to a social event, a dinner [in Washington], I would not fit in because they have an attitude that they are better. Financially, they are better, but are they happy? . . . They're too busy out there trying to lie and cheat and steal."

Government, to her, is Big Brother, going its way outside the electoral process and making decisions regardless of citizens' opinions.

At age 42, she's voted in a presidential election only once: In 1972, she voted for Richard Nixon in the first election after she turned 18. In 1996, she considered registering so she could vote for the Republican ticket because of vice presidential nominee Jack Kemp, whose work while head of the Department of Housing and Urban Development from 1989 to 1992 she admired, particularly in facilitating home ownership. But she missed the registration deadline.

However, even if she had been registered, her lack of faith in the power of her vote to influence the political process makes her appearance at a polling place on Election Day unlikely.

"If I could see a change, then possibly. But there are no changes made, and that's just like [the 1996] election. Here we go again," she says, mimicking politicians: " 'We're going to decrease your taxes.' I'm sorry, I can't figure out if you decrease taxes and we owe X amount of dollars, where's all the money coming from that's going to pay that deficit? Stop lying to us and telling us you're going to decrease [taxes] when we all know down deep that it's going to be another fight [in Congress].

"They already got 38% of our money, and they're going to continue on with it."

Ryan also disapproves of the way votes are counted in presidential elections—the use of the electoral college, which allots all of a state's electoral votes to the candidate who wins the state and determines the next president to be the candidate with the most electoral votes.

"You should take one day out of the year and you tell everybody, registered or not, this is the law we want to vote on. Go to your precinct and vote, and then we'll do the 'people count' vote. And I bet they'd be real surprised as to the answers. I think you should not have to register. All you should have to do is prove you're a U.S. citizen. . . . I think the reason behind registering is for the government to keep track of us and control us altogether."

She believes those in power will never agree to a popular vote for president because "they don't want that control taken out of their own hands. I am so convinced in my own mind that they already know who the next president's going to be and it's already set and it's already decided. They've already got the wheels in motion."

The idea of government as Big Brother comes through strongly when Ryan talks about the Oklahoma City bombing.

She believes the men convicted of the crime, Timothy McVeigh and Terry Nichols, were guilty, "but there's an underlying current. What was going on during that time was Whitewater. They were going after the Clintons hot and heavy. Where were their records kept? Their records were kept in that building, up there in the FBI quarters."

National leaders should be providing role models for the country, she says, but too many don't measure up, particularly because they often fail to accept blame when they make mistakes.

In 1996, Arizona Governor Fife Symington was investigated on charges of lying to a federal court about his finances and trying to extort concessions from a lender in 1991 related to government leases. He was convicted of seven felony charges in 1997. "He was trying to figure out what is the best way to fill out his paperwork to get my money," says Ryan. "Well, he figured it out . . . and the deal went belly up and he still stands back and acts nice and innocent."

She says she knows as a mother that she has to be responsible for her actions, good and bad, to be a good role model for her two daughters.

Her first daughter, Chasidy, was born when Ryan was 18 and still in high school in Phoenix, where she's lived most of her life.

She was 7 months pregnant when she graduated and credits supportive teachers for helping her get her diploma. They even gave her a baby shower.

"I did not marry her father, not because I didn't like him or anything. I just felt one responsibility was enough to handle at a young age."

She had been working at a title company since she was 16 and, after Chasidy was born, went to work there full-time. She got an apartment, and her mother helped care for Chasidy, now 24 and a newlywed, while Ryan was at work.

"When I hear women that say 'I cannot do it,' I look at them [and think], 'Uh-huh.' I've been on my own. . . . You can do it. When it comes to children, you can do it and provide for them even if it means taking from yourself to make sure they're fed, they're clothed, they have a roof over their head."

She got married in 1977 and had another daughter, Karine, who's now a 19-year-old college student. The couple moved to Hawaii to start a tavern but moved back to Phoenix after about 5 years, disillusioned with the cost of doing business in Hawaii.

Eventually, she went back in the lending business. Her marriage became too acrimonious, she says, and she divorced in late 1987.

"You kind of get lost thinking security is a material possession. I came out of that marriage thinking material possessions don't mean nothing. Happiness, true love means it all in the end. I had to sit down and do a lot of soul searching and think, 'Do I really have a marriage? We fight, we yell, we can't stand to be in the same room. I run out and I buy something and it just adds to the debt.'

"That's not happiness. Then you stop and look at your children and think you should stay in it for them, but if you really stop and look, it's really hurting them more. Because you're teaching them that's how life is.

"And if you want your daughters to have a good role model, you need to furnish it yourself first. I felt like at that age, I was teaching my daughters that all men were bad."

In July 1988, about 7 months after her divorce, she married Jim Ryan, a realtor.

"When I was 18, I had goals in mind and I was very self-sufficient. And then I got married, and somehow in the shuffle, I lost it. After I had met Jim, I took a real good look at myself and at the divorce and wanted to have my self-esteem back and to make my own decisions."

She credits her husband with helping her regain her self-esteem, forcing her to make decisions when she would try to defer to him.

Now she teases him about her restored independence, pretending to argue about restaurant choices.

She believes she has taught her daughters that self-reliance. "I've taught them, 'Don't be fake, don't be phony, but don't be hurtful toward people.' And they've both taken a very realistic look at life."

Chasidy didn't much like school and skipped 45 days, but Ryan pushed her to get her diploma. Now she's a manager at the YMCA. Chasidy's husband, whom she married in September 1996, has an office job at a Phoenix construction company.

Karine was a member of the student council and a self-starter who was placed in advanced classes in school and made the honor roll every year. She's enrolled at Glendale Community College in a suburb of Phoenix.

Ryan has an oversized bulletin board in the hallway crammed with pictures of her two children, and plaques from Karine's high school accomplishments adorn the walls.

Karine is paying her own way through college by working at one, sometimes two, jobs. When Ryan tried to get federal aid to help with the $700 per semester cost, she was turned down. The same thing happened when Ryan tried to get unemployment insurance for a few months in the 1980s when she was between jobs.

And when she reaches 65, she says, she doesn't expect the Social Security system to be solvent enough to provide retirement income for her or her husband.

"I hope one day to get a savings account and then I won't be afraid of retirement. Right now, I live from paycheck to paycheck, but the way they keep increasing taxes, there's no way to do it." Ryan and her husband earn about $40,000 a year.

Her firm has a retirement savings plan, but Ryan says she can't afford to contribute to it because she's trying to help Chasidy, as a newlywed in her first home, and Karine, still living at home and going to college, meet their bills.

"Whenever we buy anything, it's when Jim gets a commission, and we pay cash for it. There's no such thing as charging in this household."

Ryan is proud that she has never had to take public assistance, saying she would rather work and do without some things than take welfare. She says it would be too embarrassing to accept a welfare check. And she has no respect for the welfare recipients who she says "go out and brag about it."

The ex-wife of her husband's son and his granddaughter came to live with the Ryans a few years ago. The former daughter-in-law, who was 26 at the time, was receiving public assistance on the condition that she stay in school, but she dropped out, Ryan says. "She prefers to live on welfare. . . . And that's why I disagree with welfare—because it lets them be lazy."

"I think the welfare system should be eliminated." She recalls that President Bill Clinton had signed a welfare reform law in 1996 that required recipients to find jobs after receiving benefits for 2 consecutive years and capped welfare payments at 5 years.

But she has no faith the law will work as intended because recipients "know exactly how to play the game. You and I would go in there with nothing because we're conscientious people and will answer all those questions honestly. They have learned to beat the system through their lies. And we are the ones who get stuck paying for it. I think they should have to get up and go to work."

She also believes welfare hurts more than just the recipients because too many children see their parents getting public money and then spending it on drugs, creating another generation of welfare recipients. "Children do what they've learned and what they see."

Aid to illegal immigrants is another area in which Ryan believes the government is too lenient at the expense of taxpayers. A lot of illegal immigrants from Mexico, only 3 hours away from Phoenix, cross the border to have babies in U.S. hospitals, she asserts, so their kids can get the benefits of U.S. citizenship. But she hasn't followed the news about restricting welfare or increasing border patrols to block the flow of illegal immigrants.

"I don't make it my life [to follow the news]. If I'm surfing the channels and it happens to be on, I'll listen to it just to hear what's being said. But as far as making it a point, I can't even tell you what time the news comes on. I can't even tell you what channels." She does like watching C-SPAN because it shows Congress without any journalistic comment.

Her biggest complaint about the news media is that "there's an editor telling you the right thing, the wrong thing . . . how they want us to react."

She subscribes to *Time* magazine but has only read one article from the stack of magazines piled in the family room.

In the Medill News Service article, she said her local newspaper and TV news shows are biased. From the story, her view of the media as part of the Big Brother problem came through.

It reported,

"They all like to tell you, 'This is what my opinion is, and this is the way you should vote,' she said. They say it very stern, like, 'You better go out and do this because I say so and I know better.' Well, excuse me, but I'm a human being, too." Ryan said she trusts her own judgment and wants to form her own opinions.

The news she cares most about is what is happening in her neighborhood, a quiet middle-class street of one-story homes with well-kept yards.

She and Jim often spend evenings talking to neighbors on their front lawns.

When she thinks about who or what she can rely on other than family, it's her neighbors, certainly not the government.

Their neighbor Wade mowed the grass without being asked when Ryan was at work and her husband was recovering from heart surgery. If one of the neighbors with kids has an emergency, she will go over and baby-sit.

Jack, another neighbor, bought his house a few years ago simply because he liked the neighborhood so much, Ryan says.

"If we need something from our neighbors, we borrow something. And we help them out. . . . I'm not moving. I'll never be able to find a house for this price, and it's a good neighborhood."

The Medill News Service article highlighted Ryan's ties to her neighborhood:

> On Election Night, Ryan's 53-year-old husband, Jim, stood on the front porch talking to Jack, his next-door neighbor. Paula was across the street talking to Pam, who was paying the pizza deliveryman.
>
> Jim, who is recovering from open-heart surgery, took a drag of his cigarette. "I heard the whole East Coast went for Clinton," he said matter-of-factly.
>
> When word got around that Ohio went for Clinton—and probably the election with it—Jim shrugged his shoulders.
>
> He didn't vote. Neither did Karine, whose boyfriend had just dropped her off at home. She decided not to vote because "I just didn't feel I was informed enough."
>
> She said she would study the issues more during the next four years and vote in 2000.
>
> Paula came back from across the street and shook her head. "I don't understand it," she said. "Everyone I know is voting for Dole. I've only met one person who likes Clinton."

Her Election Night poll of her neighborhood confirms her belief that she cannot affect decisions in Washington.

However, daughter Chasidy broke the family tradition of nonvoting by casting a ballot in 1996. Ryan said Chasidy's management position at the YMCA, which necessitates involvement in the community and meetings with community leaders, pushed her to the polls.

She's comfortable with each daughter's voting decision. And with her own choice not to vote. "Their opinions are their opinions," she says. "And I just stick with mine."

———— ◄o► ————

Steve Gordon

Tuned Out From Politics

Nestled in the rolling hills of west-central Wisconsin lies the small community of Sparta, a mix of farmers, small businesses, and some manufacturing companies, whose residents are close enough to the Mississippi River to go bass fishing on Saturday afternoons and within a 2-hour drive of northern Wisconsin's campgrounds.

The town, which is the county seat for Monroe County, also is close enough to the huge Indian casinos whose signs dominate Interstate 90-94 for residents to substitute blackjack and poker for church bingo games.

Less than 10 miles outside Sparta, population 7,788, is Fort McCoy, a military base used by Army reserve and National Guard units for training—and for the occasional rock concert.

When he was 18, Steve Gordon spent 2 weeks at Fort McCoy for a reserve training camp. He fell in love with a girl named Peggy and never returned to his hometown of Bloomington, Illinois. He's spent most of the past 15 years in Sparta. He and Peggy, whom he married 14 years ago, now have three sons and a collie named Blossom.

He enjoys the small-town atmosphere, being able to go fishing for bass or walleye in the Mississippi or in the La Crosse or Black rivers. And he likes the uncrowded, unpolluted, and safe atmosphere. "I can leave my keys in the truck at night," Gordon says.

They've lived in the same one-story wood house on the edge of town for 12 years. Gordon would like to move out into the country, but his wife doesn't want to leave Sparta.

Now 33, Gordon describes himself as laid-back but not mellow. He gets "hyper" sometimes, he says.

"I'm happy most of the time, until we start talking about politics."

He makes sure that doesn't happen much. He and his family or friends rarely discuss what's going on in Washington. He's never voted and doesn't show any inclination to change.

"I don't pay attention to it, but I do listen to some of the stuff that's being said about it, you bet, because I watch CNN. I'm a channel flipper so if I see something interesting that they're talking about, then I'll stop—for *Crossfire* [a debate-format talk show] or something. I'll sit and watch it for a while until I get bored of what they are saying."

Boredom isn't the only reason he tunes out the news. Too often, as he hears the latest developments in Congress, watches commentators argue about which party is winning, or sees reports that treat what he considers trivial issues as scandals, "I get all upset."

So, to prevent boredom or anger, he simply limits his exposure to the news. He will leaf through *USA Today* at work and read the local weekly newspaper, but otherwise, current affairs are not on his mind. His wife maintains the computers for the school system, and the family has an Internet hookup at home, but Gordon doesn't go online for news either.

One reason why he steers clear of national news is the kind of news that's presented. Too often, he says, the news media focus on the trivial, the sensational. He wonders why there were so many news stories in 1992 on President Bill Clinton's statement that he smoked marijuana but didn't inhale it and, in 1992 and subsequent years, on the Clinton sex scandals. He also thinks the news coverage devoted to independent counsel Kenneth Starr's investigation of the Whitewater land deal from Clinton's days as governor of Arkansas was a waste of everyone's time.

"Why even bring up Whitewater and make a big hassle out of it? Maybe they should be punished for their wrongdoing, but why did it come up now and not before? I'm sure people know about that. . . . It's just that now he's president of the United States and it's big news."

However, it's more than lack of information or lack of interest that keeps him from voting; it's a perceived lack of impact.

"It isn't going to change anything if I don't vote or I do vote. What's it going to change?"

As an example, he says he almost voted on a local school construction issue, but he figured his wife would have voted in favor of it and he would have voted against it, so they would have had no effect on the outcome. Neither he nor his wife has voted in the time that they've known each other.

He grew up in a family of nine children. He can't recall whether his parents voted, but he well remembers how life got tough after his father, a printer who worked for the Bloomington newspaper—the *Daily Pantagraph*—and his mother, a waitress, divorced when he was about 7 years old.

"When they got a divorce, there were five of us still at home—the four youngest boys and my sister who is 1 year older than me. . . . I felt sorry for my sister when I think back on it. Once Ma got a divorce, she had to live with [and help care for] four boys."

His mother continued to work after the divorce, sometimes taking two jobs, and he well remembers the times they were on public assistance. They are not memories he cherishes.

"I grew up on welfare," he says. "I'm not on welfare now."

His mother is remarried now and living in Portland, Maine; her husband is a college professor, and she works at the post office. His father has been dead a year, but Gordon has kept copies of the *Daily Pantagraph* and speaks proudly of his father's work.

Four of his siblings still live in Bloomington. One of his brothers moved his family north to Sparta. The rest are scattered in Tennessee, Kentucky, and California. They keep in touch, but sporadically.

When he came to Sparta for his summer training in 1981 and met Peggy, "I just stayed. I never went back. Nothing to go back for."

The couple married a year later, after moving to Colorado Springs, Colorado, for a year to see if they would like living in the West. But they moved back to Sparta because Peggy missed her family. He switched to the National Guard from the Army reserves when they returned and took a job as a cook, then trained to become a nursing assistant, which he did for 4 years. He left the guard in 1988.

He went back to school, to La Crosse Community College about 26 miles west of Sparta, to study tool and die making. In his second year, his employer gave him a scholarship. He enjoyed going to school, although it was difficult to study during the days and work nights.

After his company decided to lay off employees, including Gordon, Spartek Co., one of the large employers in Sparta, called him for an interview, and he's been there ever since, about 6 years. He's in charge of making and repairing the tools and dies used to create molds for the signs and other molded products the company of about 200 employees manufactures. His small office is cluttered with examples of Spartek's work—beer signs for bars, Disney signs, store signs.

He enjoys the work, even though he's always on call in case equipment breaks during the night shift. He likes figuring out how to create a die for a sign. "I'm always doing something different."

To earn extra money, he is a Tae Kwon Do martial arts instructor at night. He had always wanted to learn martial arts when he was a kid, but his mother couldn't afford the lessons. Now he's a black belt.

He wishes he earned more than his annual income of somewhat less than $50,000 but is more concerned about the cost of health care and of saving for his retirement. "I'm going to have to build my own retirement" because Medicare and Social Security won't be around when he's 65, Gordon believes.

The current system is costing too much because of the way it is set up: Wealthy retirees should pay higher Medicare premiums and get less Social Security, in his opinion.

"There's no reason for us to pay . . . for these elderly people making $50,000 a year," he says. "I consider myself impoverished when compared to people making $100,000 a year who are considered middle class."

But particularly on national issues, even those that concern him, such as the federal deficit and a balanced federal budget, he has decided his vote won't make a difference.

"It doesn't matter what I think because they're going to do whatever they think."

But not voting does not mean he won't express his opinions on the way things are going in the United States: "I don't think that's right [that you have no right to complain if you don't vote]. I pay my taxes just as well as they [voters] do."

His biggest complaints close to home concern the large casinos built and operated by the Ho-Chunk Indian tribe at several locations around the state and the taxpayer money used to support the Hmongs, Laotian refugees who settled in Wisconsin in large numbers after the Vietnam War.

He's concerned that the Ho-Chunk Indian casino down the interstate from Sparta may bring crime to the town because the casino employees are outsiders and there's a lot of turnover.

His biggest concern, however, is that the Ho-Chunk are raking in millions of dollars in revenues tax free because of old agreements with the federal government that treat the tribes as separate governments. The Ho-Chunk earn about $120 million a year from their casinos and other businesses; several other tribes also run profitable casinos in the state. Gordon believes the Indians should be paying taxes like everyone else.

In fact, he says he refuses to patronize the casinos because he won't contribute to their profits.

Much the same issue—getting something from the government without paying taxes—colors his opinion of the Hmongs, Laotian refugees who fled their country after the communists took over because they had helped the CIA disrupt North Vietnamese supply routes during the Vietnam War. Census figures show Wisconsin has at least 15,000 Hmong refugees.

He says the federal government is helping people who come here from other countries before helping native-born Americans.

"How can these people get all these things that I can't get? I've lived here all my life. These people just came over here." When he was in community college in La Crosse, where Hmongs are the largest minority group, he says he would see Hmongs driving expensive cars while getting free schooling. He remembers one Hmong student saying he had already gone to school for two degrees and was studying for a third. "And we're paying for all this," Gordon says with feigned disbelief.

Gordon says he does sympathize with the Hmongs for having to flee their country, but now that they're here, they should have to live with no more privileges than Americans.

He feels just as strongly about Americans who have spent their lives on welfare. Remembering his own youth, he knows that welfare is vital to keeping families together at times, but he believes that getting public assistance should include a payback from the recipient. Otherwise, he says, a culture of dependence is created that goes from one generation to the next.

"I think they should work for the money. What would be wrong for them to go out and clean up our highways and that kind of stuff?"

Wisconsin Governor Tommy Thompson instituted a welfare-to-work system, one of the first states to do so, but Gordon isn't convinced that it will work.

"I think that he is out for himself, to go to his political height. W2 [the nickname for the Wisconsin plan] is not going to be the answer. I guarantee you that."

His opinion of politicians in Washington is no better, particularly because of the way they spend federal money.

"How can we be so far in debt? How can a government with the knowledge that the government has, for example, to build all these nuclear weapons, how come they can't manage money? . . . They can't have everything that they want. I can't get everything that I want, so why should everybody else?

"I mean, look at Social Security. Social Security was supposed to be meant for the retirement of American people. What's it being used for now? Everything else but," he says, referring to the use of the Social Security trust fund to report a balanced federal budget.

Part of the problem, he believes, is that elected officials who have been in Washington for a while start to think they're above the law, not answerable to those they represent. Instead, they listen to special interest groups with money to spend, and that's true for Democrats and Republicans alike, he says.

In fact, he sees little difference between the two parties.

"One's an ass, and something else, an elephant, is the other. See, that just shows you how much I really care about stuff like that. Ross Perot might have been a good president. Then again, he might have been just like all the rest, who knows? I don't know if I would have voted for him or not."

Gordon has an admittedly outrageous idea that he got from watching a rerun of a TV sitcom called *Three's Company,* in which the character played by John Ritter somehow became president by winning a lottery, he says. Of course it's not realistic, he says, but it would be no worse than the current system of electing presidents.

"I always thought we ought to have a lottery for the presidency. I mean, that may not be a very good thing to have. . . . I think if you got somebody in there who doesn't know anything and let them do what their point of view is, it may get totally screwed up, but at least it's something different than what's been going on for years and years and years."

His point: To be president, a politician has had to work up through the political system for years, compromising more with each step up the ladder. Someone without those compromises in his background could follow his convictions.

Gordon knows his idea isn't in the realm of possibility, but that's not what keeps him away from the polls.

"I really don't feel like my vote makes a difference. I know what's going on, but it's not going to change."

Iris Llamas

Politics Are Outside Her World

On most Sundays, Iris Llamas goes to church with her aunt and cousin near the west Austin, Texas, neighborhood where the three of them live in a comfortable, one-story brick home. Her parents often make the 30-mile drive north from Lockhart to join them, sometimes bringing her grandparents. They spend the day going to church, having lunch, and talking.

When her parents don't make the trip to Austin on a Sunday, Llamas will drive down Route 183 to Lockhart on Monday to spend the day back home with her parents and younger brother and visit friends from high school.

Either way, the family is at the center of her day, which is the way she likes it.

But just as the members of her family take care of each other, Llamas thinks elected officials should take care of citizens who need help, such as single moms and struggling families.

"They spend all of this money to see if people can go to Mars and live there and for what? That money they could use here to help someone. . . . I believe that right here needs a lot more help. The single lady with two kids, let's just say she has a job, she can't afford rent, a car."

She says politicians are more interested in getting elected—and then staying in office—than in helping people.

And they don't know or don't remember what it's like to have to struggle to survive.

"They're always saying they're going to do something. But when it comes down to it later, nothing actually happens."

Llamas, who is 23, is registered to vote, and she knows her parents vote, usually for Democrats. Llamas registered almost as part of the process of moving to Austin, not because she wanted to be eligible to vote.

In 1992, the first presidential election in which she was eligible to vote, Llamas stayed home.

In that election, Bill Clinton's campaign slogan was, "It's the economy, stupid," and he presided over a booming economy during his presidency. Llamas, however, says financial security still eludes many Americans. She says she can't afford a place of her own, and many of her young, single colleagues at work are in the same financial boat.

But she doesn't follow what's going on in national or even local politics. She says she tries to keep up with the news, but she doesn't read the newspaper more than about once a week and only watches TV news on her days off.

Part of her lack of interest is that the news she sees in her community, she says, never shows up on television.

"The stuff we talk about we don't see reported."

She and her friends rarely talk about what *is* reported, particularly if the topics are politics or public policy. The same goes for her family.

Llamas, a petite blonde with braces, says she's more interested in going to the beach in Corpus Christi for a weekend or planning family get-togethers. What's going on in Washington is not significant in her life.

"Family is important," she says with finality. "We're not a big family, I guess, so we're a little more bonded."

She liked growing up in Lockhart, although she remembers that there wasn't much to do in the town of 9,000. "Everyone used to hang out, rent movies. Once a month we used to come to Austin and go to movies after dinner and stuff. Shop." When she graduated from high school and was looking for a job, Austin seemed to offer more opportunities than Lockhart.

While she was working at a small electronics company, she took some community college courses in advanced typing and other secretarial skills. She tried nursing courses but decided her real interest was in medical laboratory work.

Then, about 3 years ago, she got a job offer from her current employer, a semiconductor manufacturer, and now works as a materials handler, tracking the firm's inventory.

She feels lucky to have found the job and likes what she does. But she doesn't feel secure, noting her firm had layoffs recently.

"I don't think any kind of job is secure. That's just the chance you've got to take."

She works three 12-hour days every week, with a fourth 12-hour day thrown in every other week. "I'm usually so drained [at the end of the day]. Twelve hours, that's almost 2 days of work."

She started in an entry-level job but now has responsibility for the audit of computer chips the company makes, mainly for use in personal computers and communications systems. The chips are for audio—"sound chips."

As she enters the nondescript one-story building where she works, which is surrounded by similar blocklike manufacturing buildings, she grabs one of the blue smocks employees are required to wear to reduce static. She doesn't like them and thinks they're ugly, but notes she would have to wear something similar in her dream job of lab technician for a pharmaceutical company.

Because of her long hours and frequent schedule changes, going back to school to get the education needed to realize her dream isn't likely right now.

"It's kind of hard to go to school and then work. It just didn't work out. I ended up taking one class for about 2 days. . . . But I'm getting experience. So when I go to school, I'm going to have not only schooling but experience. It will be easier to get a better-paying job."

Her schedule also makes it hard to get together with friends, most of whom work at the same company.

"My friends have different schedules than I do, so sometimes I don't get to go out. I just kind of hang out at the house. We go out here in Austin. We go out to the movies and things, out to dinner, to the beach, and a couple of times we went to Louisiana to gamble."

They also like to get together for bowling or miniature golf games, but they rarely go to downtown Austin, preferring to stay in the western suburbs.

"When was the last time we went downtown?" she wonders aloud. "I think it was for Chinese New Year. We went out to the temple, had dinner, and we watched their pageant."

But she also enjoys spending time with her 7-year-old cousin, Michael. She acts like a doting aunt toward him and, in fact, calls him her nephew. She picks him up from first grade frequently and often takes care of him on her days off. Her aunt works long hours, Llamas says, and just went through a tough divorce from Michael's father.

"The whole thing has just been really sad." It's during tough times that family should help out, Llamas believes. "When they have hard times like this, you don't want them to get depressed."

She, her aunt, and Michael live in a brick ranch home in a quiet subdivision with numerous shade trees called Emerald Forest on Austin's west side. She's clearly very close to Michael. "He's something else," she says with a big smile. "He's a really nice kid."

Llamas has never felt that caring for Michael was a burden.

"Michael and I are pretty close, so I would hurt his feelings if I decided to leave. It would have been way too much for him."

Her eyes cloud over when she thinks about Michael being hurt. And she knows his father's departure continues to bother him. It pained her to hear him, with his little, high-pitched voice, tell a relative who didn't know about the divorce and asked where his father was, "My daddy left us."

"It was terrible," she says simply but with deep emotion.

Llamas says she knows immigrants from Mexico who talk about how much easier life is in the United States, but she doesn't see it that way. She thinks most Americans have to work hard to make a living and keep their families together.

"Is there ever going to be one [president] to say, 'Yes, the public can have it where everyone is comfortable'?" She's pretty sure the answer is no.

Her boss, an ex-serviceman, says he votes, although he thinks "idiots" are running the government. But despite his disdain for elected officials, he believes voting is important because there's "no bitching if you don't vote."

Llamas disagrees. "I have a right to have my own opinion even if I didn't vote."

She can't pinpoint what it would take to get her to vote. It's not getting older, or having a family, or buying a home.

"We talk about it at work, about voting," Llamas says. "We discussed who was running [in 1996], but I never got around to voting."

"Once I get into politics more, hopefully I will."

She remembers a discussion with a friend in which the friend said one vote counts. Llamas says she believes that's true, and she intends to use her vote someday. But she quickly adds "hopefully" with a rueful laugh.

———— ◄o►— ————

Serena Slaton

"The Word" Is Not Politics

Serena Slaton does not like the image she thinks society has of 24-year-olds, an image of frivolity, of partying, of letting themselves go, of doing drugs and alcohol. She sees herself as different, more serious, and mature. Spiritual. "I think more of taking care of myself. I don't need to party, to hang out," she says. "I stay at home and I read . . . and I work, I read, I work, I read, I stay at home. I'm a loner." Her grandmother, with whom she and two siblings lived on weekdays until she was 7 years old, would tell her, "You're an old lady trapped in a young body."

Slaton's 24 years have been spent in Atlanta, growing up, going to school, working, and making church and God her foundation. When she was 16, she went with a girlfriend who lived on her block in southeast Atlanta to the friend's church in the economically depressed neighborhood of Vine City a few miles away. She had found her spiritual home. At 18, Slaton became an official member of Mount Gilead Baptist Church. She is at the church three times a week: Wednesday nights for Bible study and a prayer meeting, Thursday nights for choir rehearsal, and every Sunday morning, except once when she was recuperating from an auto accident.

"I'm a Christian and I believe in church and I believe in the word of God, and I study it and I teach Sunday school and I love the fellowship," Slaton says. She looks to the Bible, to the word of God, for guidance in her life. It is the prism through which she sees politics. "I've found that if there's any problem that you have, you can go to the Bible. It's like an instruction book, and it has stories that will help with whatever you've been through.

"We've learned in the Old Testament that you need a head. So you need leaders. If you read the Old Testament, you'll find out that the people asked God for a king and they were just asking him for a leader," she says. "I think that's needful, but to a certain extent they were wrong for asking, and God was upset with them for asking for a leader. But once they got a leader and he got in, that was King Solomon. He strayed away from the word of God. So I believe we need a leader, but we need a godly leader, and it's hard to find today."

The lesson Slaton takes from scripture is that political leaders should not be trusted just because they seek or gain positions of leadership. They must earn the people's trust. They have not yet earned Slaton's.

"I really don't believe in politics. I don't believe you can find an honest, honest, honest person. I think situations change people. When you have a person who's a candidate," she says, "once they get into the hustle and bustle of the grind of it, they can change. I don't believe that someone in politics can be straightforward and honest because situations are going to change their point of view or there are going to be situations that they cannot control or handle. So while they make all these promises at the jump, once they get in, it's just something totally different, and they can't handle it or they can't control what comes out of it."

Slaton has yet to vote in any election, though she's open to the possibility that she might vote in the foreseeable future. She registered to vote in high school shortly before she turned 18, and she can identify many of her elected officials, national and local. But she believes she will be hard to convert into a partici-pating voter. She doesn't trust politicians, and she's set in her ways, she says, even if she were to find out she is wrong about a person. "I stick with my opinions no matter what. My mom says I'm hard," Slaton relates. "Usually, I'm right."

Slaton lives with her mother and her older brother and sister in a middle-class neighborhood just inside the city limits, a short drive from Atlanta's Hartsfield International Airport. Their large, six-bedroom split-level house is dwarfed by the woods and huge pines that envelop it. Even when they were kids, Slaton and her siblings wouldn't venture into the woods for fear of snakes, possums, raccoons, and lizards. The family moved there in 1986 from a house a few blocks away when Slaton was a high school freshman after their entire block was condemned to create an industrial park adjacent to the airport.

Slaton's most vivid memories as a small child are living during the week with her 80-year-old grandmother "on the other side of town," closer to downtown Atlanta. She doesn't know why the arrangement was needed or why it was discontinued when she was 7 and her brother and sister were in fifth grade. Her parents both worked, her dad as a trucker and her mom as a dietitian and caterer for Clark Atlanta University. The kids went home to be with their parents on weekends. The grade school she and her siblings attended was within walking distance from her grandmother's house. Once they returned home for good, they and most of their neighborhood friends were bused to school.

Slaton did well academically and socially at George High School, one of Atlanta's magnet centers that was established to link the core educational curriculum with specialized career courses and work opportunities. Qualifying students could frontload their courses in the mornings and leave school at noon to begin the work component of the curriculum. Slaton chose not to participate in the program, instead taking the core courses and participating in multiple extracurricular activities. She was captain of the marching band's flag corps and played basketball. Her senior year, she won second place in the competition for school queen and served as first attendant to "Miss George." She was elected secretary of the student government association. "I don't remember why I ran. It wasn't the political side of it. I think I did it just to see if I could win. Would I, could I, and I did," Slaton says triumphantly.

Slaton's mother arranged a job for her when she graduated from high school in 1990. She started immediately cutting salad full time in the kitchen at Clark

Atlanta, the historically black private university where her mother had worked for more than 20 years. By the fall, Slaton had enrolled in the Atlanta College of Medical Careers in a certificate program to become a pharmacy technician. For 2 years, she went to school, continued working part-time, and immersed herself in her Bible study. She began reading the works of mesmerizing Christian preachers such as Bishop T. D. Jakes, the Reverend Carlton Pearson, and the Georgia-based Reverend Creflo Dollar, who founded World Changers Ministries. Their teachings, delivered through television and speaking engagements as well as books, emphasize practical living skills and self-esteem.

Slaton graduated and began working at Southwest Hospital and Medical Center, dispensing drugs. She lasted only 6 months. "Sickness, illness, all day long was taking a toll on me," she says. "I got burned out, and I really didn't want to do it anymore." She went back to school, this time in social work. She reveled in it but withdrew after 1 year because she was not receiving financial aid and couldn't afford the tuition.

Slaton got to talking with one of the parishioners at her church who was the market manager for Cash America, a Texas-based corporation that runs more than 450 pawnshops in 16 states, as well as in Britain and Sweden. She began work in March 1996 as a clerk earning $15,000 a year with benefits, and within a year she had completed the company's management training program and increased her salary to $22,000. She is learning the trade and picking up "product knowledge" about jewelry, electronics, computers, tools, and musical equipment by sifting through the computer databases in the store and comparison pricing in the Sunday newspapers and at the area Wal-Mart. Her customers are mostly people who need up to $200 in cash or those who come to Cash America's retail side to take advantage of the layaway program to buy jewelry or electronics. She likes her work but considers it a "rest stop" en route to completing her social work degree.

Slaton is insecure about her knowledge of politics. "Right now, I'm not even keeping up with it. I'm watching the news and I'm hearing this and I'm hearing that. But I'm not keeping up with it," she concedes. But she is more aware than many voters. She reads the *Atlanta Journal and Constitution* about three times a week and is impressed with the depth of its coverage, often spending 2 or 3 days on a package of stories. She watches television news every night and is so devoted to WAGA/Channel 5 that she recites its motto from memory: "dedicated, determined and dependable." She can identify the potential mayoral candidates long before the city's November 1997 election campaign gets in full swing. And she has strong feelings about the choices. She prefers incumbent Mayor Bill Campbell to his archrival, City Council President Marvin Arrington. Slaton's mother, in her job at the university, has even catered some functions for Arrington over the years. Yet Slaton doesn't trust him. She says he keeps changing his story about potential conflicts of interest involving concessions at the airport. She doesn't recall the specifics, but in 1994, an Atlanta businessman was convicted of bribery in a case in which two city council members were also convicted, and Arrington was caught on an FBI videotape receiving $500 in cash from the man. Arrington was never charged.

Slaton knows something about another city council member, Gloria Bromell-Tinubu. Tinubu lives in the same neighborhood as one of Slaton's good friends, and Slaton has met Tinubu's children in the neighborhood. Still, Slaton is hard to win over. She thinks Tinubu, elected to the city council for the first time in 1993, is too new to the political game for Slaton to trust her.

Except for the city council, which she says is "a mess" and could use someone to "come in and clean it up," Slaton is favorably disposed toward much of what she observes politically. She is quite impressed with Benjamin Canada, Atlanta's superintendent of public schools, for opening new schools, enlarging others, and initiating innovative programs. She has a positive impression of the Democratic and Republican parties and believes Democrats are more support-ive of poor people, but overall, she doesn't see much difference between them. "They spend, act, and say the same things," she says. "They're the same person, to me they are."

Slaton's family never discuss politics much. They are close-knit, but they talk about daily affairs and about each other, not about public affairs. She and her siblings, all in their twenties, still live at home. They are close to their father, who divorced their mother and moved to another part of Atlanta when Slaton was a high school sophomore. She knows her father and brother don't vote but she isn't sure about her mother. She thinks her mom might vote sometimes because of her mother's position at the university. Her sister, Carla, voted in 1996. She's sure of it because she recalls getting home from work and seeing her sister wearing an "I voted" sticker. She assumes Carla voted for President Bill Clinton but laughs at the thought of her sister voting. "My sister watches a lot of TV, and I think the MTV Rock the Vote thing kind of got her, to be honest," Slaton says, "because I don't think she really knew what she was actually doing."

Had Slaton voted, she would have voted for Clinton over Republican Bob Dole or independent Ross Perot. But she wasn't sufficiently motivated to vote, not even by her pastor, the Reverend Dexter Johnson, who encouraged his congregants to vote.

Slaton thinks of her church and its pastor with reverence. "It's like the church on the hill," she says, "there for everyone to see as an example for people to emulate." Mount Gilead Baptist Church is located in one of the poorest sections of Atlanta, situated in jarring contrast down the hill from the Georgia Dome, the 72,000-seat, $215 million stadium completed in 1992 to house the Atlanta Falcons and be in place for the 1996 Summer Olympics. In May 1994, Louis Farrakhan, leader of the Nation of Islam, delivered a eulogy at the church for

Corey Johnson, a high school student who was shot to death by another teenager after attending Farrakhan's "Let Us Make Man" speech in Atlanta the week before. The *Atlanta Journal and Constitution* reported that Farrakhan told the overflow gathering, which included Slaton, that the youth's death was a symptom of the failure of society and its institutions, including the church. Slaton was nervous in anticipation of Farrakhan's eulogy, not only that the church would be crowded with people coming just to hear Farrakhan but that there would be friction between Farrakhan's Muslim beliefs, derived in part from the Koran, and the teachings of Christianity. She was relieved. "He actually delivered 'the word,' she recalls. "He showed respect for me and what we believe, and I respect him for that."

Every once in a while during election campaigns, Slaton says, politicians visit the church to pray and to leave the subliminal message that they are worth voting for. "They tend to want to get up and talk and say little things about God and their belief and how they're happy to be here and stuff like that. They stop by." But Slaton is dubious that they're sincere. "Your mouth can say anything. Actions speak louder than words. If you're saying you're going to better this or you're going to better that. You can say anything but what you do is actually what really determines. Like the Bible says, 'Faith without works is dead.' What that's telling me is, 'I can have all the faith in the world, but if I don't put it to work, it's dead, it's nothing, it's just chatter.' "

Slaton listens, but none of it—not her pastor's sermons, not the words of politicians, not the exposure she gets to public affairs from the news media—is enough to get her to vote now. Maybe some day, but Slaton is pretty stubborn. "I really just dislike politics. It's needful," she says, recapitulating scripture. "The word says that we're supposed to have leaders in these positions, but they're really going to do what they want to do."

In one sense, what politicians do in Washington and locally affects her, but in another sense, it doesn't, Slaton says. "What God has for me is for me," Slaton says, referring to a song they sing in church. "You control your destiny through faith, prayer, and work. No outside person can determine what you're worth or what you can do. No one can determine it, no one can deter it, no one can change it."

———— ◄○► ————

5

Irritables

Cynicism and disenchantment are hallmarks of Irritable nonvoters. Just as important, however, are their habits of keeping informed politically while believing their opinions are not valued by those in power. Like some Doers, a number of Irritables believe they are making a political statement by not voting—by, in effect, withholding their votes.

Henry Montoya is the classic example, going to the election booth and pulling the lever on a blank ballot for the past 20 years. Now 68 years old, he's switched his attention from the two parties to political extremist Lyndon LaRouche.

Extreme action, he believes, is the only way to fix a system that has become beholden to moneyed interests and impervious to those in need of help, such as minorities.

But he doesn't want to give his vote to anyone because he doesn't like the choices.

Michael Keegan also uses his nonvote as a weapon. He deliberately registered to let politicians know his vote was available but just as deliberately stays away on Election Day to make a statement. He's infuriated at what he believes is an attitude common among elected officials of feigning concern while avoiding controversy or action.

A stonemason and hunter, Keegan dreams of leaving the crime, dirt, and incivility he experiences in his Philadelphia suburb of Norristown for the uncrowded country of upstate New York. But he will take with him his deep skepticism of all things political: "I'm not voting because there is nobody to vote for."

Montoya had voted for a number of years before giving it up. Melody Lewis also used to vote regularly out of a sense of obligation, knowing little about the candidates. But the sense of duty waned as she was bombarded by recurring images of posturing candidates, she says, abetted by the news media and financed by powerful special interest groups. She's angry at the lack of heroes. When she moved from Memphis, Tennessee, to West Plains, Missouri, the 31-year-old office worker's sense of obligation to become a registered voter evaporated.

Caren Freigenberg also lost her feeling for voting when she moved. She had always voted in New York and worked on a campaign or two, but Cliffside, New Jersey, didn't feel like her community so she didn't register. Her community still centers on her emotional home: New York City.

But she follows national news and doesn't like what she reads: "There are so many who I think have a hidden agenda. And I don't trust them. I don't believe in them."

Henry Montoya

On Election Day, He's Voting—For No One

When he turned 21 in 1949, Henry Montoya was in the Navy on board a ship in the Pacific. But he wanted to vote so he got an absentee ballot and continued to do so for every election until he left the Navy in 1961.

He remained a regular voter after he returned home to Denver. In fact, he became active in the Democratic Party, serving as a committeeman and as delegate to the state convention, among other duties. At the 1968 convention of Colorado Democrats, Montoya and other Chicano leaders wanted to send delegates to the national convention who would make sure Chicano voices were heard. He didn't go to the contentious convention in Chicago, but afterward, Montoya recalls bitterly, he and the other Chicanos were told by state Democratic Party leaders, "We are going to do the things that we've been doing and to hell with you."

"So I said, 'Well, time for me to change forces here,' so I quit the Democratic Party and registered as an independent."

Montoya, who still lives in Denver and manages a 12-unit apartment building on the city's west end, remains a registered independent. But just as the Democratic leaders soured him on active participation in politics, the candidates running for office and the Democratic and Republican parties they represent have soured him on voting.

The last time he voted was in the 1968 presidential election. When the next off-year election came, he went, as usual, to the neighborhood polling place he had gone to since moving to west Denver in 1961.

"I went to vote one day and I got to thinking . . . I walked in and I closed the curtain, you know, and I was looking at the candidates and I was looking at the amendments and I was looking at all this junk. And I thought, 'Why do I want to vote? None of this is going to be of any value to me or anyone else, except the politicians.'

"So I just opened the curtain and walked out. And it dawned on me: 'That is what you can do from now on. You can come in here and still remain a registered voter, do your duty, close the curtain, and get the hell out.'

"You don't have to vote. Nothing in the world says that you have to vote, you know. But by the same token, they can't say that I didn't go vote because I was there. They got me on the register. I signed my little slip. So that's what I've been doing ever since."

Every Election Day, Montoya goes to his polling place and pulls the lever on an empty ballot. He deliberately votes for no one.

"In any election, there's no one worth my vote. . . . When you get sick of doing the same thing every time, you've got to look for alternatives. I know there are no alternatives within the Democratic Party or Republican Party."

He said 1992's most visible third-party contender, Ross Perot, doesn't represent a viable alternative either because he was mostly "hurray for me and to hell with you."

The candidate that would get him to cast a vote again in a presidential election is political extremist Lyndon LaRouche, who has campaigned for the Democratic nomination for president in each election since 1980. In 1976, he ran for president as a Labor Party candidate. LaRouche's far-right beliefs include the theories that the federal government should file for bankruptcy to rid itself of national debt and that there's a conspiracy to cover up the facts of President John Kennedy's assassination.

"Oh yeah. I would vote for him. . . . He tells it like it is. He is not afraid to tell this government, that government, or any other government what it's all about." Montoya became interested in him around 1993; LaRouche was not on the general election ballot in Colorado in 1996, but state election records show he did make it onto the ballot in 1992, when he got 20 votes statewide.

Montoya subscribes to LaRouche's newspaper, the *New Federalist,* and believes, as part of the LaRouche political outlook, that U.S. political leaders such as President George Bush and officials of other governments, particularly the British government, are part of a conspiracy, called the New World Order, that involves billions of dollars in drug money.

"Certain politicians throughout the world are getting together to control the world. Politically, money-wise."

They (and that includes President Bill Clinton) jailed LaRouche on phony charges to keep him quiet, Montoya says. LaRouche was paroled in 1994 after serving 5 years of a 15-year sentence for his mail fraud and conspiracy convictions related to a deliberate default on $30 million in loans to one of his political campaigns.

Montoya is pessimistic that any change will occur in the political system that would provide Americans with real choices among good candidates.

"The candidates that we have had running haven't been defining what they stood for. They are too wishy-washy." Money plays too big of a role in elections for change to occur because rich special interest groups will continue to control candidates, he believes. He advocates stringent limits on how much candidates can spend to get elected—half of what their annual salaries would be in office. For president, that would be $100,000; for a senator, $66,800.

"If you are running for senator and I give you a million dollars, you're mine. You're mine whether you like it or not, whether you say you are or not. You're mine because when I gave you that million dollars I bought you like a pair of shoes."

Montoya, a thin whip of a man with a ready smile beneath his trimmed mustache who looks much younger than his 68 years, talks knowledgeably about current affairs, the result of his daily reading of newspapers. He follows politics closely—"So I will have a very good idea as to why I don't want to vote for them," he says with a grin—and worries about the future of Chicanos in this country, the issue that first got him involved in politics 40 years ago.

"You remember in the '60s when they had the Chicano movement, the black movement? Well, I was involved in that. We gained a lot of ground, but the leadership of blacks and Chicanos grew greedy, too. Then everything started reverting back the way it was before. People were getting political positions and ignoring the needs of the Chicano community."

Even as the Latino population in the United States continues to grow rapidly, he predicts Chicanos—a term he always uses to differentiate Mexican Americans from other Americans of Spanish descent—will not have improved their socioeconomic status in 10 years. The culprit, again, is politics.

"I don't think Chicanos have that much to be able to buy in. . . . You don't contribute to their political campaigns, you aren't going to get anything. Sure, they tell you, 'You vote for me and I'll look out for you,' but it's to hell with you."

He says the two major political parties ignore Chicanos except on Election Day. "They are not responsive to any of our needs. They want you on Election Day to go vote for them, but when issues come up concerning Chicanos in this country, nobody would get into that."

His negative attitudes go beyond the treatment of Chicanos. He believes the country is headed in the wrong direction and that the news media get in the way of society solving its problems. He also thinks politicians don't care to hear his opinions, and it makes no real difference who is elected—things go on just as they did before.

But probably as a result of his close attention to the news, he knows that most issues discussed in Washington affect him, and he endorses an active role for government in improving housing, health care, and education.

Although he quit school to join the Navy in 1944 toward the end of World War II, one of the first things he did after enlisting was get his general equivalency diploma. On the cluttered bureau in the small manager's apartment of his building is a framed certificate of appreciation for his financial help and encouragement from his granddaughter, who graduated from San Diego State University with a degree in psychology.

He explains that he left school at 16 to enlist in the Navy during World War II because he didn't want to be drafted into the Army later.

"I said, 'I don't like neckties so I'll go into the Navy.' They [his superior officers] found out that I wasn't old enough in 1945, but by then I was already 17," so Navy officials let him stay.

One of his most searing memories—which convinced him that racism will never end—occurred while he was on leave in 1946.

He was going home to Denver and had a 30-minute layover in Colorado Springs so, still wearing his uniform, he decided to go to a bar for a bottle of Coors and a hamburger. "The lady said, 'Sorry, we don't serve Mexicans.' I looked around because I thought there must be some other Mexicans." When the bartender reiterated her comment, he threw an empty beer bottle at her, but she ducked and it hit the mirror behind the bar, shattering it.

Two police officers who had been called were holding him by the arms when a military police officer arrived and told the cops to let Montoya go.

What he also remembers about the incident is that the military police officer was a huge man who looked like a redneck but who closed the bar down and told Montoya to go to another bar and use his name to get served.

"I am looking at this guy who looks like the biggest racist around, but he was the nicest guy you'd ever want to see."

Montoya married and had four children during his more than 17 years in the Navy. He enjoyed the Navy, went around the world twice, served in two wars—World War II and Korea—and finished as a boatswain's mate.

Nevertheless, when he thinks about his years of service to his country, he notes, "I spent the better part of my life defending a country that is still racist and political."

When his wife divorced him, he was given custody of his children, and although he had hoped to complete 20 years in the Navy, he got a hardship discharge in 1961 because his three daughters and one son would have been separated and sent to foster homes for the $2\frac{1}{2}$ years he needed to make the 20-year mark.

His mother took care of the two youngest kids while he worked as a garbage truck driver for the city of Denver. He would finish work and pick up the two youngest in time to be home when his older children, his only son and one of the daughters, got back from school.

"My son was pretty close to my mother, and he learned from her how to cook, which is something that I never could do. I was never around the kitchen so I never learned to cook. He was good. Even at 10 years old, he could whip out a meal in no time flat. He was the cook in the evening. I set up the cereal in the morning."

That son, his only boy, was killed in 1992 at age 43 when a police car broadsided his son's car as his son was driving on a city street. Montoya doesn't believe the cop's story that he was driving so fast—60 miles per hour–and ran a stop sign because he was responding to a fellow officer's call for help. Montoya says the police car wasn't using its lights or sirens, which is what several witnesses told police. Police also said at the time that the officer requesting help was not in an emergency situation but just needed help transporting a suspect he had arrested at a convenience store.

The son, Enrique, was a well-known Denver choreographer and playwright who had been appointed by the mayor to the city's HIV Resources Planning Council.

Montoya's three daughters and four grandchildren all live in Denver, and he sees them regularly, although the grandkids are at the age "where they don't want fogies around. They come over and visit, but it's 'Hello. How are you? See you later.' That's fine with me, too, because I'm not used to having kids around anymore."

Fogey isn't the word most people would use to describe Montoya.

"I'm 19 going on 69. People tell me I don't get old. I tell them I'm not supposed to. If you want to get old, that's your problem."

His hair and neatly trimmed mustache still are more black than gray, his step spry. He walks 5 miles a day and eats lots of protein and very little fat. He stopped drinking because alcohol was giving him headaches. He listens to self-improvement tapes and reads lots of books.

He retired from his job with the city in the mid-1980s and didn't do anything until 10 years ago, when he was offered the position managing the apartment building. He handles the leases and rent, but others do the maintenance.

"It's good because I can do my own thing. If I want to go on vacation, I just go and I let them [the owners] know."

He likes going to Las Vegas, a 10-hour drive from Denver, to gamble, mainly blackjack. In Colorado, the casinos have a $5 limit on blackjack bets—that's too tame and you can never get ahead, he says.

He also likes football but stopped being a Denver Broncos fan after the team lost the Super Bowl in 1977. Now he supports the Oakland Raiders. "Basically, their owner and their coaching is getting controversial just like I have."

When he worked for the city, Montoya stirred controversy by organizing city workers in 1969. He says the city was not treating employees fairly because there was no seniority or legal redress against managers.

"It was like slave labor. The first meeting we had was in November of 1969. Believe it or not, we had 80% of the drivers, the city drivers, the drivers in the sanitation department, which is crucial to the city during a snowstorm. That night, there was a blizzard . . . and we were all in this action center holding our meeting.

"I said, 'Okay, it's starting to snow. Now let's see how the city moves without you.' So we all stayed there. . . . Nobody was home to answer the call to go sweep the snow or sand the roads or anything."

City officials threatened him with dismissal, saying he had instigated the incident, but in the end didn't retaliate against him, he says.

The City Employees Organization was formed shortly afterward and bargained with the city to improve the rules for employees, including getting seniority used in salary and promotion considerations, Montoya says. He also pointedly notes that the group's bylaws clearly stated that it would not support political candidates or parties. He says it was a "labor organization" but not a union and that it was not affiliated with the AFL-CIO.

"We would not allow any administrative personnel in the organization. You see that's what the unions do. They get the laborers, they get the foremen, and they get the superintendent. They get everybody in the union, so who in the hell are they going to represent?"

The organization lasted 5 years; now many of its employee protections are gone, he says.

Montoya doesn't expect that to change, nor does he expect changes in the political system or the racism that he believes pervades much of society.

"I don't think that in my lifetime I will see a change."

And so he'll keep pulling the lever on a blank ballot, registering his disdain in the only way he can.

———— ◄o► ————

Michael Keegan

He Wants to Get Away
From the Lies and Incivility

The stone and wood house in upstate New York has been Michael Keegan's dream for more than a decade: a safe place for his family and an escape from encroaching development, a distressing increase in the level of public incivility, and constant political chicanery.

He decided to register to vote for the first time in the fall of 1996 because his wife and others had told him that "if you're not part of the system, you can't complain." By registering, he says, it will be clear that his refusal to go to the polls is a deliberate turning away instead of a sign of indifference to the outcome of the presidential election.

"If you don't agree with the system and you vote, then you're voting for your best choice instead of who you think should be president. You are buying into the system. You are going along with the flow."

In the 23 years since he was old enough to vote, he never has cast a ballot because he never has seen a candidate he liked enough.

"We don't have to vote. In fact, by not voting, you should be saying something. Politicians should turn around and say, 'I may have won, but I only got 52% of the vote. And there were only 60% [of the voting-age population] who voted. If that other 40% doesn't like me next time and votes, then I'm out.' "

He wants elected officials to know his vote was there to be had, hence his decision to register, but they blew it.

"Politicians say they make an effort, but they don't really listen. They say it's not their problem. 'Not my problem' is the problem." That attitude infuriates him because he has a strong sense of responsibility for himself and his family. He calls it his "John Wayne attitude."

So, on Election Day 1996, Keegan was up early with his sights set, not on the voting booth but on his hunting blind. He's been deer hunting since he was a kid and shot his first buck when he was 13.

It was archery season and a 10-point buck had got away from him a few days earlier.

Medill News Service reporter Julie Fustanio was with him. Her report read as follows:

> He woke up before the sun rose, drank chocolate milk, hunted, smoked a pack and a half of Marlboros and went to bed early after a long day's work.
>
> Eager to escape the pressures of life and the incessant drum of political news, Keegan listened to Arlo Guthrie instead of the morning news on the way up to the woods. When he reached the blind he built, a squirrel rustling in the leaves

and some geese honking overhead were the only sounds as he crouched behind his blind and pointed his crossbow into the darkness.

Camouflage-clad from head to toe, his long brown hair pulled into a ponytail, Keegan waited in silence for more than two hours. But even after he planted scents, cooed and rattled antlers together, no deer appeared.

As he left the woods, Keegan's silence turned to rage when he was reminded that the polls still were open. "[Bob] Dole is a screw-up and [President Bill] Clinton is a liar, drug addict and a thief," he said.

A week later, he bagged the buck.

"That is my escape. Mother Nature is the most calming thing on me."

His other escape is his work as a stonemason. When he was almost 13, he walked onto a job site and was hired to work summers and weekends, whenever he wasn't in school in nearby West Chester, Pennsylvania. He speaks fondly of his Italian American boss who taught him the craft of stonemasonry, the art of a few well-placed Italian phrases, and the discipline to control the Irish temper he inherited from his father.

He loves handling stone and shaping it into walls and fences.

"I'm a perfectionist. The stone has to be a certain way. I like building, creating things. I like to be able to use my mind and create something from nothing."

He chips his name in the corner of each wall he completes so his stepchildren and their children will be able to point to his work. He considers it his legacy.

"I was always beat down when I was a kid. I was not allowed to be proud of anything. So now that I can be proud, I don't want to be, at least not publicly. I prefer to say to myself that I did a good job and leave it at that."

He's particularly proud of his restoration work on a 200-year-old farmhouse that is surrounded by a new subdivision.

"When I grew up, none of this land was developed," but the county government isn't trying to stop the growth of new construction.

"Nah, they want the taxes."

He says the increasing population density of the area is getting to be too much for him, particularly because people are becoming less civilized, ruder by the day. "There's an extreme lack of responsibility and of courtesy." And because crime in the area is increasing.

"I'm tired of fighting crazy drivers to get to work. A few weeks ago, on Route 202, a guy came up to my car with a gun to my head and took my money. He was going to kill me over $24. It was three in the afternoon. No one helped me. No one picked up their cellular phone to call for help.

"But then look what society's done to me. I reached for my piece the minute he turned his back. I was going to blow him away over $24.

"It seems that everybody's patience has gotten really thin. Some of us are going to have to start blowing some things off or we're going to have our own little war here between our own people."

But in upstate New York, his dream home beckons as the answer. "People even leave their cars unlocked up there."

He carries the architectural plans for the house with him; it will be set on 10 acres he bought years ago surrounded by woods and a stream. He plans to build much of it himself, certainly all of the stonework. A painting of the home adorns the rear gate of his pickup truck.

He says his work is just as valuable as that of doctors and lawyers, but he makes only $15 an hour and can't afford health insurance. Although he enjoys all of his masonry work, restoration is particularly satisfying because he makes the stone look like it has been there for years. "There's nothing more satisfying to me than adding my work to stages of a stone house built 200 years before I was born, and it looks exactly the same."

As he works, he thinks of the generations of families that lived in the house.

"They were together from birth to death. And everything was tight-knit. Now, most of the time families are like 'Get out of my house.' I always thought living was having your family, watching them grow, and making you proud."

Sitting in the old house in the midst of construction materials, Keegan talks matter-of-factly about his own turbulent childhood. He says he and his older brother often ran afoul of their father, whose outbursts could turn ugly.

His parents divorced when he was 10, but "I only noticed that he wasn't coming home" because he wasn't fighting with the two boys. He was put in foster homes for several years when he was in junior high school. His parents still live in suburban Philadelphia, and Keegan keeps in touch with them.

Although raised as a Roman Catholic, he no longer goes to church, and again anger over politics is a cause. "Right about the time that the priest started telling me how to vote on abortion is the time I said church and politics are supposed to be separate. Good-bye. You're supposed to tell me how to save my soul, not cast my ballot."

At 17, he joined the Marines and was sent to Vietnam as a sharpshooter. He suffered a wound to his right arm, which still is lame, and came home to a country that derided the military service of which he remains proud. "I don't like to talk about [Vietnam], it gets me upset. Way upset."

In fact, he says he spent 9 months in a psychiatric facility after his discharge.

He wandered up and down the West Coast for several years, stopping in California to go to a community college, then taking whatever jobs he could find to support himself. He married a woman he met in Oregon; they returned to Norristown in 1985.

Because of rheumatic fever he had as a child, he required open-heart surgery a few years later. With no health insurance, he lost all his savings, and his wife left him.

Now, after 5 years of marriage to his second wife, Nancy, family is the most important thing to him. Nancy's two children, Denise, a 23-year-old medical transcriptionist, and 21-year-old David have lived with them, although Denise soon will be married. He carries her engagement announcement with him, obviously proud.

Taking responsibility for your actions and taking care of the family are two of Keegan's fundamental tenets.

"Family is the only thing in this world you can trust 100% of the time, other than yourself."

He worries about his family's safety and is insisting his wife and stepdaughter learn to shoot guns. He carries one with him most of the time.

"What matters most is my family. I worry about someone shooting my kids and that they will have the opportunities" for success that he never had.

He also values honesty, and the decline of ethical behavior in America, particularly among politicians, is what he considers the biggest problem facing the country today.

"Anyone had the chance to win my vote this election," he told Fustanio of Medill News Service on Election Day. "They all blew it."

He cites Abraham Lincoln and Ronald Reagan as two presidents who were honest.

"Everybody in politics has lost the reality that the public wants to hear the truth and not the bull. I want an individual in there who will take responsibility for what they do."

He believes retired General Colin Powell is honest and admires his military service. He suggests Powell, with Ross Perot as a running mate to provide business acumen, would be a ticket he could vote for.

"Powell's got the stamina and the truth to stand there and do what the people want, all the way."

The idea of reflecting Americans' opinions is lost in Washington, he believes.

He suggests more issues ought to bypass Congress and be put to votes directly by the people, referendum-style.

He also doesn't think party affiliation means much. He registered as a Republican but says he would just as easily vote for a Democrat.

"I've never been in a voting booth, but I'm saying something by not voting. Your vote is the only power that you have in this country . . . and not voting was just as important as voting."

He doesn't believe in compromising his vote by electing the better of two candidates when he doesn't really support either.

"If everybody who voted this last election, but voted for the better of two choices, did not vote, I would have liked to have seen how many people actually would have voted," he says. "That's the number I want to see—people who voted for who they wanted to, not who they thought they should."

One of the many things that angers him about politicians is the constant stories of philandering or rumored philandering.

"If you can't commit to your wife, why should I believe you?" he says. "I don't want a sneaky president. Somebody should believe in their vows."

On the other hand, he thinks the media hype such stories too much when there are more important issues that should be addressed, such as the state of U.S. education.

"We've got to equal out every education system so that we know every system in California is teaching exactly what the system in New York is teaching."

An avid fisherman as well as a hunter, he worries that the environment is not being protected and that too many government agencies have succumbed to developers' demands.

He's very patriotic and believes in the United States' authority to lead the world but says the country's leaders are squandering the moral authority America should have.

"If this country could get together on one thing, it could be a start. But [President Bill] Clinton won't do it because he's a liar."

He wrote to state and local officials in 1996 to urge them to oppose a new wing being built at the Veterans Administration hospital in Coatesville, Pennsylvania, for veterans' families, saying veterans should have top priority. He's written a lot of letters to politicians but hasn't heard back from many of them.

The unanswered letter that most bothers him is one Nancy wrote to New Jersey Governor Christine Todd Whitman after Whitman spoke out against fathers who don't pay child support. He says his wife had a judgment against her ex-husband for delinquent support payments totaling $25,000, but the New Jersey state agencies were not trying to pursue him because he no longer lives in the state and her children are older than 18 now. She asked Whitman for help, mentioning her support for Whitman's stance on deadbeat dads. She never got a response.

"If you get someone to help us on this, I'll start believing in government," Keegan says. No one, despite letters to state law associations, the administrative judge, and various state agencies, tried to find the former husband.

"This is one of the issues she talked about. So a former constituent, somebody who was wronged while in the state of New Jersey, writes and asks the governor for help and doesn't get a response."

He believes Whitman's attitude is common among elected officials. Politicians don't listen even if you vote, as his wife does, he says. "I told Nancy, 'The next time you go out and vote, tell me what it does.' Here's a perfect example of why people say, 'The hell with it.' It's all talk. It's what you needed to say to get the vote that you needed to get into the position that you're in."

He says the New Jersey Republican's lack of response also reflects the "not my problem" syndrome plaguing election officials.

He says in the future he will be hunting and fishing and working with stone, but on his own terms in his own home.

And politicians looking for his vote will have to prove themselves to him. "They'll have to be someone I could trust."

Although he says he looks forward to voting some day, he's skeptical any candidate will move him to go to the polls.

"I registered. Doesn't mean I have to vote. Give me somebody I want to vote for. I'll vote."

But he expects it will be a lot harder than finding that 10-point buck.

———— ◄o► ————

Melody Lewis

Hollow Faces on Parade

It wasn't too long ago that Melody Lewis voted. She sensed, though, as the 1996 presidential election approached, that she wasn't going to vote because she had moved to the small town of West Plains, Missouri, from Memphis, Tennessee, only about 2 years earlier and hadn't yet gotten around to registering to vote. No reason to register, no reason not to register. "It's all a circus," the 31-year-old Lewis says of politics. On Election Day, she was back in Memphis, visiting her family because an aunt was in the hospital. She didn't vote and didn't think twice about it.

Lewis had voted fairly regularly when she lived in Memphis, where she had grown up. But each time she voted, Lewis was pulling levers for candidates she knew nothing about. "I remember going and standing in the booth and just picking buttons, and I didn't know who John or Joe was or what they did or did not believe in," Lewis says. "It was just feeling like that was your obligation to vote and maybe that's part of the reason why I don't [vote] since I'm not that involved in it politically." She remembers the booth but not any of the candidates.

"If I saw their names on a list, maybe I'd come up with one." Being from Tennessee, she knows that Al Gore is a Tennessean, but she doesn't know if she ever voted for him or what he ran for, other than for vice president.

Lewis never has paid much attention to political affairs or election campaigns. Whenever she does, she feels what she observes is phony and artificial. "It's just for a face out there. You hear all these things they're gonna do, they're gonna promise," she says. "In the end, usually, it seems like all the things they promise don't get followed through on."

The recurring image that sticks with her is one of posturing in which candidates, propped up by moneyed interests and goaded by the news media, vie for the spotlight only to sling mud at each other. "Everything you hear or see is him on vacation or him with that person," Lewis says. "We hear about who he's sleeping with or what money he's hidden in the past or how many girlfriends he's had, and it's that way every year no matter who it is, and then when it comes down to the election, the two people end up going at each other's throat and cutting each other down."

Republican or Democrat, conservative or liberal—Lewis refers to the terms as labeling. "I'm this, I'm that, so what?" she asks. "When it boils down to the candidates, they're all fighting for the same issues. One might have a little different way of looking at it here or there, but to me, it just seems like they're all alike," Lewis says. "Parties are nit-picking this and that and avoiding issues." She recently consulted a dictionary to figure out if she was a liberal or a conservative. She says she read the definitions. A liberal is "open-minded or not strict in the observance of orthodox or traditional or established forms or ways"; a conservative is "tending or disposed to maintain existing views, conditions, or institutions." The definitions didn't get her anywhere. "I don't know where I would fall. You tell me," she says.

For Lewis to believe that anything in politics is real, she would have to see it for herself. She has never met a politician. "It is just someone standing for the United States, but it seems that that person isn't the real person. I don't know what his actual day-to-day, everyday job is.

"I wouldn't mind being the fly on the wall, listening to what he did that day, from the time he got up and had his coffee to the time he went to bed, how many issues he did look at or read about or discussed," Lewis imagines. "Or did he have his morning coffee and go out and play golf 'till dinner and come home and talk with his family and go to bed?"

Lewis's family didn't talk about politics or political affairs when she was growing up. The men closest to Lewis—her father, her ex-husband, and her husband—have voted. She's not aware that any of them favored a particular political party or ever strongly supported any candidate. She's not sure about her mother, whom she describes as reserved and nervous when it comes to politics. "She feels like if you have any kind of political belief, one way or the other, then if somebody disagrees with you, you're liable to have a maniac knocking at your door, wanting to kill you because you believe differently than he believes."

There is no political figure, historical or contemporary, that Lewis admires. The closest is President John Kennedy. "I feel like I don't know a lot about them, but I respect a lot of what I hear about John Kennedy, and even his family after that," Lewis says. "It seemed like everyone was so emotionally attached to him. I was so young. I hear people really respected him and followed him."

"I liked [Bill]] Clinton when he came around. I agreed with some of the things he said, and he was down-to-earth for our times." Lewis says. "But maybe that wasn't such a good thing now that you see all the dirt that's comes out about him." She voted for him in 1992, but then she lost interest. "I'd rather hear what they're doing to make a difference, instead of where they're going on vacation or where their daughter's going to college," she says. "One of the problems is you get clouded with all that other stuff that you forget about what he ever stood for," Lewis reinforces later as she tries to specify what Clinton has accomplished in his first 4 years in office.

The issues Lewis cares about are welfare, immigration, and the possibility, even if it's remote, of a government conspiracy. She mentions the Oklahoma City bombing, for which two men, Timothy McVeigh and Terry Nichols, have been convicted. "For whatever reasons, the government may be involved," she says of the April 1995 bombing that resulted in the deaths of 168 people and injuries to another 500. "I mean they're [the government] supposed to be protecting everyone, not killing them off even if they're having to cover something to protect their own butts. I hope and pray that they weren't involved. That would be just horrible. There would be no place to go."

Lewis graduated from high school a year early by taking an English course in summer school and took a full-time job doing order entry for a vending supplies company "to get on with my life, whatever that would be." Lewis was married by the age of 20 to a man she had dated since she was 15; she was divorced at 23. She remarried in 1990, and with her husband, Chad, their two dogs and two cats, she moved to West Plains, where Chad's grandparents retired 2 years before. He loved to hunt and fish there and got an optician's position at a Wal-Mart.

When they moved, Lewis's hourly wage dropped from $11.60 an hour in Memphis as a customer service phone operator to $4.70 as a cashier at a convenience store. The best she's been able to do since, she says, is $5.50 an hour, doing accounting work for a small-chain shoe store. Every other Saturday, she cleans houses to earn some extra money. Her work goal is to find a job in which she can put her skills in customer service to better use.

The couple rents an A-frame house that is built into a ridge, nestled in the woods and a few unpaved roads removed from the nearest rural route. The landlord owns 50 acres and rents out five houses on the property. The neighbors guard their privacy. One told Lewis when she introduced herself that he hadn't met any of his neighbors in 3 years.

Lewis watches television news every night and the television newsmagazine programs regularly. In her rural location, she receives only two stations, both out of Springfield, 85 miles northwest of West Plains. They do not have cable. When she lived in Memphis, Lewis read the newspaper almost every day. She now reads the local paper about three times a week. She wasn't very interested in local affairs when she lived in Memphis. She says she's even less interested in West Plains.

To Lewis, politics never mattered. Whether she voted or not, she felt uninformed and uninterested. Now she's also turned off. Even the most concerted efforts to draw her back into the electoral process would be futile, Lewis thinks, even if she voted. "I don't have the time," Lewis says she would tell a candidate if one came personally to her door. "It would probably be a way to get rid of him. The person might be able to get me to vote, depending on my mood and what he said. A lot of it, boiling down to why I do or don't vote, may be ignorance," Lewis suggests. "That I don't know a lot about it."

She senses that every time she checks to find out what's going on, she picks up mostly rumor, meaningless catfighting, and "hollow faces on parade" whose names she cannot remember. "I keep thinking it's not really the person, not really how they feel, not anything about what they intend to do. They're just telling you what they want you to hear," she says. "Who cares about it? I don't."

——— ◄o► ———

Caren Freigenberg

A New Yorker at Heart, She Won't Vote in New Jersey

Caren Freigenberg had been a registered voter most of her life, participating in every national election and most local ones since she turned 18. But in 1994 she moved to New Jersey, and she stopped voting.

When she left her tiny flat in Chelsea in lower Manhatttan and crossed the Hudson River for a spacious apartment in a luxury high-rise in New Jersey near Fort Lee, she lost her connection to the community she lives in. After more than 2 years, she's still more likely to know what's going on in New York than in her New Jersey suburb of Cliffside Park.

"It's like . . . registering in New Jersey is admitting to living in New Jersey when I look at myself as more of a New Yorker."

Even after several years in New Jersey, she knows little about the state—by choice.

"I used to vote a lot. When I lived in Manhattan, I voted in every election. I had an ex-roommate who was a schoolteacher, and I voted in school board elections. And it's only since I've been in New Jersey that I haven't voted."

She also says her nonvoting is part laziness, part a sense of impermanence—a feeling that New Jersey is a temporary stop. "Partly it was, when I moved, the laziness of never getting around to registering or figuring out where to register," although on Election Day there was a polling place in the children's playroom in the basement of her building, she says. "It was partly the whole change in what I was doing in my life and where it was going. Was I staying? Why change your driver's license to a new address? And why change other things like that?"

In the 1996 presidential election, she wanted to vote, as she had in every presidential election after she turned 18. Freigenberg, then 40, tried to vote in Wesley Hills, a suburb of New York in Rockland County, because her mother thought she might still be registered there from her college days, but she wasn't.

"That was the fault of listening to my mother say, 'Oh, yeah. You're still on the books here.' And I wasn't. They had finally taken me off the books after years without being there."

She now is among those Americans who, in her opinion, don't have much right to complain if they don't like the way things are going because they didn't register their choices at the polls.

But although she may not complain about today's public policy decisions, she has strong feelings about today's politicians. "That's probably why I don't [vote]. Because there are so many who I think have a hidden agenda. And I don't trust them. I don't believe in them."

Her disdain for politicians and other institutions associated with elections and the political process, particularly the news media, also is part of the equation for Freigenberg's nonvoter status. "Don't blatantly lie. And if you make a mistake, be upfront about it instead of always twisting things. If you're not upfront, then you only end up with lies. You keep trying to balance it out.

"A lot of it has to do with the press taking something and twisting it around." She also believes that the news media manipulate information and report things people don't need to know. The sex lives of politicians are irrelevant, but they're reported because the media want to provide "too much sensationalism," she says. "It's not like he's going to destroy the country if he has an affair or he doesn't have an affair. . . . It's his and his wife's problem. It's not my problem."

But she also faults politicians for bringing up such personal issues for political purposes under the guise of family values.

"When [former Vice President Dan Quayle] preached about family values and the whole thing he brought up with *Murphy Brown,* I thought what she [Murphy Brown actress Candace Bergen] said in response was really good. What constituted family? And who's preaching about family values? [Bob] Dole was divorced. And Newt Gingrich left his wife while she was in a hospital bed. It's like, 'Excuse me, who's preaching family values? Who are you to say what's right and what's wrong?' "

Although she has clear opinions on how politicians ought to act, she rarely discusses them with family or friends. "My family means a lot to me. But we almost never have political conversations with each other. And part of the reason is that my sister is a lot more conservative, and I know I'm not going to agree with [her]. So instead of having a discussion, we've just avoided the subject."

She says she's even less likely to bring up politics with friends.

"Very rarely do my friends and I ever have these conversations. . . . I think the reason I don't want to discuss it is because we have differing opinions, and rather than bring them up, we choose to ignore them."

She adds with a smile, "I don't talk about it with anybody. I have arguments with the TV."

The family has regular get-togethers. Her brother in Utah and sister in Ohio, their children, her parents, and Freigenberg vacation together at least once every year: Recent trips included Aruba, Disneyworld, and Lake Tahoe. "It's an unusually close family."

In fact, although her parents have moved to Florida, her father stays with her during the week because he still practices dentistry in the Bronx and flies up each Monday to see patients at his office.

Freigenberg was born in the Bronx and lived there until she was 8 years old, when her parents moved 35 miles north to the suburbs in Rockland County.

"My father is a phenomenal dentist and a terrible businessperson. But he loves what he does. He's very content. Someone described him as a gentle giant because he's 6 feet, 4 inches and he's quiet unless you rile him up."

Her mother is the more vocal of the two. She admires her mother for going back to college and starting a career after being a homemaker for nearly 20 years. "My mother went from being a housewife to getting her bachelor's [degree] 1 month before I did. To getting her master's." Her mother became a weight control counselor for several years before becoming a realtor.

Freigenberg got her bachelor's degree in 1977 from Florida State University, majoring in interior design.

"Even as a kid, I always loved putting together spaces and rooms and colors. You don't go into interior design to make money. You go into it for the love of doing it and for the sense of pride you get in creativity." Her first job after college was in interior design working on office spaces, but she switched to the textile industry in 1991 because the interior design industry "took a nosedive" and she wanted more stability. She began selling fabrics for furniture and wall coverings to businesses and, in 1995, decided to leave her company and do the same type of work as an independent contractor. She now represents fabric lines to businesses all over Manhattan, northern New Jersey, and Westchester and Rockland counties north of New York City.

"I like being my own boss. . . . You work hard, but you're working harder for yourself instead of anybody else."

She's very self-assured as she moves from sales call to sales call. Although she pulls a large suitcase on wheels that's filled with fabrics, Freigenberg looks poised and professional in a tailored silk pantsuit.

"Most of the people I call on are people I've called on for 6 years. . . . I'm a soft-sell person. I'm not hard-sell at all. There's too many people in my industry that are hard-sell."

She has several suitcases filled with fabrics and paperwork or sales brochures; they took up so much space that she moved to a second, larger apartment in her building in New Jersey. They had caused the same problem in her fourth-floor walk-up in Chelsea, quickly filling all available space. "It was an adorable 450 square foot apartment that had a working fireplace and a real kitchen." But she decided to move when she was trying to decide whether to buy a vase and realized her decision was based on whether she had a place to put it in the tiny apartment.

"I looked in New Jersey reluctantly. . . . Now I'm 7½ miles from Times Square. I clocked it once. So it's faster for me to go to the Upper East Side from where I am now than it was for me to get there from Chelsea."

She describes the wonderful views of the Manhattan skyline from her full-length windows and balcony. But she has no sense of New Jersey as home, her community.

"New Jersey's got a different kind of mentality. If you're a family, there's things to do, but basically in the 3 years that I've been here I know where the movies are, I know where some restaurants are, and I know where shopping is. But other than that, there's not much else to do. The one jazz club I knew closed. Everybody just says, 'We'll just go to the city.' "

She doesn't read the New Jersey papers, favoring *The New York Times* and New York TV stations.

"I think New York gets under your skin and doesn't let you go. You can't compare any other city with it."

Her knowledge of New York is deep; of New Jersey, shallow. She can name the local New York politicians but doesn't mention those who represent her in New Jersey.

As she eats lunch at a nouvelle American restaurant on lower Park Avenue, she pauses to push back her long, curly brown hair and quickly assesses the city's succession of mayors: Ed Koch, who was in charge when she moved there, loved the city, but catered to developers; it was a fluke that David Dinkins, Koch's successor, won; and Rudy Guiliani is sneaky.

The same type of negative descriptions comes out when Freigenberg talks about senators and presidents. Although she leans Democratic in her politics, her disdain for most elected officials cuts across party lines.

President Jimmy Carter was just a peanut farmer, she says, although she admires the work he's doing now building homes for poor people through Habitat for Humanity. President Ronald Reagan "destroyed the country. The '80s for a lot of people were great, but for a lot of others, they were not. And he destroyed the whole infrastructure, built everything on a false economy. . . . I was totally opposed to Reaganomics. I don't think [George] Bush did much else to change that philosophy."

The economy is a big issue for her. Reaganomics forced up apartment prices in New York, she says, making it difficult to afford a roomy apartment even on her annual income of more than $50,000.

She volunteered in the 1992 campaign of Democrat Robert Abrams, but "it was more working against [Senator] Al D'Amato," whom she considers the worst politician in Washington. D'Amato won that race by a narrow margin.

She also went to a national rally in Washington in the 1980s to support the right of a woman to choose to have an abortion. "I'm a strong believer in choice. . . . I wasn't supposed to go. I took the bus." She says she has given money to and done volunteer work for Planned Parenthood and the National Abortion and Reproduction Rights Action League.

"You have an individual right to choose what is correct for you. Nobody else can tell me what I can do with my body."

In the 1996 election, conservative Christians controlled the Republican National Convention, and the party platform opposed abortion. But despite her strong pro-choice sentiments, she wasn't moved to go to the polls on Election Day.

"I guess I was just showing my belief that it wasn't going to be in jeopardy."

The Washington figure from this century whom Freigenberg most admires is Eleanor Roosevelt, a strong woman who didn't run for office. Her husband, President Franklin Roosevelt, did a lot of damage, in Freigenberg's estimation, because he initially didn't support Jews fleeing Hitler. "He told Jews that he was their friend when he wasn't."

One of the few politicians Freigenberg talks about positively is New York Democratic Senator Daniel Moynihan. "I just like the fact that he's upfront."

He's one of the few, she believes. "They all justify themselves—can we make concessions to this? You're electing them for their beliefs, but you want them to listen to who they came from [in their home districts]. With Dole, he's preaching he's a small-town Kansas boy. Well, he hasn't lived in Kansas in 40 years. Clinton—he's not from Hope, Arkansas. He hasn't been to Hope, Arkansas, in 40 years. Don't think everybody's stupid and naive. That's how a lot of politicians frame people to be. They try to feed you what the public wants to hear. I would rather you tell me the truth."

She says U.S. Representative Carolyn McCarthy, the Long Island nurse who ran for Congress after her husband was killed and her son was wounded in a shooting spree on the Long Island Railroad, is admirable because "she's fighting for what she believes in"—gun control—and she's willing to admit the issues she doesn't know.

"She wasn't letting the political powers that be control the way she spoke, what she talked about. It's hard to know whether big bad Washington will corrupt her or not."

"Big bad Washington" has little impact on Freigenberg's daily life, she says, and thinks that's true for many other Americans. However, she realizes decisions in Washington in the long run will affect her. And she may get back to voicing her opinion about it through the ballot some day, particularly if she sees someone running for president who, like D'Amato in the Senate, makes her want to say, "No way."

"Up until [1996], I voted in every election and I never voted *in* a president. . . . I guess I'm not so much voting for someone as against someone else."

But first she will have to register as a voter. In New Jersey.

——— ◄◦► ———

6

Don't Knows

Voting is considered by many the simplest, most minimal of political actions. Susan Godoy of Rosemead, California, thinks otherwise. "Voting is a very responsible thing to do." Going to the polling place is easy, she agrees, but becoming informed so her vote has meaning takes time and effort.

Godoy kept herself deliberately uninformed about politics until a family problem brought her into contact with government. Now, at age 41, she's trying to pay attention to the news, but her interest level is low. She's concerned about gangs but says politicians aren't doing anything substantive to help kids stay out of gangs.

Elizabeth Baxley doesn't trust elected officials or government agencies. They lie, she's convinced. Even though her family receives financial aid from the government, she only counts on family, fearing any government help will be taken away. She doesn't keep up with political news because she would rather not hear empty promises. In fact, every 4 years, the Scranton, South Carolina, native refuses to watch TV on her birthday. She was born on January 20, the same date as Inauguration Day. "I hate my birthday on those years. I don't even put on my TV on that day because I'd just have to watch the man who lied become president."

George Perez watches TV news every night and knows the names of a few politicians. But he doesn't know what a senator or U.S. representative does. The 36-year-old lifelong resident of El Paso, Texas, doesn't work and lives in the past much of the time, watching reruns of old TV shows and listening to music from the 1960s. His biggest concern is that his Social Security payments not be reduced. Whatever happens, however, he assumes will be beyond his control.

Erica Smith may be uninformed about most political issues, but one—domestic violence—got her involved in politics briefly, when she called a campaign office to find out the candidate's position. That involvement convinced her to stay away because no one from the campaign returned any of her calls. The 29-year-old resident of Lynn, Massachusetts, is hiding from her son's father, who used to beat her.

Like many nonvoters, at least one of her parents voted. Her dad still badgers her to vote, but she says it's a waste of time. If she wanted to, she says, it's an easy process but one with which she doesn't want to connect. She gives another example of how politics doesn't work for people like her: When Hillary Rodham Clinton visited her son's grade school in 1996, the kids sat in the cold, targets for snipers, while they awaited the first lady and her police-protected entourage.

Susan Godoy

Cracks in Her Fairy-Tale World

Susan Godoy always has felt insecure about voting. When she turned 18 in 1973, voting didn't matter to her. She was living in her parents' protective bubble in Rosemead, California, near Pasadena, about a 20-minute drive from Los Angeles.

Her parents voted. That mattered to her because she respected them. They didn't discuss politics at home, and Godoy assumed her mother voted however her father did.

She was born Mary Susan Sanchez, Hispanic by ancestry but American by birth, like her parents, and speaks no Spanish.

"I always had this thing that I was stupid and that you had to have intelligence to vote," Godoy says. "When I was 18, I lived in a fairy-tale world. My mom and dad protected me. There was no violence, no trouble, other than no date for the night."

By the time of the first presidential election in which she could vote, in 1976, Godoy was married and a mother. For a few years, she stayed home to care for the children. She began working in the early 1980s, earning $10 an hour at Caltrol, a control valve company near her home. She still works there after six promotions and, as a sales engineer, she now earns more than $35,000 a year. She has three children, one grandchild, and another on the way and still lives near her mother and siblings. "To me, being a mother is the greatest thing in the world," Godoy says of the one task that "doesn't come with a set of instruction manuals." She asks nothing in return and is buoyed that her children are proud of their mother's accomplishments without a college education.

She doesn't vote, isn't registered, and never has registered to vote. Neither has her husband nor her two children who have turned 18. She explains her civic lapse as a reflex conditioned by compounding resistance. First indifference, then preoccupation with home and job. "I never kept up on issues. Government issues are not my problem. My problem is working and taking care of my kids," Godoy says. "The last thing I want to do is think about going somewhere to vote . . . or reading the pamphlets on issues."

Godoy worked at staying uninvolved until she got yanked out of her bubble. Her oldest son, Guy, was being drawn into a gang and getting into deeper and deeper trouble. Petty crime, juvenile camp, attempted murder charges. "It all changed when my son got in trouble," Godoy says of the collapse of her fairy-tale world. "Having a child go the wrong way is the most dramatic thing in the world. I had to become smarter, I just had to."

Godoy stopped looking the other way. She discovered officials and agencies that came through, others that she had to fight. She started paying attention to television news. She gained confidence, only to realize how little she knew. She doesn't know who the governor of California is, who the state's U.S. Senators are, the names of local politicians, or the differences between Democrats and Republicans. She says she's closer to registering and voting now than she ever has been, but something else troubles her. "Voting is a very responsible thing to do," Godoy reflects. And she's not there yet.

Godoy's son was 16 years old when she first became aware of his gang involvement. "At first, I didn't want to believe it," Godoy says. Guy was getting arrested periodically for petty crimes. Godoy would pick up her son from the police station. Her first challenge was to get Guy back in school after he had dropped out. She succeeded.

The next summer, it wasn't so easy. Guy had stolen a pizza from a delivery-man. "The cops came with guns drawn. My 5-year-old witnessed it," Godoy recounts. "It was too far out of hand." When police took Guy to the station, Godoy decided that time, she wouldn't go down to get him. It was time for tough love. Guy spent 8 months in a juvenile camp.

While he was in the camp, Godoy visited him every Saturday. She heard parents say that they were not coming to visit anymore. "I would think, 'If I give up on him, how does he keep making it? Does he give up on himself, too?'" Godoy recalls. "I just don't think you give up on your kids."

Her encounters with officials at the camp and with those in the criminal justice system were mostly favorable. "They'd try hard to lead the kids down the right path," Godoy says. Godoy's father died while Guy was in a transitional home following the juvenile camp. The camp wouldn't release him to attend his grandfather's funeral. The public defender who represented Guy agreed to meet Godoy in court right away. They convinced a judge to release Guy on a 12-hour leave. "I'll always be grateful for that," Godoy says. "I really didn't expect for it to happen, and I needed that kid home."

"People see gang members as hard core. It isn't the case with all of them," Godoy says. She stuck with her son and began thinking ahead about her younger son. She tried to find an organization to help out but got nowhere. "'What do you want, lady?' was the attitude," Godoy says of the boys club, the church, and the police. She wanted to find a way to have kids be in a controlled environment, and she offered to watch them.

Guy was arrested again, this time charged with attempted murder. He spent more than 4 months in jail before pleading guilty to lesser charges based on an admission that he was at the scene but not involved in the crime.

Guy was leading two lives: one as part of the Bartlett street gang, the other as a young father, living in Godoy's home with his girlfriend and daughter. Godoy watched as her son fanned his girlfriend while she was in labor. She saw him playing with children and telling his younger brother, Rudy, not to go the way he did. "He'd imitate what gangs say," Godoy recollects. "'Where you from?' he would ask Rudy. Rudy would say, 'Nowhere.' 'That's right,' Guy would say, 'Nowhere.'

"A lot more attention has to be paid to gang members as people. If somebody could understand they're people with feelings, looking for a way out. It's so hard to find a job once you're in a gang. Not a single politician speaks to that. They all say they want to get the gangs off the streets, 'three strikes and you're out,' " Godoy observes. "If someone campaigned in a way that dealt with gang kids as people, I'd not only register and vote, but I'd ask 'What can I do to help?' "

The problems Godoy has had with her son have mixed with her accomplishments at work to give her confidence in unexpected ways. Her son told her once that he turned to a gang because he needed someone to rely on. He didn't have much of a relationship with his father. "What about me? I'm here constantly," she thought. "Of course, I'm a woman and he needed a man." Godoy says she learned to be more independent.

Her husband has gone through prolonged periods of unemployment. She has become the financial and emotional backbone of the family. Godoy's sister was 16 years old when she had a baby and 23 when her husband, a private detective, was shot and killed. Her sister has had a difficult time supporting herself and her daughter. "I'll tell my husband, 'Watch me,' if he tells me not to do something," Godoy says of her changed attitude. "I don't feel that anybody has the right to tell somebody else what they can and cannot do."

When she was in high school, Godoy reflects, her goal was to be a secretary. She took typing and shorthand. She didn't associate with anyone who talked politics and didn't know anyone who was in politics. Her biggest mistake in life, she says, is not going to college, not even considering it. If she had a chance to do it all over, she would be a lawyer, helping people with their problems and knowing how to solve them.

Before her father died, Godoy felt he would keep her informed. She didn't read the newspaper or watch television news. Her father did. After he died, Godoy had a conversation with her mother about the election campaign pamphlets and sample ballots her mother would take to bed with her and read. She reminisced with her mother about how her father would complete the sample ballots for her mother. Her mother told her she would always take the completed ballots and throw them away. She would then vote for whomever she wanted.

Godoy is confident about her career, less so about her political involvement. "I'm going where I'm headed," she says of her plans to stay at her employee-owned control valve company until she retires. Her professional goal is to "engineer any valve by myself without asking." Her civic goals are more complicated. One of her goals is to vote. "I always say I want to [register], that is just one of the things I want to do. I just haven't done it," Godoy says.

The acts of registering and voting are the easier steps for Godoy. The harder part is being sufficiently apprised of issues or candidates to feel comfortable voting. Her experiences with her son's gang activity have made her recognize that political decisions affect her life directly. She appreciates the connection between her problems and those she believes the country needs to face: crime and violence, education, and homelessness. She even believes that elected officials care about the same problems. "I think they do care. I just don't think they take the time to find out everybody's thoughts," Godoy says. "I think they have to care about what people think. Otherwise they're not going to get elected."

She is tough on herself. "I don't know what's going on [in Washington] so it can't affect me," Godoy starts to say. "I mean, I'm sure it does, but I'm naive to it." A few years ago, a work colleague expressed amazement that she did not watch the news on television. She has watched the news ever since, for an hour every morning before she goes to work. She no longer flips the radio dial away from the news. But when the president comes on, she spaces out. "Nothing sparks my interest in what he says so I don't listen," she admits.

Bob Dole, who ran against Bill Clinton in the 1996 presidential election, piqued her interest favorably. She was doing a crossword puzzle and "Dole" was one of the answers. His name became familiar to her, and she came to think of him as more honest than Clinton. "If I voted, I would've voted for him," she says. She also thinks favorably of Ronald Reagan. "My parents liked him so he must be good," she says.

Godoy still doesn't read a newspaper. Her son Rudy does as part of a school assignment, and they talk about some of the current affairs. One of Rudy's teachers is a councilman in Rosemead. Godoy says her inclination is to call him and become more active, though she hasn't. She is intent on keeping Rudy away from gang activity.

Her daughter, who has turned 18, lives at home, as Godoy did when she became old enough to vote. Her daughter is not registered to vote, and neither Godoy nor her daughter thinks she will vote in the foreseeable future. It's not something they talk about. What Godoy wants for her daughter is that she go to college, get an education, and know that she can have "a say-so."

"A lot of people don't vote because 'What's one vote? What's it gonna matter if I don't vote? I'm only one person,' " Godoy suggests. But people need to know, she says, reflecting on her children, "they do have a say-so in what goes on. So I'd like to see my kids vote. I'd like to see them take an active interest in government, be aware of what's going on, and what their rights are."

She comes back to Guy. "I guess I have gotten fed up with the government. You're only helped if you're on the good side. If you're on the bad side, then you can't have help, you've got no say-so, and you've got no rights, and I don't think that's fair," Godoy says. "In some way, why bother? Why go through this?"

———— ◄o► ————

Elizabeth Baxley

Family Matters, Politics Don't

Every 4 years, Elizabeth Baxley hates her birthday. On her January 20th birth-date in those quadrennial years, a president is inaugurated, which she says ruins her celebration.

"You go through the whole election year and you look at all these campaign things and say 'Well, you know which one is going to get it [the presidency] because you know which one is lying through his teeth.' Every 4 years that's what you're going to see.

"I don't even put my TV on that day unless I'm going to watch a movie. Because every 4 years all you're going to do is watch that president go into office after he's lied. I say 'I didn't help him get in there, and I'm surely not going to help him get out of it once he gets in trouble.' "

Baxley has no kind words for anything related to politics or government. Although her family receives federal financial assistance because of her husband's disability and her mother supported her children with the help of welfare, Baxley has a profound distrust of government. She accepts as gospel that any help given by government agencies can and, at some point, will be taken away at a moment's notice.

Her opinion of public officials is just as distrustful.

"They can make some pretty speeches now and promise you a whole lot. But I don't think there's any change, I really don't, because the government has been one way for so long. It's like a married couple. They get set in their ways and ain't nothing going to change."

Elections don't make for change, she says. "Voting? The only thing that it is—an opinion poll. I just don't feel like what you vote for will really make a difference because they are going to do exactly what they want with the government to start with." Elected officials only listen to those who have contributed to their campaigns, she says, and the agencies set up to help those in need often don't provide the kind of help necessary for people to keep their lives or families together.

Baxley doesn't listen to the officials either, turning away from political or public policy news at both local and national levels. National politics are particularly outside her interest. She knows that if she watches the news too often or reads the paper too much, she can count on tales of political doings that will never affect her and on which she can have no impact.

The only thing Baxley counts on is family.

"People tell me not to look at it that way, but I've seen people who need help, I mean honestly and truly need it and cannot get it. I know from experience. I've been through a lot of things because my momma had her children taken from her."

Baxley, who is 43, has lived in the country outside the tiny town of Scranton, South Carolina, population 820, for 21 years, surrounded by family. She and her husband of 26 years, Willard, live with their two sons, 24-year-old Brad and 20-year-old Robert, and Brad's wife, Tracy, in a blue, vinyl-sided home to which they've added rooms over the years. Her husband's brother and his family live next door on one side, and his other brother's widow and children live on the other side.

The shed behind her house is dominated by a large pool table she bought, used, a few Christmases ago for her kids. She said she could afford the $800 because the former owner let her pay in installments.

Outside the shed is the 20-foot Wellcraft she uses for fishing south of Myrtle Beach in the Atlantic Ocean, about 60 miles away.

The house is cluttered with photos of the boys at various ages, and she likes to kid them about staying out too late or working too hard, but her pride in them is evident. "I'm very protective of my children. I say 'God gave 'em to me, and I'm going to do my best to take care of 'em.' "

She calls herself a "plain Jane" who doesn't need much to be happy, just her family.

She has spent the majority of her life in South Carolina, although she was raised in upstate New York near Schenectady until she was 18 years old.

After her father and mother divorced when she was about 3, she and her mother left South Carolina and moved to upstate New York with her mother's second husband. Her mother and stepfather had six children, five boys and a girl, before they split up. Baxley was 15 at the time.

From the time she was 13, her mother started keeping her home from school to help take care of the children. As a result, the local authorities eventually put her in a foster home. "School was the one thing I enjoyed. I loved school, but momma would call them up and tell them to send me home. I reckon the school board had enough of it, and they took us to family court. And I was put in a home for a year and a half."

When she was 17, she was going to be transferred to a second foster home, but she rebelled because she knew her mother needed her help at home. The authorities finally allowed her to return home. Shortly after, the family moved back to South Carolina, but the oldest boy, Al, was left behind in a foster home where he had been placed after a shoplifting incident.

"He never came back home. He moved to California to be with his daddy, which killed my mother. And after I got married, the youngest were taken away again. Mark was in one home, Dale and Billy were in another, and Kenny and Mary Ellen were in another."

Her mother died at age 39. The children's father, still in California, sent for Kenny and Mary Ellen. He then tried to get custody of Dale and Billy, but Baxley convinced the welfare agents that the two boys should stay in foster homes because she said the two kids who had moved in with their father weren't happy.

"Dale and Billy blame me for not being able to be with their daddy. But I tell them, 'Look, you've graduated high school. You've made something of yourselves.' Don't get me wrong. I love my stepfather to death. But there was no way I was going to let those children get away from me. Now they have nothing to do with me. . . . That's a burden I have to live with." The youngest child, Mark, was put up for adoption; she never saw him again.

The only one of her siblings with whom she is close is a stepsister from her father's first marriage who lives in Dillon, South Carolina, near the border of North Carolina.

"I took care of the kids ever since my stepfather left. My mother had a cerebral hemorrhage, and she was sick all the time.

"She needed help. She got some, but she didn't get that much. They come in and they put the kids in what they call a children's shelter, and I went to that children's shelter one time and I didn't like what I saw. But there wasn't any way to do anything about it. I couldn't take care of the kids by myself.

"There are things that the government could do to help, but instead of helping they are hindering. Things could have been better for momma if there had been some help. I've seen caseworkers come into momma's house and momma have one of her seizures that she'd have [because of the hemorrhage]. And momma wouldn't be able to sleep or move her right side. And they'd come in and upset her, threaten her."

Baxley remembers neighbors who helped her mother get groceries and other necessities. The memories reinforce her belief that reliance on the government is chancy, but family and friends come through.

"I've just seen so many people promised so much, and they don't get anything. The harder you work, the less you're going to get. If you get a raise in Social Security [payments], then the insurance goes up. So you fight a little harder. Dig a little deeper. Get a little stronger."

She had to find that strength early in her marriage when her husband, now 50, was seriously injured in a construction accident.

She married at 18 and lived in nearby Lake City with husband Willard, who was a construction worker. Two years after their marriage, when Brad was just 1 year old and Baxley was pregnant with Robert, a block wall fell on Willard while he was working, causing serious injuries to his head and the fingers on one hand. He was in the hospital for several months, mostly in intensive care, and it took nearly a year at home before he was able to do much for himself.

"It was a very long haul. It was 6 or 8 months before we could get Social Security [disability payments]. It got rough on us. They threatened to come take the clothes we were living in. If it hadn't been for churches and family members, we'd have lost what we had."

Her husband hasn't been able to work since the accident because he's deaf in one ear, suffers from double vision and blind spells, cannot keep his balance, and has limited use of his right hand. "He's not able to work because they don't want him around machinery, and he only went through sixth grade because he had to work. That's a hard thing because he worked since he was 13. It drove him nuts."

She says the disability checks and payments she received for her kids, which stopped when the boys turned 18, were hardly enough to cover the costs of raising her family.

Her husband didn't want her to work, but she got a job in 1991 because "I had to do something to keep us going." She went to work at the clothing plant in Hebron after getting job training through the state. She earned a certificate as a sewing machine operator. But she had to leave after 2 years because her allergies flared amid all the cloth and dust.

Now she works in Lake City at Godwin Brothers variety store. Her daughter-in-law works at the clothing plant, Brad is a mechanic for John Deere, and Robert works for a company that builds swimming pools. "We work hard for what we've got. I just wish the system worked better."

Although she rarely follows national news, she remembers a TV newscast about a year and a half ago that scared her because Social Security was being threatened—an entitlement she had counted on.

"They had it on the news where Social Security had gone broke, and they were going through and reviewing papers to see those who could do without Social Security. And we didn't know if we were going to get a check that next month or not. It really makes you sweat bullets because you don't know if you're going to be able to make a light bill or buy groceries to put on the table."

Mainly she tries to ignore the news. She doesn't see a connection to reports from Washington and her life in Scranton. She cannot avoid some of the "big headlines," she says, but she doesn't spend time trying to catch up on the news, particularly if it is from Washington.

She calls herself a worrier, always fretting about how to pay the bills, whether the kids are okay, making sure everybody's as healthy as possible, looking out for her family. She worries that they won't be able to afford the medical care her husband needs. She says Medicare covers most costs, but they have to pick up some of the expenses. And they have to pay for his prescriptions, so he's not taking some pills the doctor recommended because they cost $2 each. Her health insurance is provided through her employer, but it has a clause prohibiting coverage of preexisting illnesses, so it's no help for her husband.

She worries that her married son and his wife cannot afford to buy their own home because prices are too high and they don't have enough credit. "So we're trying to help them, too, and ourselves. This is a tight family, I reckon. See, out here there's nothing but family." She points to the white house on one side where her sister-in-law's family lives and the gray house on the other, owned by her husband's younger brother. "We fight and squabble between us, but we will stand up for each other."

That attitude of cooperation is what's lacking in Washington, she believes. "Phooey with the guy who needs help because he can't put money in their pocket.

"If they are honest when they go in there and they honestly give it a try, it's not long before they are thinking the way everybody else is. The government is more for the richer man, the man who can put money in a pocket or give something impressive. Where's the little man?"

She has never voted because she believes it doesn't change what is going to happen in Washington.

Of those presidents who served during her lifetime, John Kennedy was the only one she liked. "Things seemed to work better then. It was almost like he had walked in my shoes. When he was shot and killed, I even cried."

But Jimmy Carter grinned too much, she says, George Bush sugarcoated what he had to say too often, and Ronald Reagan "wasn't too bad." Bill Clinton gets the harshest critique: "I didn't like that man. He's the biggest liar of them all. Can we not find someone that really wants to help? They say they are going to do their best to help this one or that one, but no. Uh-uh."

The only time she got involved in politics was when her fishing was threatened. She likes to take her two-person aluminum boat to Lynch's River 3 miles away, but recently a plastics company in Lake City wanted to dump waste into the river.

"So far, we've been able to stop it. I signed every petition I could. It would have ruined the fishing and game around the river."

She says she would sign a petition again if the issue was worth fighting for, but with her ingrained skepticism toward politics, "first I'd read the fine print."

— ◄○► —

Erica Smith

Living in Fear

"First Lady pays first visit to Lynn. Hillary Clinton campaigns here Friday."

So read the headline in the *Lynn Daily Evening Item* on October 2, one month before the 1996 presidential election. The story, positioned under a photo of Hillary Rodham Clinton waving as she toured a medical center earlier in the week, announced that the first lady would visit students and teachers at Ford Elementary School in 2 days. The next day, the newspaper ran a reminder: "Hillary here tomorrow."

"First Lady's visit is first rate. Hillary enjoys meeting Ford faculty, students." The story that accompanied the Saturday headline informed the paper's 28,000 readers in the blue-collar town north of Boston that the "first-rate" visit was about both education and politics.

Erica Smith did not read any of the newspaper accounts. She found out from a friend the day before the visit that the first lady was coming. When she was told, her reaction was guarded. She didn't know much about the first lady, but she was favorably inclined and believed Clinton was more sincere than most people in political life. But she thought her 7-year-old son, who was in the school's second grade, wasn't likely to get a chance to meet her.

Smith seldom reads a newspaper. In this case, she didn't have to. She was there. But her account of the event differed markedly from what others read in the paper.

To Smith, the visit turned out not to be an expression of concern about education but the epitome of phoniness and arrogance.

Smith lives with her son and her fiancé across the street from the school. The morning of the visit, she was awakened by a loud bang at the door. She had gotten her son off to school and gone back to bed. It was the Secret Service telling neighbors to move their cars.

" 'Move that car or it's gonna be towed,' " she recalls them yelling. "I thought, 'How rude!'

"Now all of a sudden my mind kicked in that that's my son. The first lady's coming, and what if somebody decides to shoot her or something? They advertised it in the paper. My son might be in the middle of the action."

When she walked outside, she noticed police cars everywhere in sight. She didn't take comfort in it.

"I saw all of these Secret Service everywhere, ready to shoot at anything that moves the wrong way and I just got nervous, you know, if something went wrong. I just thought, 'Why my kid's school?' "

She recalls thinking, "This is Lynn. Anything can go wrong. It's a low-income town; 80% of Lynn makes under $15,000 a year.

"All of a sudden my son is my main priority. He's my thing, and I believe in God well over what I believe in politics or anything."

She joined her neighbors, two older women who were sitting on their porch drinking coffee, cameras ready to capture the once-in-a-lifetime event and maybe, just maybe, to get a shot of the first lady as she entered the school. That irritated her more. "I said, 'I'm not taking pictures, I'm just watching for my child,' " Smith says.

"All of a sudden all of the children came out of the school. They put them behind a rope and made them stay there. There were so many of them. I couldn't even see my child, and I looked and I looked, but they wouldn't let me cross the street."

It was chilly. Smith remembers that she could see her breath. The first lady arrived eventually, went into the school, and spent time with some of the students, teachers, and selected parents. For those 90 minutes, as Smith recalls, the students were shivering outside in the cold, first standing, then sitting. When the first lady emerged, she waved, and the students waved back. Smith's older neighbors watched it all as Smith fumed.

" 'How dare they?' " she told her neighbors. "They were more concerned about her than about the children.

"The people reading about it in the paper who weren't there that day [think], 'How nice of her to come in and teach that first-grade class.' Nobody saw the whole thing. Nobody saw what I saw."

She doesn't blame the first lady. She assumes her advisers told her what to do. She figures it would be the same with any politician.

"That's probably another reason why I won't vote," Smith concludes. "How can you vote when that's happening? Why would you want to vote for these people?

"We're all adults, and the children are our future, so if we put them in danger, then how can they be our future if they're not there anymore?"

Smith has reason to fear. She cloaks her identity, doesn't tell people where she lives, and has asked that her real name and her son's name not be used. She counts how often she has moved since her son's father went to prison for manslaughter for killing one of his childhood buddies: 15 times, and she's preparing to move again when her lease is up. Her son's father used to beat her, and she went public about it in April 1995 when she agreed to be profiled in a story in a local free weekly newspaper about her attempts to have a law enacted that would take away custody and visitation rights from fathers who beat their child's mother. She allowed her name and a photo of her and her son to appear in the story. She regrets the exposure but feels good that the story prompted discussion of domestic violence. She sometimes goes by Erica Smith, one of her stage names. She moonlights as a singer, working late at a seafood restaurant and bar, in addition to holding down two part-time day jobs to make things easier for her son.

At 29, Smith is a single-issue nonvoter. She has convinced herself that if any politician were to sincerely care about her issue, domestic violence, she might vote. She hasn't yet, and she's never been registered because "basically there's nobody that I've seen yet that I'd vote for."

She recounts that during a political campaign a few years ago, she called a few campaign offices to register her views. She refers to the campaigns as "offices of politics." She wanted to know the candidates' positions on custody and visitation rights for men who batter their mates.

"I called four or five times so it wasn't that the message was lost or eaten in the tape." She had taken the phone numbers from campaign literature that was dropped off at her house. She recalls one pamphlet in particular telling prospective voters if they have any issues, the candidate would be more than happy to take time out to discuss them. She can't remember the candidate but recalls the campaign literature had a family photo on the back.

Nobody called back. "It was the straw that broke the camel's back," Smith resolved. "That was it. I was done."

Smith recognizes that if she registers to vote, it will be easier for her son's father to track her down. She's afraid to register but acknowledges that's not why she hasn't registered.

She has no faith that elected officials will confront her issue. "Nobody's dying because of welfare and taxes being raised. It's not a life-or-death problem. Battered women and the crime that's there is a very big issue. It may seem like it's just one woman, but nobody deserves to be hit. Nobody."

To Smith, politics is empty rhetoric. Politicians talk about cutting welfare costs. She observes the problem firsthand.

"I have two friends who are on welfare, and I would say to them, 'Why don't you go to work?' because they're always bored and they don't have any money. They're always complaining about how much the kids are driving them crazy, and they don't have a car because they can't afford one, so I always say, 'Get a job.' [They say], 'Well I can't because I'm on welfare.' And I say, 'How much do you get from welfare?' 'Well I get four something a month plus my rent paid plus this plus food stamps plus child care, and I lose everything if I make this much money. How am I supposed to afford to live?' "

Smith concludes, "Welfare makes it so you can't afford to be off of it. So they stay on it. So how can you cut costs if you don't make these women work? And they say they're going to make them work or only pay for one child and do this, and they never cut costs, and there's still billion of dollars spent." Smith knows better, even though she realizes she doesn't know much.

The news stories on Hillary Clinton's visit identified a slate of officials the first lady was there to support or oppose: Democratic congressional candidate John Tierney, Republican Congressman Peter Torkildsen, U.S. Senator John Kerry, Massachusetts Governor William Weld, and Lynn's Mayor, Patrick McManus. Smith's heard of only John Kerry, but she's stopped listening to anything that they say about each other.

"Every time you turn on the TV during voting season, somebody's on there saying, '[So-and-so] is running for office and he has all these skeletons in the closet.' They go back and forth saying who's bad. Oh, he smoked a joint when he was 17 or he got a speeding ticket or something really stupid that they're digging up." When candidates do talk about an issue, Smith says, they say they're going to take care of it, but they don't.

Smith isn't embarrassed about not voting. She feels that part of the problem is a political system that doesn't care about her and other nonvoters. "If they're only going to cater to those who vote, then they're going to cater only to those who give money," she reasons. "Maybe you didn't vote because you were misled because of all the lies that are being told on TV."

Smith regards the news media with much the same passing disdain she gives politics—something to not pay much attention to. She reads a newspaper about once a week, sometimes the *Boston Globe,* sometimes her hometown daily. She doesn't read magazines, switches the radio dial from news to easy listening music unless "they start out with something really good," and watches television news for the weather. Some news seeps in that way. Her filter is dense and discriminating.

During the O. J. Simpson case, she avoided the news accounts, believing that "everybody's gonna lie at trial," so she wouldn't know for sure what happened and what didn't. She does know that "money talks." Her feeling is that Simpson deserves what he's gotten because he beat his wife, and pictures were found that showed it. She isn't bothered that Simpson was acquitted. "I don't *know* the truth if he really killed her; there were so many mistakes at trial," Smith says. "His name got scattered all over the news, and everyone knows he's a woman beater. Right now, I wouldn't go near O. J. Simpson."

She can't recall the name of Simpson's wife, or much about the recent bombing of a federal building in Oklahoma City, or the name of baby Jessica, although the 10-year-old saga of the child trapped in a well in Midland, Texas, sticks with her. "That [case] shows you that somebody has to be literally near death—a child has to be in a hole, almost dying—for people to turn on the TV, actually say a prayer, care and take time out of their day," Smith says. "Then after it was all over and she was safe and warm, nobody cared anymore, except maybe to write a book or movie." All she can remember of the Oklahoma bombing story was that a day care center was involved and that she felt sick thinking about the people suffering.

Another news account sticks with Smith: the story of a 2-year-old boy who was strangled to death at a local day care center when the drawstring on his windbreaker caught on a tot-lot slide. She had seen something flash across the television and checked for the story in the morning paper. What sticks with her is how incomprehensible it was for people not to have noticed more quickly that the boy was being choked, yet people were blaming the company that made the clothing. The *Boston Globe* had reported that a state lawmaker was considering introducing a bill to ban the sale in Massachusetts of children's clothing with drawstrings.

Smith learned the little she knows about politics from her father. They didn't talk politics at home, but at the age of 16 or 17, Smith would accompany her dad to The Post, a social club he frequented regularly. There, talk would turn to politics.

"I think he was independent. I wouldn't say he was a Democrat or a Republican by any far stretch. He was always looking at who was going to lower taxes. That was his issue," Smith says.

But over time, her father stopped voting too. "Lately he's been saying the same thing as me, that there's nobody good in office right now, there's nobody to vote for," she says. "The last time he voted was for [Jimmy] Carter. He may have voted for [Ronald] Reagan. I remember him saying [Reagan] was a working man, and he was probably going to win because he had so many fans, but he liked Carter," Smith recollects.

Her father tried to convince her when she turned 18 to vote. "He was very into politics and always talking about it, so it wasn't anything I didn't hear," Smith says. "So I knew I could vote if I wanted to, but at that time I think I was too busy to vote. I didn't think about voting until I was about 22. I was too busy dancing and being a kid."

Smith took after her mother. She can't recall her mother ever voting. "She doesn't know anything except about her immediate surroundings. She's oblivious to anything outside," Smith says, adding that her mother has never been out of Massachusetts, except possibly to New Hampshire.

"If you asked her who the president or the first lady are, she wouldn't know," Smith believes. "My mom is just who she is. I don't think moms had to [know anything] back then."

She assumes her older brother doesn't vote. "He's probably afraid of jury duty or some such myth," Smith figures. Her friends don't vote. Her fiancé doesn't vote either. His attitude, like Smith's, is "give me something to vote for." Neither is checking whether a candidate's views reflect their views, and no candidates are seeking them out.

When she was growing up, she lived in Ward 1, where everyone knew everyone, where the precinct captain came around, "where the mayor put his mother to live." "When there is a hole in a street in Ward 1, it's noticed and fixed," she says. In Ward 5, where she lives now, no one comes around to register people because "they don't think we're worth the vote in that neighborhood. I'm surprised that Hillary Clinton came to that school. I'm so surprised," she marvels.

She still argues with her dad. "My dad always says, 'Just register to vote. You never know when you want to vote on something.' And I always say, 'When I want to vote on something, I'll register to vote. It's not all that hard to do. You can do it any time you want. You don't have to. It's not a law.' "

Smith also argues about it with her son. She considers him a keenly observant child. "You have to be very careful how you phrase things 'cause he's going to bring it up again," she beams.

The 7-year-old knows his mother doesn't vote, and that doesn't bother Smith. Her son overheard a conversation she and a friend were having about Hillary Clinton's visit. He chimed in that the visit was the best thing that ever happened to him, having someone so prominent come to his school. Smith wondered why. She reminded her son that he didn't even get to meet the first lady. But he remembered the first lady was wearing a brown outfit. His only disappointment was that he didn't get a chance to talk to her. He told his mom that he had some questions for the president's wife. He didn't like how negatively his mom reacted to the visit and told her, "Well, you don't vote anyways."

Smith is prepared to take him up on his challenge. If the issue of voting comes up again, "I'd tell him I haven't seen anything done, so why vote?" She is sure they will understand each other.

"He's my son, and he knows that if he chooses to vote, that's not a problem with me. If he chooses to be independent, Republican, anything that he chooses to be, is okay with me."

———— ◄○► ————

George Perez

Right There in Spirit if Politicians Touched Social Security

George Perez keeps to himself. The 36-year-old lifelong resident of El Paso, Texas, rarely goes anywhere and doesn't own a car or read a newspaper. But he watches TV every night, including daily viewership of the evening news. He shares a house with his brother in the Lower Valley, a Hispanic neighborhood this side of the Rio Grande River from Cuidad Juarez, Mexico's fourth largest city.

Perez often sits in his sparse bedroom with the blinds fully drawn over metal-grated windows. He refers to the furnishings as "basic, nothing too fancy." The basics are a bed, a dresser, a few music cassettes, and a photograph of his mother. The stereo and VCR that were there a month earlier are now in the pawnshop. He says he is starting to collect movie videos. So far, he has one. His dresser drawers are empty. Nothing is on the walls except a time management chart. It reads

   6—wake, shower

   7—breakfast

   12—lunch

   5—dinner

   10—sleep

The lawn in front of the house has caked away, leaving behind clumps of brittle dirt. "I get paranoid just going out to water the lawn," Perez says nonchalantly, so it mostly goes untended. Perez and his brother Luis have schizophrenia, a chronic brain disorder that afflicts more than 2 million Americans. Perez is on medication and has not worked full-time since shortly after he was honorably discharged from the military more than 15 years ago. "I would take these odd jobs, but they never lasted too long. I could never hold onto a job," he says. He receives a monthly Social Security disability check of $461 and a supplemental payment of $43. His brother receives $484 a month. He says they are having a hard time making ends meet.

He says that Social Security is about all he has. He has never voted. "I don't see how one vote's gonna make any difference unless I knew that it would directly affect me," he says. "I get Social Security and if [a candidate] said, 'We'd give these people a significant increase,' I'd probably be the first one there [at the polling place]." That would take more effort than Perez is accustomed to exerting.

Perez is not registered to vote, and he never has seriously considered registering. "I don't know how the process works," Perez says. The only person who has ever tried to get him to register to vote is his father, a Mexican American who was born in Arizona, drove a garbage truck for the city of El Paso, and voted regularly.

Perez had a hard life, even before he was diagnosed in the military as having schizophrenia. When he was growing up, the conditions in his house were so embarrassing to him, he recalls, that he stopped having his friends over. The toilets didn't work, and the family had no shower. He and his six brothers and sisters bathed in a large tin tub.

Still, he did what kids did back in the 1960s, he says. "I had to do without a lot of things, but I had a lot of fun," he recalls. "I was too busy being a kid and having fun to notice how bad."

He watched a lot of television. "It had a lot of novelty. It had *Ed Sullivan,* Beatlemania, *Laugh-In,* Dick Clark's *American Bandstand.* The one I was most fond of was *Lost in Space,*" he recalls. He recently found and bought a battery-operated toy robot that's a replica of the *Lost in Space* robot at a downtown store in El Paso. He now watches 5 or 6 hours of television a night. He seldom watches during the day. He has stopped watching *Nightline,* the late-night news affairs program hosted by Ted Koppel, in favor of reruns of *Hawaii Five-O,* a show he watched when he was younger.

Perez listens to music from his childhood—Jackson Browne, Neil Young, Bob Dylan, Aerosmith, Alice Cooper, and Elton John. He remembers fondly from childhood days that a delivery truck would bring groceries to the house, and he recalls hitching a ride on the back bumper of ice cream trucks. "I remember that neon light with an ice cream cone painted on the side of the truck. I was not aware of the Vietnam War. I would play soldiers, but I was not aware of the war. Like I said, I had fun.

"I think I had faith in America in some way, I don't know how," Perez says. "Maybe I got it from my dad. Every time they had those military parades here in town, he was there marching along with all the veterans. He was very proud about having served in the war." Perez is not sure which war, but he thinks his father fought in the Philippines and in Pusan. "He was in an artillery battalion."

Perez enlisted in the military when he was 19 to get away, have something to do, make something of himself, and get paid. His brother Richard was already at the end of a 7-year military service. Perez hadn't done well in high school. He drank, smoked marijuana, and dropped out in 10th grade. He took job-training courses and worked in a convalescent home and in shipping and receiving at a department store. "I felt like such a loser," he recalls. "I never had the temperament to go and study."

After basic training in North Carolina at Fort Bragg, he went through advanced individual training in Virginia and then was assigned permanently to Fort Carson, Colorado. He remembers the stress of dealing with dangerous situations as unbearable. "It was like I was there and like I wasn't there. It's hard to explain. I'm glad I didn't do anything crazy," says Perez.

Perez lasted only a year in the military before he was diagnosed with schizophrenia and honorably discharged. He returned to El Paso and moved back in with his family. In 1988, a year after his father died, Perez, his brother, and his mother bought the house he now lives in for $60,000. They had the house retrofitted with a large extra bathroom to accommodate his mother's wheelchair. His mother suffered from diabetes and heart disease and had both legs amputated due to complications from her diabetes. Until she died in September 1996, Perez helped take care of her.

Perez thinks periodically about looking for work. He recalls a line from the comedy movie *Ghostbusters*: "I've been in the private sector, and they expect results."

"It sounds pretty scary," he says. "I've got a mortgage, and if anything goes wrong with the job and I lose my Social Security, I'm really in trouble," Perez says. "If you work for more than 6 months, they automatically take away my checks. To me that's pretty scary. I wouldn't want to risk it for just any job. In fact, I wouldn't want to risk it at all."

Whatever Perez knows of political affairs, he knows from television. He watches the local news on Channel 9 and knows the names of the anchors, Erica Castillo and Nick Miller. He hasn't read a newspaper in years. "It would be nice to buy the paper once a month," he says, "but not every day." He is more apt to say "I don't know" to questions than to pretend he knows something.

Perez doesn't know what a senator does, but he has heard of Phil Gramm, who is one of Texas's two U.S. senators. He doesn't know what a congressman is or does, but he recalls the name Silvestre Reyes, who was elected as his district's U.S. representative in 1996. "I saw some of his advertisements when he was running, saying Vietnam veteran . . . to represent El Paso. I can't even remember the position," Perez says. He doesn't know who the governor of Texas is, nor does he know anything about the Democratic or Republican parties or the difference between a liberal and a conservative. All he knows about Bob Dole, the Republican candidate who ran unsuccessfully against Bill Clinton for president in 1996, is that he was the butt of jokes on *Saturday Night Live*.

He volunteers some names. "Ross Perot. He's rich, but that doesn't necessarily mean he knows what's best for the country. [Secretary of State] Madeleine Albright. I think she went somewhere to try to solve some kind of conflict. I don't know what it was. Attorney General Janet Reno. I'm not sure. I think she was investigating some contributions."

He knows Clinton has been criticized for taking campaign money improperly, particularly from Asian contributors, and for inviting people to stay at the

White House. He also recalls Clinton saying he wanted to balance the budget, but he says he cannot begin to comprehend what that means. "It must be quite an undertaking. They're talking about billions and billions of dollars," he says. "I don't know how they go about doing those things.

"Every time I see a president, when they're running," Perez adds, "it's like watching a high school pep rally, these speeches of how good things are going to get."

Perez doesn't expect things to get much better for him. He has dreams that he knows are unattainable. "Dreams of doing important things," he muses. "Dreams like working for the Central Intelligence Agency, investigating or spying or protecting." He corrects himself. "That would be more the Secret Service, not the CIA." He envisions himself in real-life roles like those in the 1994 movie *Guarding Tess,* in which a Secret Service agent guards a former first lady, played by Shirley MacLaine, and another movie, *In the Line of Fire,* in which Clint Eastwood plays an agent who is haunted by the memory of the assassination of John F. Kennedy and tries to protect a president against a madman.

Perez does not associate his daily concerns with those of the nation. The biggest problems facing the country are "terrorism and disruption of life the way we know it, undermining the government," Perez believes. "It could be anything—a bomb, a forest fire at a strategic point, things that would disrupt our orderly way of life, not only that, but hurt people."

But his main concerns are the solvency of the federal program that affects him directly—Social Security, his ability to eke by financially, and his efforts to cope with his disease. "I don't know what chances I stand in this world," he says, resigned to get by as best he can. He is resigned also to an abiding belief that whatever chances he gets will be determined by others, beyond his control.

—— ◄o► ——

7

Alienateds

Neither Kathy Smith nor Alma Romanowski, the two Alienated nonvoters we tracked, has voted. Smith isn't registered; Romanowski, thanks to the so-called motor-voter law, is.

Making registration easier moved Romanowski to register, if not to vote. But ease of registration will not move Smith even to register because she's convinced there's no point in registering for a futile action. That's her definition of voting. The 31-year-old resident of Olympia, Washington, recalls as a kid watching the election returns with her dad, a lifelong Democrat, when the television network announced who won before the polls in their neighborhood had closed. "Your vote didn't really count, did it?" she thought. She hasn't changed her mind since: She has never registered or voted.

The system only works for the well connected, she believes, and her cynicism toward civic life is deep.

Romanowski, on the other hand, says she means to vote but just doesn't make the connection on Election Day. Romanowski, who lives in Flint, Michigan, has registered three times in her life. Each time she has almost voted. When she was 18, she wanted to make sure they didn't raise the drinking age. In 1992, her husband talked a lot about Ross Perot. In 1996, when she was 36, she registered by mail as she was renewing her driver's license. Each time, she never quite made it to the polls.

Although her list of reasons for not voting grows with every election, her stated intent to vote remains strong.

Nevertheless, her connection to public affairs and politicians is faint and mostly negative. "I don't trust them."

Kathy Smith

Doesn't Count and Doesn't Care

Kathy Smith recalls as a kid watching the election returns with her father, a lifelong Democrat. "How could that be?" she asked him when the television network announced the winner before the polls in their Tacoma, Washington, neighborhood had closed. "Your vote didn't really count, did it?" She hasn't changed her mind in the ensuing years.

At 31 years old, Smith has never voted or registered to vote. She says she never will. She spent much of November 5, 1996, volunteering at the Washington Soldier Home in Orting—driving more than an hour from Olympia, baking cookies for the veterans who live there, and talking. Not about politics, though, even though it was Election Day, "because my father always told me that politics don't mix in some circles." Medill News Service reporter Michael Fielding accompanied Smith that day and wrote that one veteran tried to draw Smith into a conversation about her responsibility as a citizen.

" 'Why don't you vote, Kathy?' the vet asked. 'If you don't, you've got no room to complain.' Smith just smiled and tapped the edge of her cigarette into her ashtray," Fielding reported in an Election Day chronicle of Smith and other nonvoters that ran in newspapers around the country.

Smith wants as little to do with politics and elections as she can. That night, even before the polls closed on the West Coast, television newscasts were proclaiming that Bill Clinton would be elected to a second term as president and were turning their attention to the congressional and gubernatorial races. Smith and her family didn't watch. Instead, they turned to a movie. "I'll end up finding out who won one way or another," Smith was quoted as saying. "People are going to be talking about it anyway."

People taking action and standing up for what they believe are what matter, Smith says. But to her, the electoral process and voting do not. She cites example after example of lessons she has learned in how the system works for the privileged, how individual rights are being eroded, and how money, not the citizens, matters to politicians.

Smith grew up in Tacoma, an only child to a single parent. Her mother, who was an alcoholic, walked out when Smith was 6 months old. Smith has not seen her since. Her father raised her. "We were best buds," she says. Her father did road construction work for the county. After some years, he developed back trouble and hardly could walk. He applied for Social Security benefits.

Smith recalls him applying three different times. "They kept denying him. They told him to get a lawyer," she recalls. "He did, and the lawyer finally got it for him." She says the experience made her cynical about how government works. "A person should be able to get [Social Security], especially after paying into it for all those years. They should be able to get their Social Security without going through all that hassle and getting lawyers and then having to turn around and pay the lawyer part of whatever you get."

That's it in a nutshell for Smith. The government doesn't care about people, and votes "just don't count." "These veterans out here . . . they've tried and tried and tried to get their Social Security, and it takes them forever to get it when they do get it." She is particularly cynical about Social Security "because when I get older, it might not even be there."

In contrast to Smith, her father was politically involved. He voted Democratic "because he thought the Democrats were more for the poor people, the working class, more blue-collar people," Smith says. As a road construction worker, he had an opportunity to know the county commissioners and, Smith says, he made his beliefs on issues known to them. "He really felt strongly about smoking. He didn't feel it was right for [the county] to put a tax on cigarettes so only the people who smoked got the tax," Smith says. "One year they taxed cigarettes so they could clean up the lake, and he didn't feel that that was right." The tax stayed in effect.

Smith's father died in 1992 but not before passing on his independent streak to his daughter. Smith recalls having faith in the political system when she was in public school and losing it with each exposure to the political process and to bureaucracy. In junior high school, she responded negatively to the student government elections. "I thought they [the students who ran for office] were stuck up. They were just trying to be popular. I didn't get along with them," she recalls. "That is what the voting process meant to me in my head."

Smith dropped out of school when she was 16 years old to run off with the guy she was dating. She left a note for her father as her way to say good-bye and moved to Coeur d'Alene, Idaho, just across the Washington border, where her boyfriend had family and where they would have a place to live until they could make ends meet. Within a year, she and her boyfriend moved back. They married a few days after Smith turned 18. "We were flat, flat broke and we went in to apply for welfare and food stamps, something to help us get up on our feet until my husband got a job, and they denied us because we had no children."

Smith believes that even now, with her second husband working, her family of six is caught between a rock and a hard place, a dilemma perpetuated by a government that makes it hard for people like her. Because she receives child support from her ex-husband and a $440 monthly check from her father's retirement benefits, her family cannot qualify for public assistance, she says, no matter how tough times get, no matter that her husband also has to pay child support, no matter that they live in a trailer home that is in need of repairs they cannot afford.

To Smith, her experience with the Internal Revenue Service (IRS) is another case in point. "They put themselves way up there on pedestals, and they make mistakes just like anyone else," she says. Both her cousin and her husband have had problems with the IRS—her cousin because someone used her Social Security number without her knowledge, and her husband because he and his ex-wife both claimed their son as a deduction. "We ended up having to prove to the IRS that we had him the whole time, and we had to come up with all the paperwork and get character witnesses and the whole shebang just to prove that he had custody of his son," Smith recounts. It left her bitter.

She draws another lesson from the intrusive and disparate way the government treats alcohol. "They had Prohibition way back when, and now it's legal, yet you get in trouble for drinking and driving, and alcohol's still legal," Smith says. "Some people can get by with stuff, and other people can't. The law should be made so everybody has to do the same thing and not because one person has more money and another person doesn't have enough," Smith says. She was arrested a year earlier for driving under the influence and was ordered to undergo a treatment program to defer prosecution. "These public defenders should represent you better than they do. They should actually try to fight for you and help you, instead of just doing the paperwork and getting it over with," she says of her experience. "There are other people out there that get [caught, too] and they get off, totally." The difference, she says, can be summed up in one word: money.

Smith says she and her husband agree on most issues. He, too, never has voted. However, he may be getting closer. He registered to vote for the first time before the 1996 presidential election because, Smith says, there are too many issues he cares about. He opposes gun control and feels strongly that health care costs and the costs of raising children should not be allowed to go up. Smith agrees, but she intends to "go about my business" just as the public officials do because they don't take her into account anyway. "They care about their money and how they can make more. Little people don't count," she says. "It's kind of like when you were in school. You had the popular kids and, if you weren't one of those, you didn't really count. It didn't matter if you weren't wearing the hundred dollar jeans and the two hundred dollar shoes."

There is no good reason *to* vote and, in Smith's mind, there is at least one good reason *not to* vote. Smith doesn't want to be called for jury duty. She is unaware that as a licensed driver in the state of Washington, she is as likely to be called for jury duty as a registered voter. Even if she were convinced that voting wasn't tied to jury duty, she says she still wouldn't vote. "Voting won't help," she says with conviction.

If she voted, she says, she would vote Democratic, as her father did and as her husband would, but there is no one in the Democratic Party or in politics she admires. She says unapologetically that she doesn't have time to follow government affairs. She reads newspapers less than once a week and then mostly for the ads. She watches television news about three times a week, mostly for the weather and because the television is on. She volunteers at the veterans' home and at her children's school, and she's looking for work, possibly as a part-time cook for the school district.

Smith's goals in life are mostly short term. "Day goals," she calls them. "I am happy if I get things on my list done. And if not," Smith says, "there's always tomorrow."

Her long-range goals are "to raise my kids and do right by them." To Smith, doing right means supporting them and always being there for them. She tells them what counts "is to stand up for what you believe in." Voting couldn't be farther from her mind. Smith's oldest daughter, who is 12, is beginning to study history and social studies in school. She has asked Smith why she doesn't vote for her beliefs. Smith tells her because it won't do any good. Politicians will do what they want regardless. Vote if you want, she says, but "it doesn't count."

———— ◄o► ————

Alma Romanowski

Registration Is Only Nine-Tenths of the Vote

Sometime in 1996, before her 37th birthday and half a year before the presidential election, Alma Romanowski registered to vote. She hadn't given it much thought, and she wasn't sure if she already was registered. But it was easy. The registration material came by mail with her Michigan driver's license renewal form. "I just filled it out and mailed it in," Romanowski recalls.

Romanowski appears to be the ideal beneficiary of the national moter-voter law that streamlined the voting process by allowing registration by mail and at multiple government offices. She is so busy volunteering, running about, helping out, and being a "taxi mom," shuttling children to and fro, that any effort to ease the voter registration process might be just the incentive it takes to get her to the polls. However, Romanowski is not the intended target of the law. When President Bill Clinton signed the National Voter Registration Act in May 1993, saying under a tent on the White House lawn that "there is no longer the excuse of the difficulty of registration," it was believed that it and similar laws at the state level would be most helpful to those younger than 30 years of age and those who move around a lot.

At 37, Romanowski never has left Flint, Michigan, lives a few blocks from where she grew up, and tends not to use "the difficulty of registration" to excuse her failure to vote. In fact, Romanowski has registered three times in her life. Each time she has almost voted. But to date, her slate is clean. She has never voted, and neither has her husband. Her list of reasons for not voting gets longer with each election she passes up, although her intent to vote stays true. "I keep meaning to [vote]. I have good intentions," Romanowski says.

The first time she intended to vote was the first election after she turned 18. She was attending high school, working at Hudson's department store, and beginning to drink alcohol with her friends. It was 1978, and the state of Michigan had a referendum on the ballot to increase the drinking age from 18 to 21. She registered to vote. "I felt like it was taking one of my rights away, and it made me mad. At 18, I was gonna go and have a fit and vote against it," Romanowski recalls. "But I didn't."

She cannot recall why she failed to vote that first time, but the referendum passed, and after an unsuccessful court challenge, the law setting Michigan's drinking age at 21 went into effect on December 21, 1978. Two years later, with the 1980 presidential election at stake and another referendum on the drinking age up before Michigan voters, Romanowski again took a pass. "Young voters who are more likely to support the lower drinking age are less likely to turn out on Election Day," predicted a United Press International wire story days before the election. Romanowski was one of them.

It was not until 1992 that Romanowski took the step to register again to vote. She wasn't passionate about an issue. This time, it was a candidate. Ross Perot had caught the attention of her husband. He and a cousin of theirs would talk about Perot. They liked his image. "He had a good head on his shoulders, and he was rich," Romanowski says, but she cannot recall much more than that about him. It didn't matter. Neither she nor her husband voted in 1992.

Nothing changed in 1996. Romanowski's polling place is conveniently located at the end of her block in an adult education building. She recalls watching the cars come and go on Election Day. "I bickered with myself back and forth about going down to the school [to vote]," she says. Something kept her from following through. "Maybe it's just the fear of going in that little booth and not knowing how [to vote]," Romanowski muses.

She fishes about to understand why. Maybe she doesn't know enough, she thinks. "I wouldn't feel comfortable voting for someone I don't know much about," she says. "I guess I'm not real sure about who I'd like to vote for. You hear the person talk and they sound really good and then you hear their opponent talk and they put them down, twist things around, and you don't know what's true and what's not. I'd just be real unsure of myself."

Romanowski's connection with political affairs and public officials is faint, mostly tangled images that leave her unsure of what or whom to trust. To Romanowski, Clinton is little more than a man who plays the saxophone and was honest about trying, but not inhaling, marijuana. Her impression of recent presidents is similar: cast in positive but vague images. For Ronald Reagan, it's wife Nancy's red dress and the notion that someone suffering from Alzheimer's disease must have worked pretty hard; for Jimmy Carter, it's as a peanut farmer and the favorable image of farmers in her family history; for Lyndon Johnson, it's a face that looked like her grandfather's.

"I have no bad feelings about any of the presidents," Romanowski says. "I think if you're going to run for president, you're going to do the best job you can do because you're going to be under the public image and public eye all the time. Anything you do is going to be heard about. I don't think it's a position I would want to be in, and I have to admire anybody who would go for it."

Yet presidents and all other politicians are too remote for Romanowski. "Maybe it's just that I don't trust them, maybe I don't trust what they're saying, the politicians," she says as she tries to understand why she hasn't, in 20 years, followed through on her best intentions to vote.

Something failed to take root in Romanowski that had existed in her parents. Romanowski always considered her parents politically involved. They were solid Democrats, especially her mother. "It went back to my grandfather who was from Missouri," she says. The family revered John Kennedy. Romanowski remembers that after her mother-in-law died, her mother was tickled to receive a box of magazines about the Kennedys that her mother-in-law had stored as a keepsake. "Whoever was running in the Democratic Party, that was who [my mother] voted for," Romanowski says, adding that she picked up none of the allegiance to the Democratic Party or to politics.

"My parents would sit around and watch the . . . negotiations," Romanowski says, forgetting the word for campaign debates. "They always watched all that and they'd speak their opinions, but I wasn't into politics and when that stuff was on, I'd say, 'See you guys later.' "

Her parents divorced when she was 3 years old and remarried when she was 9. While her parents were divorced, her father would see Romanowski and her five siblings three times a week, mostly to take them to church. She remembers being "independent and responsible" until the fourth grade. "My trouble started when my dad moved back home. I was always a pretty good kid and I did what I was supposed to do and stayed out of trouble," she says.

Romanowski rebelled in response to her father's return. She stayed away from home as much as possible. Her grades suffered. Her poor health made matters worse. Bouts with diabetes made her miss weeks of school. She recalls a mock election the school held when she was in sixth grade. "I hadn't even heard of elections before that and didn't know how someone becomes president," Romanowski recollects. "We all got to vote, and who I voted for lost, and I lost interest."

In high school, Romanowski partied. She hung out at parks or apartment complexes, smoking, drinking, and spending time with mothers who smoked dope with them. She indulged in more potent drugs. In her senior year, she had to repeat civics because she couldn't graduate without passing it. She was getting by in school; working; going to clubs, bars, and discos; and getting stoned every day.

She smoked marijuana regularly from her senior year through her first pregnancy 7 years later. Romanowski and her husband had people partying in the house all night long. She stopped using cocaine once she got pregnant, but her husband was hooked. It took another 7 years and an episode in which she locked her husband out of the house and threatened his supplier before her husband entered a recovery center and gave it up. "Life's goal was having fun," Romanowski says of those days.

Today, her husband owns a company that designs conveyor belts. They are doing reasonably well financially—$737 a month, after taxes, she says off the top of her head. But she began having pain in her arms in 1994. Still undiagnosed, she can't raise her arms above her shoulders. The pain forces her to soak in a tub daily. She is "ready to scream" from the pain.

Romanowski's goals are to get healthy, return to work, and make successful people out of her two children. She spends most of her time being a mom not just to their two children but to nieces, neighbors, and friends. "I give a lot of my time to people, volunteering," she says. When her children were younger and the family was financially strapped, the kids were enrolled in Head Start, the federal enrichment program for preschool children from low-income families. She thought the program was wonderful and an example of the system working when parenting sometimes didn't. "Head Start may be the only hug [children] get in a day," she says.

What if something happened to put Head Start in jeopardy? "I would say, 'It figures that that would be something they'd cut out,' " Romanowski says, and then regroups to summon her best intentions. "I would go fight it. I really would. That would irritate me more than the drinking age [did]."

Now that her children are in school, the same public schools she attended, Romanowski has turned her attention there but only to a point. She avoids school board meetings. She attended one a few years back because she thought that if she knew more she might be more persuasive with other parents. "I was going to be involved more. But I wasn't impressed with the way the meeting went," she says. The issue was potato sack races. The school principal had discontinued them because they were too dangerous. "The head honchos blew off the ideas people had. Their minds were already made up." She left the meeting resolved: "Just call me if you want something and I'll do it." No one called, and she never went back. Curiously, it has left her doubting herself. "I don't feel like I know enough about how the school is run and kids are educated to make a final decision on how they should be taught or why they should be taught that way," she says.

Romanowski believes the nation is suffering in areas she feels she knows something about: schools, drugs, and crime. She sees children "ruling the teachers." "There's no discipline at home, there's no discipline at school," she observes. "The kids are raising themselves because both parents have to work to support the family, and the kids are just unsupervised."

She recognizes that drugs have left her at a tremendous disadvantage. "Before I got into them real bad, I was working, I felt better about myself, I was doing okay at school, somewhat, in the classes I liked," she says. "Then I lost interest in school, didn't care if I passed or failed. Just get me up on stage to graduate and out of here. I had no desire to go to college." Once she's healthier, she wants to go back to school to take college courses. "I don't know for what, though," she concedes.

Romanowski thinks about the crime problem often. She has stopped reading the daily newspaper, but she watches television news every evening, mostly for the crime reports. "It's getting closer to my neighborhood all the time. The place that I used to go visit my dad, I wouldn't send my dog to live today," she says. "I want to know how close it is."

As with the school board, Romanowski attended one meeting of her neighborhood's crime watch program. "They didn't get back to me to pass out flyers, so I didn't go back," she recalls. "I figured it was just another disorganized group."

She can't ignore the gang graffiti in the school playground. Her 13-year-old daughter tells her that classmates are adopting gang signs, wearing one pants leg up, the other down. She has told her daughter to stay away from a girl who told her she would take care of her.

Guns hit very close to home. In 1983, Romanowski's brother held police at bay with a shotgun after barricading himself inside her parents' house. The front page of the *Grand Blanc News* read, "Six Hours: Gunman Holds Police At Bay." Romanowski recalls that the prosecutor played politics with her family tragedy. "We saw [him] straightening his tie and saying 'Where's the camera, where's the camera?' because he was going to give a report for the news before he even told the family anything," she says.

The prosecutor's photograph accompanied the front-page story. Romanowski says the incident undermined her confidence in public officials. She saw the prosecutor priming for the camera "so people will think he did something wonderful" and give him their vote. That's how Romanowski views elected officials. They appear to care about what she and others think but only to get people to like them and vote for them.

After the incident, Romanowski wrote a letter on behalf of her brother to the county board of commissioners in Flint. She wanted the board to place him in a controlled environment rather than jail or prison so he could take medication to treat his psychiatric problem. She still has the letter. "I don't think I mailed it," she says.

Romanowski is aware of her pattern of not following through. She wants her children to be different. Her older daughter, Ashley, participated in a mock election at her grade school before the 1996 presidential election. The candidate Ashley voted for lost. "I try to encourage her to keep active and find out what's going on in politics and hear about the different people who are running," Romanowski says. "I was glad that she did take part in the mock election and voted for who she thought would make a good president."

Ashley remembers the mock election, but she cannot immediately recall for whom she voted. After prompting, she recognizes the name. Ross Perot. Why him? Her father liked him. She knows her mom doesn't vote. "She wants no part in it," Ashley says. She doesn't think she will vote when she gets older. "It takes too much of your time," she says. How does she know that? "It's always on TV. It takes an hour to get in the booth," she says. "It took 15 minutes at my school just for the mock election."

As for Romanowski, although she's registered, she says she still doesn't have enough confidence in any particular candidate to prompt her to vote. "If they came by and talked for a while, maybe," Romanowski muses. "I'd probably have to sit down and have a personal interview with them, and they'd really have to sell themselves to get me to go vote."

That reminds her. A woman came by before the 1996 election and gave her campaign literature. "I remember. She came to the door, and she said she was running and she handed me a flyer and encouraged me to get out and vote," Romanowski recalls. "We didn't chitchat or nothing." She even remembers the candidate's name and how it is spelled. Debbie Stabenow. But she can't recall what she was running for. Stabenow was the Democratic candidate for U.S. representative, seeking to unseat the Republican incumbent. She won, with 54% of the vote. Romanowski almost voted for her.

——— ◄○► ———

8

Can't Shows

Three of the nonvoters we followed represent a segment of the voting-age population that has sparked considerable debate—those who are of voting age but cannot vote. Most statistics on voting trends include these nonvoters in the voting-age population, although some critics say they should be excluded, which would make the nonvoting trends less ominous.

Peter Bruce, a research analyst at the University of Connecticut's Roper Center for Public Opinion Research, wrote in the October/November 1997 issue of *The Public Perspective* that including those legally excluded from voting inflates the voting-age population by 10%. If they were excluded, he wrote, 54.5% of eligible voters cast ballots in 1996. But Curtis Gans, whose Committee for the Study of the American Electorate's figures are the most often cited, scolded Bruce in the same magazine for ignoring factors that offset the legally excluded nonvoters in the voting-age population: U.S. citizens living abroad, the U.S. Census Bureau undercount, and naturalization.

Can't Shows comprise about 17 million people, or 8.5% of the voting-age population. About 14.5 million are legal immigrants who are not citizens, and 4.2 million are convicted felons.

When James Ayarkwa-Duah, now 34, came to the New York as a teenager, he fell in love with the United States and decided to stay, even without proper papers. He became an illegal alien and got a job making jewelry. He tried to get amnesty under a 1986 law but missed the requirements on what he calls a technicality. Now a United Parcel Service employee in Dallas, Texas, he wants to become a citizen and would consider it a privilege to vote. He cannot understand why so many Americans ignore that privilege. In our survey, he was in the Alienated cluster, mainly because of his antipathy toward government because he feels he was treated badly by the Immigration and Naturalization Service.

In 1959, Estela Crespo was 2 months old when she arrived in the United States in her mother's arms, missing automatic citizenship by months. Now 38 and living in northern New Jersey outside Union City, she says she wants to become a citizen but hasn't applied. However, even if she became a citizen, she doesn't think she would vote—politics are of no interest to her, and she tries to ignore them. Her lack of interest in politics and annoyance with political and government institutions placed her among the Irritables.

Keith Roberts, whose survey answers showing knowledge of public affairs helped place him among the Doers, is no longer sure he would vote even if he could. When the former deputy U.S. marshal pleaded guilty to felony drug charges, he lost both his right to vote and his confidence in the government and its officials. Attempting to regain both, the 39-year-old is taking graduate political science courses at Pennsylvania State University, hoping to teach about "an American political process that tried to throw me away."

James Ayarkwa-Duah

He Knows a Vote Counts—And Wishes He Had One

In 1981, James Ayarkwa-Duah arrived in New York at age 19. He had traveled from his native Ghana with his father's friend on a business trip. He decided he liked America so much that he moved in with relatives in the Bronx and got a job making gold jewelry.

But his visa was temporary, and soon he was living in the United States illegally. In 1986, President Ronald Reagan signed an immigration law that included an amnesty offer for illegal aliens who had lived in the country continuously since 1982. The offer lasted for 1 year, starting in May 1987.

Ayarkwa-Duah applied for amnesty at the New York Immigration and Naturalization Service (INS) office but was denied because he had left the country for about a month in June 1987 for a trip to Canada to visit friends.

"I break my chain for living here. I didn't know or I wouldn't have gone. . . . I want to become a citizen. You want to become part of the society when you fall in love with a country. Since I'm here working hard, paying taxes, staying out of trouble, why can't I be part of it?" He wonders if he will ever be accepted as a U.S. citizen.

After he moved to Dallas in 1990 to be near his sister and other relatives, he checked in with INS officials and was given a 1-year work authorization card. Each year, he goes to the INS office to get it renewed. But he says more recent immigrants have less trouble getting green cards, which provide permanent residency, but he cannot get past the bureaucracy. The New York INS officials, in particular, soured him on the politics of getting green cards. He says they treated him like a criminal when he tried to appeal their rejection of his amnesty application.

"I was very hurt, and I tried so many times, and I said, 'Why should this happen? Is it because of the way that I talk?' I can't talk like an American. But that shouldn't be the point."

Ayarkwa-Duah, now 34, says his dream is to become a citizen some day because he finds America "wonderful." And he's surprised at Americans who don't exercise their citizenship by voting.

"I am supposed to vote if I become a citizen because that's the voice of the people and the voice can make changes," he said. "It's a privilege. Voting to me is an essential thing for everybody to do because it shows what we stand for. It's the only way the government can hear the voice of the people."

Ayarkwa-Duah, a short, muscular man with a ready smile who makes friends easily, works hard to improve his life. He holds down two part-time jobs, getting up around 2 a.m. to get to his job at United Parcel Service, where he loads trucks for deliveries until it is time to go home and grab a quick nap before heading to the community college near his home. After classes in English, math, or biology in the afternoon, he spends nights at the Kroger in his North Dallas neighborhood stocking the shelves with groceries. He gets another nap at midnight before starting the routine all over.

He would like to finish school quickly but cannot afford to quit his jobs. He was offered a scholarship by UPS, but it would have required him to quit his jobs to go to school full-time; he says the scholarship wouldn't have offset the losses of his working income.

"My goal is to finish school, to have time for myself and get married—to have time for a family," he says, "I have no life. If I'm not at work, I'm at the [college's] library."

Ayarkwa-Duah loves the time he spends on the campus of his school, Richland Community College in North Dallas. He strolls past ponds and sits on benches under shade trees to study or simply read his favorite books and magazines. He figures it will take him at least 5 years, at 6 credit hours a semester, to get a bachelor of science degree, which requires 120 credits. After Richland, he hopes to go to Baylor University in Waco, Texas, or Southwestern University in Georgetown, Texas, to complete a degree with a major in microbiology.

With his degree, he hopes to get a research job.

One of the reasons he admires President Bill Clinton is his focus on education. Ayarkwa-Duah also praises Texas Governor George W. Bush for his efforts to improve education in the state. In fact, although the two politicians are from different parties, they both have been strong proponents of setting educational standards for children and schools and programs to improve reading scores, among other things.

His apartment is in a complex of two-story units and a short drive from the college campus. When he has time, he likes to use the complex's gym to work out or to go jogging. He also likes to spend time with friends, dancing, listening to soul or jazz, or just socializing.

But he has no serious girlfriend, he says, "because with two jobs, I've got no time for the ladies. . . . Girlfriends need attention all the time. They need someone. They are like, 'Oh, you don't have time for me.' That's how it is."

Although he hopes to marry and have a family some day, for now he spends time on weekends with his sister, Agnes Appiah; her husband, Paul; and their three children. The couple met in Ghana but didn't marry until Agnes joined Paul in the United States. Paul now is a disc jockey for a Dallas radio station. The daughter of Ayarkwa-Duah's late sister, Cecilia, also lives in the Dallas area. But his two brothers and mother remained in Ghana after his father died. His other sister lives in London.

Ayarkwa-Duah says he has no desire to go back to Ghana to live—he likes America.

And he thinks American citizens, with the right to vote, should be more interested in taking part in their democracy. "If you don't vote and you're a citizen and later on you sit back and criticize, to me that is very stupid. It doesn't make sense."

He thinks most nonvoters are just tired of the way government works and the way politicians act.

"They don't vote because they are not happy with what they're taught by most political parties," he says. "[The politicians say], 'I will do this. I will do that. I will do this.' Promises are never fulfilled. . . . That's how people see our political system."

Ayarkwa-Duah says that would not be his attitude if he had the opportunity to vote. Those who say their vote makes no difference are simply wrong, he believes. "I have the impression that any one vote can make a difference in this country."

He does have some sympathy for women and members of minority groups who don't vote. He says they were excluded from the vote originally and still may feel less a part of the political process than others.

Improving race relations is the biggest problem facing the country, he believes. And although he doesn't think politicians are always working to solve the problem, he believes the news media often get in the way of solving the country's problems. He reads news magazines, *Time* and *Newsweek*, faithfully and listens to talk radio to get his news. He particularly likes editorials and radio commentators who present strong viewpoints.

"I'm well-informed. I try to pay attention to what's going on. You've got to know what's going on where you're living, especially the community where you live in."

Ayarkwa-Duah remembers seeing Clinton on TV when he first ran for president in 1992 while still governor of Arkansas. "I didn't like him the first time I saw him. The one thing I did like was him reaching out to people during the campaign [by going on MTV and the *Larry King Live* TV talk show]. It lets people know who you are and what you have done so far. If you reach out to the people, it will promote voting a lot."

Clinton's appearances on MTV and *Larry King Live* were also smart strategy, Ayarkwa-Duah says, because the president—at least on those few occasions—was able to bypass traditional news outlets, which he says are too quick to look for the sensational, the bad news. Ayarkwa-Duah doesn't blame him for trying to avoid mainstream news outlets. "The media is always after negative things. It doesn't praise people. . . . It would be very nice if one day the media can say [an elected official] has done a good job."

Journalists could help Americans be better Americans, he believes. He notes with dismay that many Americans don't know the Constitution. "They don't know American writings, and that is very sad. That's what the media has got to portray [to help educate the public]."

But he would also like politics to be less divisive. Although he's Catholic, he departs from the Roman Catholic hierarchy on abortion rights in saying the abortion debate is a good example of politicians meddling in something that's none of their business.

"I think that religion and government should be apart. A lady has the right about her body. . . . I'm against someone who kills someone. But in abortion, ladies have their own rights."

He doesn't spend much time thinking about public policy, however, and rarely talks politics with friends or family. He says most of his time is spent just trying to keep up with his schedule of school and work.

It's his down payment on his future, which he hopes will be the American dream.

———— ◄o► ————

Estela Crespo

She May Become a U.S. Citizen, But
She Still May Never Vote

In 1959, Estela Crespo's mother carried her 2-month-old daughter in her arms as she arrived in the United States from Colombia. The infant missed automatic U.S. citizenship by a few months. Her mother eventually became a U.S. citizen. Estela Crespo never did.

She has spent all of her 38 years in Union City and North Bergen, New Jersey, blue-collar towns near Newark that have attracted large numbers of immigrants. "It's a nice place to live," Crespo says.

She says that she will never turn her back on the country where she was born, but despite not being a U.S. citizen, she feels like an American and intends one day to become a U.S. citizen.

"I do want to become a United States citizen. . . . I know I wasn't born here, but I was raised here. I mean, these are my [presidents]. Abraham Lincoln, he freed the slaves and all that. And George Washington. I don't know the politics and all from my country . . . maybe one day I'll decide to go find out the history."

Crespo is a permanent U.S. resident, which makes her ineligible to vote. But even if she had been born a few months later in the United States, which would have given her automatic citizenship, her status as a registered voter would be far from certain. As much as she has thought about becoming a citizen, she has never thought about voting as one of its benefits. In fact, she is unclear about the connection between citizenship and voting. "You might have to be a U.S. citizen to vote, not a resident." Later, she says she will probably vote when she becomes a citizen. "Don't they require you to?"

When informed that voting is not required of citizens, Crespo then changes her mind, saying she probably won't become a voter—a reflection of her lack of interest in voting, politics, and the entire electoral process.

"I don't like politics. I stay away from politics. I just don't like it."

Instead, she goes to PTA meetings and keeps up with what's going on at her son's school. She says "it's just part of being a mom" to make sure she knows what programs the school is offering to help keep kids out of trouble. She remembers attending many meetings at which she gained useful information from teachers and other school officials. At those meetings, she felt her involvement was direct and got results in terms of advice, information, or action.

Crespo says elections don't change things for the better or result in solutions to the problems she sees around her—homelessness, unemployment, high rents, and too many taxes. And she attributes the lack of improvement to politicians who make campaign promises that too often are not fulfilled. Elections might change things "if they [officials] do the things they say they're going to do," Crespo says. But she's not counting on it.

Although she ignores politics, her family is more involved.

"My mother votes, my stepfather votes, my sister votes, my brother votes. My boyfriend doesn't vote either, but he's not a citizen."

But she thinks their votes won't matter: "Honestly, I don't think anything changes."

She cannot explain why she's the lone nonvoter and noncitizen in her family. She is able to live her life without citizenship, so she hasn't yet taken the time to fulfill her goal of becoming an American. If she does, it won't be because she wants to vote. The action of voting seems too remote from getting results that would improve her life.

Nevertheless, she says she knows that the decisions of elected officials are not irrelevant to her life. "Oh, it does affect my life. Because there's no jobs out there. There is, and there isn't. The homeless. The rents are ridiculous. First-time homebuyers—it's difficult to buy a home. The taxes are ridiculous. Insurance rates are ridiculous."

She and her boyfriend live in a cramped two-room apartment so they can save enough for the down payment on a house. Crespo estimates they will be able to become homeowners in about a year. Then they will get married, with the wedding in their new home.

When she's at home, she has the TV set on much of the time and often catches the news. But she's more interested in news of the day's events, such as a plane accident, than in what politicians are doing. The TV set is in a large bookcase filled with her collectibles, a silver teapot, china plates, and Disney figures.

"We have all this clutter," she says of the crowded shelves and cluttered bureau in the living room, "and we don't know what to do with it" while waiting to buy their house. Despite the lack of space—her living room is crowded with a double bed, two overstuffed chairs, bureaus, and a bookcase—Crespo can't help but indulge her hobbies of craft projects and collecting. She figures she will need the decorations for the home she and her boyfriend are planning.

"My house has to look nice in order for me to feel good. It has to be comfortable."

Her first marriage lasted 15 years. She married at age 18 while she was still in school but did graduate from Emerson High School in Union City and had a son, Xavier, now 17, who's living nearby with her mother because the apartment she's sharing with her boyfriend is too cramped for her son to join them.

After high school, she went to Jersey City State College for a few years, but "about that time I had my son, and it was getting hard because he was little," so she dropped out. She held a series of office worker jobs at department stores, lawyers' offices, and a cleaning firm before taking a job working for a record company. Eventually, she used her record company connections to become a booker for Latin bands.

Her son became interested in music through her connections and now is a disc jockey at parties on weekends to earn extra money. He also butchers chicken for Chicken Delight on the weekends.

"My son came out to be a good kid. I think I did pretty good [raising him] by myself."

She says attending PTA meetings regularly and knowing what was going on at a school were worth the effort because she's sure her son will head for college or the military. She had been working for a medicinal herb company for about a year but decided to leave because she was having to leave the office late in the day, after dark, and was afraid of being mugged. Now she's on unemployment while looking for another job but earns some extra money going to women's homes to give them manicures.

Life today is more difficult than it used to be, she believes, and thinks her son has had it harder growing up than she did. "It was more innocent then than it is now. The kids now know too much."

But, again, she doesn't think elected officials can help change the situation. Crespo says she shouldn't be mistaken for a cynic or pessimist, however. "I'm an optimist. I'm not negative, I'm positive. I don't know. Maybe if I were involved with the politics or doing something regarding politics, I might be different."

She can't imagine that happening now, but she recalls getting involved in politics once, when she was a teenager.

"I helped give out flyers for this guy who was running for mayor." As she remembers it, she wasn't interested in his politics. It was a part-time job. In that case, the benefit of political involvement was tangible. And the results reinforce her belief that she can have no effect on politics.

She doesn't know the candidate's name anymore, but she remembers the outcome of the election: "He lost, poor thing."

———— ◄○► ————

Keith Roberts

U.S. Marshal Turned Felon Turning Back

Keith Roberts remembers the headline from the *Virginian-Pilot* verbatim: "Ex-Marshal Back in Court, On Drug Charges." He remembers the date it appeared, too. October 23, 1991. The day before, a Tuesday, he had walked into a federal courtroom in Norfolk, Virginia, together with a group of men, only one of whom he knew. He and seven others were charged in a cocaine conspiracy.

The newspaper story focused on him, a former deputy U.S. marshal and former deputy sheriff, and reported that he was "accused of being a low-level cocaine dealer" and that the cocaine ring he and the others operated "resorted to murder" by gunning down a construction worker with a sawed-off shotgun.

Two months later, Roberts pleaded guilty to one count of conspiracy and was sentenced to 18 months in federal prison. Roberts believes that both the federal prosecutors and his lawyer knew he had nothing to do with a conspiracy, with drug dealing, and with the men to whom the indictment linked him or with any murder. Trouble was, he had been caught using cocaine while a federal marshal; he admits to that, and that was enough.

The day he pleaded guilty and was sentenced, Roberts lost his confidence in what he believed was a government and its overzealous officials who were willing to inflate the facts. He also lost his right to vote, a right that in Virginia and all but four other states is taken away on conviction of a felony.

Before then, Roberts had been a committed voter, a hard-core Democrat. His political consciousness was first tapped in his freshman year in college when he met William P. Robinson, his political science professor at historically black Norfolk State University. To Roberts, his professor was one of a kind. A black man of prominence and stature who didn't look down on other blacks, "who could deal with paupers as well as kings," and who also served as a state legislator in Virginia, the first black ever to chair a legislative committee. "They don't make 'em like that anymore," Roberts says, recalling how he and his classmates would wait in class for up to half an hour until Robinson would walk in late from his chemotherapy treatments. Robinson died of bone cancer in Roberts's senior year, after Roberts had taken six courses from him.

When he was 10 years old, Roberts was in Little League. He was the only black in the league. As a high school freshman in 1971, he was the only black on his team, though other teams were showing signs of integrating. His senior year, he had one black teammate. He found himself playing mediator more than he liked. "I had white friends who I had been friends with for 5 or 6 years, and I had black friends who I naturally gravitated to, that were hating each other," Roberts says, "and I'm in the middle."

As a youth, Roberts saw the world through the teachings of sports and old-time religion. In high school, he lettered in football, basketball, and baseball and didn't get home most days until 7 p.m. There was enough time to have the pictorial images of the Vietnam War sink in. He would watch the evening news with his parents and browse through the stark photos of the *Life* magazines that were accumulating around the house.

His father had been a ballplayer, a good one Roberts was told, although his dad didn't talk about it much. Roberts's parents came to his games regularly and established relations with whites that way. "In the '60s in the South, white and black families didn't have a lot in common. They didn't do a lot together, but there was a common bond we had that carried on to other things," Roberts recollects. Because of it, Roberts felt he wouldn't be out of place anywhere he went in America.

Roberts's grandmother provided the spiritual core. On Sundays, the family would have a big country breakfast and plant themselves in church from 9 a.m. to 5 p.m., first for Sunday school, then for back-to-back services. In the evening, family and extended family, up to 30 strong, would gravitate to his grand-mother's house. In the year and a half he served in prison, Roberts took refuge in his grandmother's teachings and in her belief that if you "trust in the Lord and in prayer and respect people, they will respect you."

At 39, Roberts has become disillusioned by the political and civic leaders who abuse the respect people give them. He disliked student government types all through school because he felt they condescended. In the political science class he loved, he would observe them sneering at fellow students. "I used to watch their tactics," Roberts recalls. "That was my first real lesson in politics." He's convinced that arrogance has caused problems in the black community. "No matter how far they get," Roberts says of blacks he has known personally or observed politically, "they'll never be as big as they think."

He cites Clarence Thomas, the Supreme Court justice whom he regards as voting more conservatively than any other member of the court votes. But it is not Thomas's ideology that offends Roberts. It's his arrogance. "I'm not a militant, but [if] you try to hide behind your success and just try to camouflage or mask it, you can't sweep it under the rug because you're on the winning side and are liked by them, or like them," Roberts says.

Roberts began to lose respect for himself while he was in the Air Force. He enlisted in 1981, a year after graduating from college, and was accepted into officer training school. He completed the 90-day course and was commissioned a second lieutenant. What mattered most was that on completion, the president of the United States signed off on it and Congress declared him "an officer and a gentleman." Then it was on to flight school in California, where he planned to become a weapons systems officer. At 23 years old, he was making $25,000 a year in base pay, excluding flight pay and additional assistance for living off the base. He succumbed to the temptations he so disliked in others. There was a certain glamour to being a flier. "You have to be smart and tough. All that power," Roberts says, "you feel like a god." He lived the California life, drove a Porsche, partied, and went to clubs. His grades plummeted. He was put on inactive reserve status because he couldn't cut it. His 6-year military commitment ended after a year, with what on paper was an honorable discharge but was to him a personal humiliation.

By most appearances, Roberts bounced back. He married his college girlfriend, had a son, and went into law enforcement, first as deputy sheriff for the town of Chesapeake, Virginia, and then, only 2 years later, as a deputy U.S. marshal. But what he had avoided during his mercurial year in California, he found back home. He tried cocaine for the first time at a Super Bowl party at his cousin's house. It became the skeleton in his law enforcement closet and the seed of his distrust of government.

"In the '80s there was this flood of cocaine that I always felt was very suspicious," Roberts says. "Cocaine was a drug of choice for the rich and prosperous people, but in the '80s somebody flooded America with cocaine. Middle-class people like me. People who were up and coming. It was at every party I went to."

His skeleton was still hidden when he was visited at home by federal internal affairs agents. His name had surfaced in connection with a Virginia Beach restaurateur who was apparently a member of an organized crime family. The restaurateur had given Roberts a job washing dishes back in 1981 when he was between college and the Air Force. They had remained friends ever since. The agents told Roberts to stay away from the restaurateur, and he did.

From there, he became a target of federal drug enforcement agents who, he says, pursued him to defend the honor of law enforcement. "If they had really wanted to get me, they should have gotten me on a simple possession charge," Roberts says. But the allure of nailing a federal marshal, particularly a black one who was a "fast burner," a rising star, made him an appealing target. "The criminal justice system got me before the coke did," Roberts says.

The federal prosecution of him as drug dealer and conspirator has shaded his attitudes about government. Roberts sees government as decaying under the influence of people who get corrupted by power and a public that has gotten complacent.

Something stuck with him when, as a child, he watched officials deny the body bag count coming out of Vietnam. That image kept resurfacing when he was in the military, in law enforcement, and in prison. He recounted that with his Air Force security clearance, he was aware of military actions occurring that government officials were denying publicly. As a federal marshal, he was assigned to Jose Blandon's detail for the 2 weeks in 1988 that the Panamanian official testified before Congress about the illegal activities of Panamanian leader Manuel Noriega. Roberts became disillusioned hearing how George Bush, when he was CIA chief, knew everything Noriega was doing to let drug trafficking flourish.

When he served time in Three Rivers Federal Prison in south Texas, Roberts observed drug use on a daily basis. A bunkmate did heroin regularly; another inmate died of an overdose. "They aren't keeping drugs out of prison, much less the neighborhoods," Roberts says, attributing the problem to rich and powerful people who become convenient bedfellows with government officials who find it easier to stockpile poor minorities behind bars than to provide them jobs and a chance at the American dream.

The more humble the beginnings, the likelier Roberts is to trust a government official. He regards President Bill Clinton as "a poor Southern boy who hasn't disappointed" him. He is impressed with Kweisi Mfume, the president of the NAACP and a former congressman, because he heard a radio report in which Mfume described himself as a former gang member who had fathered five children by the time he was 22. "He knows what people experience and can relate to them," Roberts says. Not so with most congressmen, according to Roberts. "Thirty percent are millionaires. They can't relate to people who can't pay insurance for their kids. They make $120,000 a year, which is probably play money to them." To Roberts, the difference between Republicans and Democrats is money. "Most of the richer Americans are Republicans. They want to cut welfare, get tough on crime, sweep problems under the rug," Roberts says. Public policy has suffered. "Either the public officials don't care or they're stupid," he continues, "and I know they're not stupid."

Roberts sees himself as embittered but enriched by his time in prison. "The most encouraging events in my life as they relate to political science were actually the negative things that happened to me," Roberts says. "Knowledge is sorrow," he adds, citing Ecclesiastes 1:18. When he watches the 10 p.m. news, Roberts notes, "it can be disturbing if you know the truth."

Roberts believes in the democratic process but thinks the public has gotten complacent. "Democracy was set up so its inhabitants would always be vigilant," he says. To him, the news media are key. Roberts reads newspapers every day and grew up with the *Virginian-Pilot, Life* magazine, and *Ebony* and *Jet*, two magazines that serve the black community. He considers television the most powerful news medium and regularly watches the evening news, CNN, CNBC, C-SPAN, and *60 Minutes*. He notices the flaws, half-truths, and distractions. "If the news media related truthful information to the American public, they could really inform a lot of people who aren't well informed. But on the other hand," Roberts observes, "if you give bad information, you have ill-informed people."

He's troubled most by the stories the news media do not tell that he has experienced firsthand. "I'm disturbed about the truths that I don't hear in the news media. They whitewash the news, military events, numbers that relate to crime and punishment, the war on crime, and the war on drugs. They tell the public what they want to hear," Roberts says. The public wanted to hear how a black federal marshal got caught up in a major drug-trafficking conspiracy, and that's what the newspaper gave them at his expense. "They knew they blew it. Even the agent [involved in his prosecution] said, 'Keith, we don't know where this story came from,' " Roberts recounts. "Some writer was hot-dogging. He wanted to make a big story out of it and got it out of his imagination that I was part of this big conspiracy."

After prison and a few tough years trying, as a convicted felon, to get a decent-paying job in Virginia, Roberts remarried and moved to State College, Pennsylvania, home of Penn State. He traded a minimum-wage job as grounds worker at his alma mater, Norfolk State, for a $6 an hour job as night monitor in Penn State's student union. Within a year, he was promoted and his income rose to $21,000. He believes the college administrator who hired him, a former professional football player, put a block on the criminal record information he put on his job application so others at the university would not treat Roberts as a marked man.

It reminded him of the measures he took when he was in prison, where law enforcement inmates are marked men. "The first thing they [fellow inmates] asked was 'You a policeman?' " he recalls. Roberts told fellow inmates he was in real estate.

Roberts says the stigma of a felony conviction is hard enough to overcome without the government adding to it. As a convicted felon, Roberts cannot vote in state elections in his former home of Virginia, his new home state of Pennsylvania, or in 44 other states, nor can he vote in national elections. He is working through a Virginia state senator to apply to have his voting right restored. He is pessimistic about the prospect because the governor of Virginia, who is empowered to restore a felon's right to vote 5 years after being released from prison or after completing probation, "is very conservative and law-and-order."

"I deserve the right to be able to vote or not vote if I do not want to vote," Roberts says. "I think I've earned back that right."

He maintains that he would have voted in the 1992 and 1996 presidential elections, even while in prison, had his right not been revoked by law. But now, he's not so sure if he would exercise that right. He has other ways he plans to be politically active.

Roberts has applied to the doctoral program in political science and is taking preparatory classes in international politics and comparative government meanwhile. "I don't want to be on the front line anymore, carrying a gun or a badge. I want to be objective and truthful and teach at the college level," he says. He would tell his students about his experiences—with drugs, in law enforcement, and in prison—and how they interrelate to make him skeptical about politics in America. "I am a person in the American political process who they tried to throw away but who won't go away," Roberts says.

———— ◄◦► ————

9

Conclusion
American Democracy Into the 21st Century

Each election cycle, the news media indulge in a familiar ritual. As the races unfold and the election nears, an overarching issue rises to the surface and shrouds the whole process. It is the issue of voter participation. It has been an issue for 20 years since it became apparent in the late 1970s that voter turnout was on a steady downward spiral since 1960, when more than 62% of age-eligible Americans voted. And before each election, the news media seize on hopeful indicators that the cycle may be broken by election-specific events that will galvanize the American public.

A high-profile race that is too close to call. Two candidates with starkly divergent positions on the issues. A third candidate or multiple candidates to shake up the Democratic and Republican parties. A declining economy. No incumbents in the race to make the results a foregone conclusion. Redoubled voter registration efforts, coupled with eased registration laws, that boost the voter rolls dramatically. Ballot referenda on hot-button issues. High absentee balloting before Election Day.

In 1998, a vote by the Republican-dominated House of Representatives on October 8, less than a month before the election, to conduct an inquiry into the impeachment of Democratic President Bill Clinton provided what appeared initially to be the optimal incentive for increased voter participation: a referendum, in effect, on whether the president of the United States should be removed from office, whose outcome would be determined by the results of contested congressional races.

A few days before the election, a reporter asked Clinton if he thought the impeachment issue would affect voter turnout. In response, Clinton tried to steer the question toward issues of Social Security, a patients' bill of rights, education, the minimum wage, campaign finance reform, and tobacco use by children. But he punctuated his answer by saying "All I can do is tell the American people: I know this is no ordinary time, no ordinary election, and they need to vote. I have no prediction about what the turnout will be, but I am confident that if people understand the stakes, it will be quite impressive."

Two days before the election, John Glenn chimed in from space. "I'd like to see a record turnout vote. . . . Every election should be a referendum on what you want America to be for the future," said the astronaut, who was ending his 24-year career in the U.S. Senate with a mission aboard the space shuttle *Discovery*. In noting that he and his fellow astronauts had voted absentee, he admonished, "If you don't get out and vote, you give up your franchise to somebody else. And that's not the American way of doing things."

Yet, in fact, it has become the American way. Half of voting-age Americans do not vote in presidential election years, two thirds take a pass in off-year congressional and gubernatorial elections, and far more fail to turn out for local elections.

The November 1998 elections provided continuing evidence that the nonvoting phenomenon has become a defining trait of American society. Americans once again chose to stay away from the polls in record numbers. The postelection report by the Committee for the Study of the American Electorate showed that only 36.1% of Americans old enough to vote cast ballots. Turnout in a midterm election had not been that low since 1942, when millions of eligible voters were fighting in World War II.

About 119.4 million Americans were no-shows in 1998, the largest number of nonvoters in any election.

In the 12 states in which voter participation increased compared with 1994, in all but one, less than half the states' eligible voters turned out. The only exception was in Minnesota, where almost 60% of the state's eligible voters turned out and unexpectedly elected for governor Jesse Ventura, a former pro wrestler and Reform Party candidate. It should be noted, however, that Minnesota always has been a leader in voter turnout, so its 60% rate in 1998 was as much the result of habit and tradition as of a flamboyant candidate, who for many voters may have been, in effect, a vote for "none of the above."

The new record for low turnout set in 1998 is not surprising because even though some nonvoters are motivated to cast ballots from time to time, most nonvoting is chronic and habit formed, not an election-by-election or candidate-driven choice.

Of the 30 representative nonvoters we tracked for this book, 27 are eligible voters, but only 11 ever have voted. In 1996, of course, when we conducted our initial survey, none of them voted. In 1998, 3 decided to cast ballots, 2 for the first time.

It's not surprising that two of our crossover nonvoters in 1998 are Doers because members of that group believe their vote would count if they voted, and their group characteristics look a lot like those of voters. The other voter, an Unplugged, is more surprising, although he has voted in the past. As a group, Unpluggeds don't follow politics.

Claudine D'Orazio, who was in the hospitality industry in Savannah, Georgia, transferred back to Atlanta about a year after the 1996 election to become a sales manager for a large hotel. In 1998, this Doer, now 29 years old, cast her first vote: for Republican gubernatorial candidate Guy Millner, who lost to Democratic incumbent Governor Roy Barnes. She had been embarrassed about her nonvoting status and now proudly says, "I told you I was going to [vote]. I didn't want you to put I still hadn't voted."

D'Orazio speaks knowledgeably about the two candidates' backgrounds and records, saying she preferred Millner's experience in business to Barnes's image. "I didn't like how Southern he was, a very heavy Southern drawl."

The governor's contest was the only race in which she cast a vote. She intends to continue to vote but only for major offices. "I don't pay enough attention to the others yet. Maybe when I get older, I'll pay more attention to the schools and education, when I have kids."

Like D'Orazio, Doer Ryan Gerali cast his first vote in 1998. On Election Day, the 22-year-old student from suburban Chicago was away at his school, Monmouth College, where the convenience of on-campus voting drew him in. "I voted at the school. . . . I don't know why. I just wanted to vote to say I did. For governor, I wanted to vote for [George] Ryan, and I wanted to vote for [Peter] Fitzgerald [for the U.S. Senate]." They are Republicans, as is much of DuPage County where Gerali grew up. He predicts he will be a regular voter from now on. He has signed up for a course in politics and is looking forward to it.

Jack Daniels, the Unplugged former musician who was slowly recovering from a major stroke in 1996, is 55 now and getting stronger from physical therapy sessions and the passage of time. He listens to music and is teaching piano to a cook at a neighborhood restaurant.

He voted a straight Democratic ticket, as he had in a few local elections decades ago. "The lady helped me out because [in Illinois] you can't just pull one lever anymore."

"I wanted [Senator] Carol Moseley-Braun to win. She lost. I like her. I like the way she talks." He also voted for Glenn Poshard for governor but only because he was a Democrat. "He's a crook like the rest of them." Poshard also lost.

In 1997, Irritable Caren Freigenberg voted in a local election in New Jersey but noted with a chagrined laugh that she couldn't remember for whom she had voted.

Two other Doers, Dr. Robert Wolkow and Nancy Smith, came close to entering the voting booth in 1998.

Wolkow, the New York doctor who works for Pfizer pharmaceuticals and now has entered a doctorate program to study environmental research and conservation, thought about voting in 1998 to defeat U.S. Senator Alfonse D'Amato, the powerful Banking Committee chairman, which is the same reason he voted 6 years ago. He even liked D'Amato's opponent, U.S. Representative Charles Schumer, although he opposed Schumer's support of Clinton during the impeachment inquiry. Ironically, in 1998, Schumer beat D'Amato without Wolkow's participation. It was more important to Wolkow to abide by his principles of not voting for mediocrity and not participating in a process that encourages it.

Smith, whose life revolves around the constant care needed by her severely ill daughter, had hoped to vote against Maryland Governor Parris Glendening, but she missed the registration deadline. It was her last chance to vote in Maryland because the family moved to a Boston suburb a few months after the 1998 election. "The potential [to vote] is there. My husband and I have talked about it, and it's one of the first things we're going to do."

On Election Day 1998, however, daughter Lyndsey, who has cerebral palsy, had a temperature and stayed home from school. "So we just hung out and did lots of Motrin and Tylenol. This is just what would have happened if I had been registered. I couldn't have voted anyway." Glendening won.

The Election Day attitudes of the rest of the nonvoters we tracked show they are more likely not to vote, despite occasionally voicing good intentions.

Doer Gene Tencza, who owns a farm in western Massachusetts and works at a machine and tool company, paid little attention to Election Day. The next day he checked the newspaper to find out who his governor would be. "Whoever got elected was fine with me."

Karen Pelling, a member of the Unplugged cluster whose chief interest is playing darts and getting a more financially secure life for her family, says, "I can't remember offhand who was running. I was listening a little closer this time." But on Election Day 1998, she was out looking for a job in Winter Park, Florida, because she had been laid off from her job at a vehicle fleet company.

"We didn't have anybody decent to vote for," says Unplugged Steve Gordon, who spent Election Day 1998 at his home in Sparta, Wisconsin. He complains that political "backstabbing" has come to dominate politics. "The only one I would vote for is me," he laughs. "I haven't seen anybody to change anything. It's the same old stuff." A local referendum to build a new school almost persuaded him to vote in 1998, but, as has been the case before, he and his wife would have voted on opposite sides, effectively canceling each other's vote, so neither cast ballots. They figure it was a waste of time.

Elizabeth Baxley, the member of the Don't Know cluster we tracked who lives in Scranton, South Carolina, also bemoans "backstabbing" by candidates. In 1998, the South Carolina gubernatorial race was particularly nasty, she says, pointing to the contest between incumbent David Beasley and Democrat Jim Hodges, who won after allegations that Beasley had had an affair were leaked to the press and gambling interests intent on getting a state lottery poured millions of dollars into Hodges's campaign.

Henry Montoya, the Irritable nonvoter who registers his disdain for politicians by voting for an empty ballot in every election, once again went to his Denver polling place in 1998 to vote, in effect, for "none of the above."

"There's nobody in this state worth voting for," he said of his November 3, 1998 choices. "If I'd voted for anybody, I would have voted for [U.S. Senator Ben Nighthorse] Campbell. But I didn't because I don't believe in politicians."

Wolkow understands Montoya's decision to vote for an empty ballot. Wolkow said two things might impel him to vote: a choice of candidates that included at least one he really wanted to see in office and, even more likely as an effective carrot, the institution of a system that would allow him to vote against all the candidates—a choice of "none of the above." "It would not only get me to vote, but I think it would get a lot of others to vote, too."

The *Wall Street Journal* makes a similar argument. In a June 3, 1996 editorial, the newspaper advocated, "It's time to consider giving voters a binding None of the Above line on ballots." The *Journal* urged the adoption of a binding vote to give people a real choice, which is particularly needed, the newspaper wrote, in races in which an incumbent has no effective opposition, in which the Democratic and Republican candidates are unworthy, or in states that do not a history of robust competitive politics.

Consumer advocate Ralph Nader has proposed a "none of the above" ballot option also, arguing that the public's ability to say no is also an opportunity to say yes to better-quality candidates and to elections dictated less by money and the advantages of incumbency.

Only Nevada residents have that option, although as a nonbinding vote, thanks to a 1975 law requiring that statewide races, including those for president and vice president, have a line on the ballot for "none of these candidates." In four party primary elections, two congressional and two for state offices, "none of these candidates" actually finished first, according to Nader. By law, the candidate with the next most votes was declared the winner in each case. Nonetheless, Nevada's voter participation rate is among the lowest of any state in the union: 39% of its age-eligible residents voted in the 1996 presidential election, and only 33% voted in the November 1998 elections. In fact, its voter turnout has declined steadily since the law went into effect in 1975.

The idea of voting for no one as a way to increase turnout shows the profound disconnect that nonvoters feel toward politics and the voting process, which for them is neither a relief valve to register discontent nor, as it is for some voters, to show committed partisanship.

Paula Ryan, the Phoenix, Arizona, member of the Unpluggeds, didn't vote in 1998 because she continues to believe that elected officials ignore voters' wishes. "You vote rules in and then they take [them] away from you. Last time, they had a proposition that gave doctors the right to give marijuana to [seriously or] terminally ill patients, but they took that right away." In November 1998, Arizona residents had another chance to vote on an identical referendum. It passed overwhelmingly, as did the measure 2 years earlier. In between, the state legislature blocked the voter initiative and deepened Ryan's distrust in government.

She worked on Election Day 1998 and says no one in her mortgage loan company talked about politics; she knows of only one coworker who voted. Her husband and younger daughter, Karine, who's now in college at Northern Arizona University, didn't vote, but her older daughter, Chasidy, did. "Probably nothing will get me to vote. She [Chasidy] believes it will make a difference."

The frustration that elected officials ignore the wishes of the people is sounded again and again among nonvoters. Often, it's tied to the belief that politicians consider themselves in a different class than other Americans, a particularly strong theme among middle-income to low-income nonvoters.

Ryan mentioned how out of place she would be made to feel at a Washington political dinner. Melody Lewis, an Irritable nonvoter who had moved to Missouri shortly before the 1996 election and now has an office job with the Howell County trash department, wants to see what a day in the life of a politician is like; she cannot imagine what such a life is like. She paid no attention to the 1998 election and, on Election Day, went home from work and watched a movie she had rented. She didn't vote and didn't care to know who had won.

Among all the nonvoters, there was near-universal belief that politicians only care about those who vote on Election Day, then go back to business as usual, and never take an interest in those who are not at the polls on that crucial day.

Because of such deeply rooted beliefs, a close race, a big issue, or a more engaging candidate isn't likely to mobilize core nonvoters. In New York state, the November 1998 turnout was low—33%—despite the hot contest between D'Amato and Schumer, for instance.

And even the lurking presence of an impeachment inquiry wasn't enough to transform nonvoters into voters.

Most of the 30 nonvoters we tracked felt, like many Americans, that it was time to end the entire Clinton-Lewinsky-Starr chapter. For the nonvoters, what resonated most was how the political dialogue over impeachment was more theater and noise than anything that had to do with them or their lives.

Don't Know cluster member George Perez, who lives on Social Security and disability payments in El Paso, Texas, continues to watch television much of the time. He is getting out a little more, although he didn't go out to vote in 1998. "I think he's a good president," Perez said of Clinton. "He's human." Irritable Caren Freigenberg called Clinton's affair with former White House intern Monica Lewinsky a private matter between the president and First Lady Hillary Rodham Clinton. "It's nothing I need to know about or anyone else in the country needs to know about."

But Don't Know Elizabeth Baxley believed Clinton ought to be punished because he was supposed to be a role model. Nevertheless, she also wanted to see an end to the investigation by independent counsel Kenneth Starr and the action by Congress.

For someone like Paula Ryan, who cannot think of anything that would get her to vote, her condemnation of President Clinton, despite its intensity, was not about to move her to the polls. "He lied to a grand jury. That is an offense according to our law. It's not just an affair. . . . What about all of his other lies?" She believes that former White House aide Vince Foster was murdered and that Clinton took campaign cash from the Chinese in return for giving them military technology they can use against the United States.

Nonetheless, she didn't vote in 1998 to show support for Republicans. "I still feel it [voting] doesn't matter one way or another." Her attitude typifies the core nonvoters; their nonvoting is a habit. And the habit of nonvoting has been formed over nearly four decades, since the peak voter turnout year of 1960. Their attitudes have hardened into a wall that shuts out the political process, the candidates who thrive on it, and the issues that spring from it.

The preelection impeachment debate among candidates, pollsters, pundits, and the news media turned on whether the public's intrigue with the Clinton scandal would translate into votes to endorse or pull the plug on the impeachment process. What was evident from the nonvoters we tracked was that the affair, whether it captured their attention or turned them off, was disconnected from the political process. What they watched on television or talked about with friends and family, although political at its core, was just the stuff of everyday conversation, not unlike sports, the weather, and which movies are worth seeing.

In the repeated refrains of nonvoters that there's no difference among candidates or no candidate worth their vote, their desire for heroes but inability to find any also can be heard.

When asked what political figures they admire, President John Kennedy was cited more than once. Almost no figure after his time was mentioned. Unplugged member Jack Daniels had intended to cast his first presidential vote for Kennedy in 1964. He had admired Kennedy and believed in his goals. After the assassination, Daniels couldn't bring himself to vote for Kennedy's successor, Lyndon Johnson.

Another Unplugged, bartender Barbara Beth of Lakehead, California, remembered Kennedy as the last president she could like. She was too young to vote for him in 1960; now, she has never voted, including in 1998. She has quit her job because she has emphysema and has moved to nearby Redding, California. Although her in-home health care worker asked if she wanted to register to vote and Beth said she might vote in 1998, the election passed her by as her emphysema and a knee operation consumed her attention.

Yet another Unplugged, Janet Shepherd, voted for Kennedy in 1960. "There wasn't a thing Kennedy said that I didn't believe. I don't remember Kennedy saying anything bad about his opponent."

Two nonvoters who weren't born when Kennedy was assassinated are saddened at the dearth of modern-day political heroes.

Irritable Melody Lewis, 31 years old in 1996, says, "I respect a lot of what I hear about John Kennedy, and even his family after that."

Serena Slaton, an Unplugged who lives in Atlanta and was 26 years old in 1998, was disappointed that Georgia state Senator Ralph Abernathy III, whom she had supported, was caught at the Atlanta airport in 1997 with marijuana, which he claimed was for his glaucoma. "I'm trying to find someone who's changed for the better or that has gotten into a leadership position where they can determine this or that and has done right by it. And I'm trying to think of one and I can't think of one. . . . I had a lot of faith in Ralph Abernathy. Wrong is wrong no matter how you do it."

But as much as they may have admired Kennedy's policies and the Camelot atmosphere he created, pointing to Kennedy is also a way for nonvoters to point to a different era whose end was tied to his death—a time before the Vietnam War created a new attitude of cynicism toward government officials and before the dominance of TV news in political campaigns changed the way elections are run.

Despite negative advertising and TV-driven campaigns that have caused some nonvoters to flee even farther from electoral politics, the idea that information consumption is an indicator of voting is not borne out by the Medill survey or our interviews. Numerous political analysts have said that those most likely to vote are those with the highest rates of news consumption. Some have even gone so far as to say that because nonvoters are not informed, it's good that they don't vote. The facts show they couldn't be more wrong about a large segment of nonvoters. Doers and Irritables follow the news, usually know what's going on politically, and have definite opinions about the candidates.

Nancy Smith, the Doer from the Washington, D.C., suburb of Silver Spring, knew who was running for governor of her state in 1998 and knew where each candidate stood on the issues. The same was true of her political knowledge in 1996. Another Doer, Wolkow, had followed his senator's career for years. Freigenberg, an Irritable, has worked on a campaign or two in New York City, is up on the national issues, and can give a political history of the past three decades.

Michael Keegan, also an Irritable nonvoter, left his hometown of Norristown, Pennsylvania, a year before the 1988 election to move to upstate New York, near Ithaca. He's working as a mason until he can start building his dream home—a log and stone house in the woods. He took his appetite for news with him and can recite the facts about the local and national politicians.

Jason Caldwell, a Doer from the Kansas City, Missouri, suburb of Belton, says he would have voted if he'd had time in 1998, but he was working 10-hour days and missed the chance. He would have supported U.S. Senator Christopher Bond because of his views on education. Now that Caldwell is married with an infant son, his interest in politicians who support education has deepened. "I probably will vote in the future."

Another Doer, carpet installer Paul Rains of Cheyenne, Wyoming, says he also will return to the polls one day, "when something sticks in my craw." Like Caldwell, he followed the issues in the 1998 election, particularly a local sheriff's race, and watched TV news most nights. "I wasn't impressed. Our little local election wasn't pretty."

Some Internet enthusiasts, including author and Internet guru Esther Dyson, believe the World Wide Web offers the best chance for renewed interest in participatory democracy. In her 1997 book *Release 2.0,* Dyson wrote, "For me, the great hope of the Net is that it will lead people first to get involved on the Net and then to change their overall experience of life."

In the 1998 election season, Web White and Blue, a campaign to promote easy access to political information, was launched by the Markle Foundation and Harvard University's Joan Shorenstein Center on the Press, Politics and Public Policy and got more than 400,000 hits on its Web site, according to a news release it put out.

Steve Gordon, the Unplugged nonvoter from Sparta, Wisconsin, spent Election Day online. He spends a lot of time connecting electronically, but he remains disconnected from politics. His Web interests revolve around fishing and other sports.

Doer Gene Tencza also has turned to the Web as his main information source. In fact, he created his own Web site devoted to his antique tractor collection and gets about two or three visits to the site every day.

Neither Tencza nor Gordon voted. Nor, for that matter, has Dyson, according to her book.

No matter where they get their information, having that information doesn't turn nonvoters into voters by itself.

Neither does getting older and settling down. Doer Caldwell, who turned 27 in 1998, has gained a house, a wife, and a son since 1996, when he didn't vote, but he remains a nonvoter. Another Doer, 37-year-old Sue Jablonsky of New Brighton, Pennsylvania, had only her youngest son living at home on Election Day 1998; the oldest moved in with his father, and the middle boy is living with a cousin. She could have gone to the polls; instead, she spent the day at one of her favorite occupations—baking cookies.

"There was nobody worth voting for," she says of the 1988 election. "I don't think I'll vote in the future. I haven't so far. I can't see it happening. I don't want to vote for the wrong person."

Like Jablonsky, some nonvoters have accumulated an insecurity that they are not up to the task of voting, that voting is something beyond the lowest common denominator of citizenship. Don't Know Susan Godoy is one of them but is gaining confidence. "Voting is a very responsible thing to do," the Rosemead, California, sales engineer told us after the 1996 presidential election, and she wasn't ready in 1998, despite the lessons she was learning from having to confront her son Guy's gang problems. On July 21, 1997, Guy Godoy was shot and killed when he got out of a car to argue with a pedestrian. The *Los Angeles Times* quoted sheriff's deputies as saying the murder was gang related. Godoy has not learned much more than that since, and no one has been charged in the murder.

A few months before the November 1998 elections, Godoy renewed her driver's license by mail. She noticed the voter registration form that accompanied it but failed to complete and return it. "I kept telling myself to get over there because it was an important election year," Godoy says, referring to the governor's race and the 12 propositions on the ballot. She wanted to vote on Proposition 5, touted as the most expensive single-issue campaign in American political history, to make sure that Indian reservations could continue to offer gaming, but she felt she didn't know enough about another high-profile proposition on whether to cut back electricity rates. She feels she's not quite there yet.

Another common misconception about nonvoters is that they would vote if only the process was easier. Some are inclined to say that. When we surveyed them initially, 14% of the unregistered nonvoters said they weren't registered because they had recently moved, 5% said they weren't registered because they didn't know how, 4% because the place they have to go to register is inconvenient, and another 4% because they work during voter registration hours. But when we probed deeper, the impediments to registration and voting became shorthand for a palpable disconnect.

Tracy Rowley, an Unplugged nonvoter who lived in Troutdale, Oregon, in 1996, registered to vote after she and her husband moved to Portland in 1998. On November 3, 1998, her husband voted; she didn't.

"I thought about it. I read the voters' pamphlet book because it came in the mail and my husband wanted me to read it. Some of the measures were pretty darn silly." After leaving her job as a tax accountant on Election Day, she picked her son up from school; he asked her if she had voted. When she said no, he said she should. But her future as a nonvoter seems pretty certain. She cannot name a reason that would get her to the polls.

Irritable Caren Freigenberg, who's now registered in New Jersey, had an excuse for not voting in the 1998 election. On November 3, she was in Utah on a family vacation and would have had to vote by absentee ballot, which she thought was too much trouble. Among her parents, brother, sister, and their spouses, only her parents voted absentee that day.

"If I was living in New York, I definitely would have found a way to vote [against U.S. Senator Alfonse D'Amato]. It had a lot more to do with what's going on in country. In New Jersey, there was nothing major in the election." So an absentee ballot would not have been too difficult if she had been living in Manhattan, the city she loves.

She had refused to register in New Jersey for several years but finally gave in when she registered her car in 1997, one of several nonvoters whose registration was due, in part to the National Voter Registration Act that made the process easier by allowing registration by mail and at government offices, particularly motor vehicle departments.

Nevertheless, ease of registration didn't turn her into a voter, except in one local election in 1997. To get her to vote again, she would have to "totally hate the person in power. Or if I really liked the candidate. If I knew what was going to be in the election . . . affects me."

Serena Slaton, the Unplugged nonvoter from Atlanta, skipped the November 1998 election because she hadn't kept up with the issues, although she remained registered to vote. She did hear the radio ads exhorting people, particularly African Americans, to vote. "There was a real need to vote, [the radio ads said]. It was urgent, it was urgent, it might be your last time." As she worked at Cash America, she noticed the customers with "I voted" stickers.

Unplugged Iris Llamas of Austin, Texas, also is registered but didn't vote in 1998. "Probably for the presidential election I will. Right now, I'm not politically educated enough." She says work—she switched from her job at a computer chip manufacturer to a secretarial position at a new company—and church, where she is helping stage a gospel play, have kept her too busy to become an informed voter. "Once I get into politics more, hopefully I will." But she adds, with a laugh, "Hopefully."

Unplugged Barbara Beth had the opportunity to register with the help of her in-home health care worker. "It's mandatory that they ask if you want to register." But she let the deadline pass.

Alma Romanowski, an Alienated cluster member, has been registered more than once, most recently in 1996, when the registration came in the mail with her Michigan driver's license renewal form. She completed both forms and sent them in.

In January 1998, she had moved to a new neighborhood in Flint, Michigan, where she felt her family would be safer. She continues to volunteer at her daughters' schools and joined Moms Who Care at the high school. But her involvement doesn't extend to Election Day participation. In 1998, she continued her record of nonvoting.

"There was nobody I was interested in voting for. I didn't like either of the candidates running for governor. I'll never do it. I'm chicken. I don't have enough confidence or trust in anyone to go voting for them."

The only way to get her to the voting booth is "someone picking me up and taking me and making me."

Romanowski is an example of the gulf between registration and voting, a gulf beyond the reach of the motor voter law, which increased registered voters in 1996 by 5 million, but the total number of actual voters dropped by 9 million to 95.8 million. In 1998, 4 million more Americans registered, but the number of voters dropped by 2.5 million to 72.5 million, according to the Committee for the Study of the American Electorate.

Columnist George Will poked fun at the motor-voter registration effort in a July 1998 column:

> In 1996 record sums were spent by parties, candidates and interest groups to excite an electorate swollen by a net increase of five million registered voters. This was partly a result of the "motor voter" law, which enables people to register when they get their driver's licenses. (What next—"pizza voter," whereby the guy who delivers your pizza will register you?) The electorate remained unstimulated.

A 1998 report issued by the U.S. Bureau of the Census, *Voting and Registration in the Election of November 1996,* said nearly 5 million Americans didn't vote in 1996 because they considered themselves too busy—three times more than gave that reason in 1980.

The nonvoting phenomenon that encompassed 100 million Americans in the 1996 presidential election and 119 million Americans in November 1998 elections is not about a busy America. It is about an evolution in the fabric of American society that has made voting neither a duty nor a habit nor a ritual for a growing majority of the nation's people.

Nonvoters may tell pollsters they don't vote because they don't like the choice of candidates. What they often mean, we found, is that they don't connect and aren't likely to connect enough with any political candidate or party or with the electoral process to become involved. Behind the answer that they are too busy to vote or that the process is too cumbersome lies the accumulated belief of a majority of Americans that a vote has lost not only its actual value in terms of influencing the result of an election or governmental actions after the election but also its symbolic value as a democratic virtue. In the simple finding that nonvoters are more likely than voters to call themselves independent lurks a profoundly deeper message: Often, they mean that they have become independent of the body politic. The vast majority of nonvoters are not turned off by a particular candidate or a certain election. They opted out long ago and generally are beyond the reach of conventional measures to bring them back.

In America today, for every voter there is a nonvoter such as Doer Paul Rains, who sees himself as the epitome of a complacent mainstream America that doesn't want to be bothered; Unplugged Steve Gordon, who thinks election outcomes are no more rational than an image he remembers from a TV sitcom of choosing presidents randomly by lottery; or Don't Know Elizabeth Baxley, who has built up a quadrennial aversion to her own birthday because it falls on January 20, Inauguration Day.

There is some debate over whether nonvoters would change an election outcome were they all to vote one mythical Election Day: those who conclude they would not argue that nonvoters have political ideologies and opinions so similar to voters that they would merely reinforce the outcome versus those who say they would rest their conclusion on the evidence that nonvoters are less affluent, less educated, younger, and more likely to be members of minority groups than traditional voters.

Nonvoters are not a monolith, however, and their disconnect is more ingrained than any predictive political leanings or ideology. In fact, the differences among nonvoters are predictive of when they are likely to cross over to vote in an election, if ever.

Civic responsibility in the form of voting tends to resonate with Doers. They are likely to vote from time to time: Only two of the eight we tracked—Gene Tencza and Sue Jablonsky—never had voted by 1998. Dr. Robert Wolkow, who won't give his vote to an unworthy candidate, and Paul Rains, who's waiting for the issue that gets him riled up, demonstrate Doers' belief that their vote is worth something—that it would count if they voted.

The Unpluggeds remain unconvinced that their votes would have meaning. And they're not sure voting is worth the effort to find out. Only two of the nine we tracked had ever voted. Karen Pelling worries about jury duty. But the Florida legislature amended its jury service law so that, by 1998, jurors were selected from driver's license lists rather than voter registration rolls. Still, she's not registered. "I never got a chance to get down there to register." Tracy Rowley was embarrassed when her son told her on Election Day 1998 that she should have voted, but she doesn't plan to change.

Irritable nonvoters don't like what they've learned—neither from candidates nor from the news media that cover them. Michael Keegan says politicians had the chance to get his vote in 1996 but blew it with posturing and lying. He followed the candidates' positions closely; Ross Perot came closest to getting his vote because he talked directly to voters through paid TV infomercials, bypassing traditional media coverage. Henry Montoya has started reading the Libertarian Party's newspaper for his information, believing mainstream news media are reporting the political establishment's line without enough skepticism.

Don't Knows aren't watching the news media. They've tuned out from political information. Elizabeth Baxley literally tunes out on Inauguration Day so that her birthday isn't ruined by news from Washington. George Perez tunes out most days, preferring sitcom reruns to the news. Erica Smith, the single mom from Lynn, Massachusetts, whose single issue is domestic violence, didn't vote in 1998 because she "didn't see anything worth voting for." But she admits she wasn't looking because she was preoccupied with getting custody of her teenage sister after her father became very ill.

Kathy Smith of Olympia, Washington, has vowed to be a lifelong nonvoter. So far, she's kept her vow.

Like many Alienated nonvoters, she believes voting is a futile exercise. Despite growing up in a household of voters, she has no respect for the election process. The system only works for the elite, she believes, and she can cite example after example of voters' decisions thwarted by politicians' post-election deals.

In the Can't Shows, ironically, the desire to vote is strong. Of the three we tracked, two appear to be likely voters if they could cast ballots.

Estela Crespo, who still lives in North Bergen, New Jersey, with her boyfriend, is studying computer technology now. In 1998, she was too busy to follow the election news.

But Keith Roberts of State College, Pennsylvania, and James Ayarkwa-Duah of Dallas, Texas, did follow the 1998 election campaigns.

Roberts, the former U.S. marshal who lost his right to vote after a drug conviction, is trying to get a pardon to restore his voting rights, a right taken away from an estimated 4.2 million convicted felons, 1.4 million of whom are black males. He has moved from Pennsylvania back to his native Virginia. If he regains his right to vote, he will exercise it, he says. "Everybody needs to get involved in the political process."

Ayarkwa-Duah also has some hope of gaining the right to vote. One of an estimated 14.5 million legal immigrants who are not citizens, he married an American in 1997 and is going to apply for citizenship.

"If I become a citizen, voting is important. It is an important thing for every citizen to participate. People are comfortable so they don't vote, but that's wrong. If you don't vote, I see it to be not a very good sign for the country. It's our way to make clear how we think the country's being run. Voting is the voice of the people."

Nonvoters often say that they agree with Ayarkwa-Duah's sentiment, yet their nonvoting behavior is chronic and habit formed. The duty, habit, and ritual of voting that many saw in their parents didn't develop in them.

Only three of the nonvoters profiled in this book—Doer Claudine D'Orazio, Irritable Caren Freigenberg, and Don't Know Susan Godoy—express embarrassment at their status as Election Day no-shows.

In fact, few of the 30 nonvoters consider voting relevant to their perception of good citizenship. Voting may be a right or a privilege, they believe, but not one with the abiding meaning for them of other rights and privileges or duties, such as obeying the law, paying taxes, volunteering in their communities, or going to church.

Alienated member Alma Romanowski says, "I don't do anything bad, hurt anybody, or break the law. I probably should run for president."

Doer Ryan Gerali also mentions his law-abiding nature. "I think I am a good citizen. I was never arrested, always obeyed the law. I volunteer my time as a Big Brother mentor to take out deprived kids, to hang out with them." He also volunteers in campus activities and donates blood.

Doer Nancy Smith and Unplugged Steve Gordon liken good citizenship to being Catholic. "It's just like being [a good] Catholic doesn't mean going to church each Sunday. How you live your life and treat other people, how you help your friends and neighbors is what counts."

Unplugged Paula Ryan agrees: "A citizen is someone who stops and helps. It's compassion, caring, and concern of what's going on. When we're forced to vote, our democracy has been taken away from us."

Paul Rains, another Doer, says, "It's a privilege. You're not bound to it. It's your right not to vote."

Don't Know cluster member Elizabeth Baxley sums up the definition: "Being a good citizen can mean a lot of things, not just voting."

But Susan Godoy, also a Don't Know, is less willing to consider herself a good citizen unless and until she attends more public meetings and votes.

Irritable Caren Freigenberg adds this dissenting opinion: "In all honesty, if you never vote, you really don't have a right to complain. One vote does sometimes count. It's not a good thing not to vote." She says she will resume voting, a habit she dropped when she moved to New Jersey from New York City, where she felt connected.

The mistake we make every election is to treat voter turnout as part of the political campaign—a phenomenon tied to that year's election. It is something more. In the 2000 presidential election, it will take a minimum of 14 million more voters than those who voted in 1996 to produce what is perceived to be a respectable turnout of 55%. Even if that were to occur, an unlikely prospect in itself, there still would be a core 90 million no-shows in America entering the 21st century. A conservative estimate is 100 million American no-shows in presidential elections, as well as another 20 million in congressional and gubernatorial elections. And the numbers are growing. For a generation to come, a vast core of America—as of 1996 the majority of America—shows little sign of opting in.

Worse yet is that the political process—its candidates, parties, and pollsters— and the news media seem disinclined to do anything about the fundamental disconnect. Their investment is tied more to the stuff of elections than to the disaffection beyond the vote. Candidates and parties seek to control or narrow the electorate to bring out only those people whose votes are predictable. Pollsters and the news media have opted to hear from those whose participation is most likely. The nonvoting majority is less likely to cross over and vote than it is to become voiceless, invisible, and forgotten.

Recommendations to increase voter participation, such as longer voting hours, weekend voting, mail-in voting, more flexible absentee voting rules, shorter ballots, and limitations on negative campaign advertising, nibble at the margins and will not draw in core nonvoters. That is why other electoral reforms—such as easing voter registration through motor-voter legislation, same-day registration, or uncoupling registration from jury duty—have had at best a negligible net effect on voter participation. Although a "none of the above" voting option, as is available in Nevada, might make the disaffection more visible, it does not address the fundamental disconnect between the public and the political process, as Nevada's turnout figures prove.

That disconnect is immune in the short run to all but the most dramatic measures. There are proposals aplenty that seek to import political realities from elsewhere.

The United States could elect officials through proportional representation, as is done in many European democracies, including Finland, Germany, and the Netherlands.

Voter registration could be automatic, as it is in Austria, Belgium, and Italy, at the age of 18, or voting could be made mandatory, as it is to differing degrees in Australia, Italy, Belgium, Greece, Peru, and Brazil. Even efforts to enfranchise age-eligible Americans—specifically legal immigrants and convicted felons, although it would increase the vote count—would do nothing to reach the vast majority of nonvoting Americans.

Mandatory voting, although it would succeed in spiking the numbers, would not produce an invested electorate or one connected other than by force of law to the political process.

For the majority of Americans for whom voting is neither duty nor ritual, a more fundamental evolution must take place if voting is to be used as an indicator of the legitimacy of a thriving democracy. The voice of the nonvoting majority, with its competing strains of alienation and complacency, political awareness and obliviousness, futility and indifference, speaks of no heroes or icons in the political landscape. Nonvoters exhibit little trust in the responsiveness of the political process, not even those who believe it is working. They get little reinforcement at home or on the job for the importance of the political or voting process. What has resulted is a generation of which half its members lives outside the conventional body politic.

It may take decades for nonvoters to change their attitudes and beliefs, to find heroes in the political world and meaning in government actions or responses. Certainly, it will take years for nonvoters to receive information from the political process with more than passing curiosity or hostile cynicism, much less to act on it by voting. The disconnect is enormous, the conviction to snub the polling place ingrained.

At this juncture, on the cusp of the 21st century, the great divide between nonvoters and voters defines American democracy and is evident every Election Day.

Appendix A

No-Show '96: Americans Who Don't Vote

RESULTS OF NONVOTER SAMPLE ($N = 1,001$)

Hello, I'm _____ from the Medill News Service in Washington, D.C. We're conducting a telephone opinion survey for newspapers and TV stations around the country. I'd like to ask a few questions of the youngest male, 18 years of age or older, who is at home now. (**IF NO MALE, ASK:** May I please speak with the oldest female 18 years of age or older, who is at home?)

A. INTERVIEWER: RECORD SEX OF RESPONDENT

    Male = 46.4%
    Female = 53.6%

1. Some people seem to follow what's going on in government and public affairs most of the time, whether there's an election or not. Others aren't that interested. Would you say you follow what's going on in government and public affairs most of the time, some of the time, only now and then, or hardly at all?

    24% = Most of the time
    33% = Some of the time
    19% = Only now and then
    24% = Hardly at all
     1% = No answer

2. These days, many people are so busy they can't find time to register to vote or move around so often they don't get a chance to reregister. Are you **NOW** registered to vote in your precinct or election district, or haven't you been able to register so far?

    36% = Yes, registered
    64% = No, not registered
     1% = No answer

IF NOT REGISTERED IN Q2, ASK:

2a. What would you say is the main reason you're not registered to vote? **(DO NOT READ LIST)**

21% = Don't care much about politics

14% = Have recently moved

11% = Not a U.S. citizen

5% = Don't know how to register

4% = Place where have to go to register is inconvenient/too far from home

4% = Work during voter registration hours

3% = Registered and vote at a previous address

2% = Don't want to get my name on the list for jury duty

35% = Other

3% = No answer

3. Did you vote for president in 1992, did something prevent you from voting, or did you choose not to vote for president in 1992?

16% = Yes, voted

35% = Something prevented me from voting

45% = Chose not to vote

4% = No answer

IF DID NOT VOTE IN Q3, ASK:

3a. What was it that kept you from voting? **(DO NOT READ LIST)**

20% = Not registered	4% = Working
12% = Didn't like the candidates	4% = Traveling
12% = Not old enough	2% = Illness
10% = No particular reason	2% = No way to get to polls
10% = Not interested in politics	12% = Other
9% = Not a citizen	2% = No answer

IF RESPONDENT ANSWERS NOT REGISTERED, ASK:

3b. Was that because you weren't old enough, or for some other reason?

6% = Not old enough

94% = Other reason

1% = No answer

4. How likely would you say it is that you will vote in the presidential and congressional elections this November—would you say you'll definitely vote, probably vote, probably not vote, or definitely not vote?

25% = Definitely vote **(ASK Q4a)**

28% = Probably vote **(SKIP TO Q4b)**

20% = Probably not vote (**SKIP TO Q4b**)
23% = Definitely not vote (**SKIP TO Q4d**)
 4% = No answer

4a. What would you say is the main reason you'll definitely vote?

SEE ATTACHED

IF PROBABLY VOTE OR PROBABLY NOT VOTE IN Q4, ASK:
4b. What would be your main reason for deciding to vote?

SEE ATTACHED

IF PROBABLY VOTE OR PROBABLY NOT VOTE IN Q4, ASK:
4c. Why do you think you might not vote?

SEE ATTACHED

IF DEFINITELY NOT VOTE IN Q4, ASK:
4d. What would you say is the main reason you'll definitely not vote?

SEE ATTACHED

IF REGISTERED AND VOTED IN 1992 OR GAVE "NOT OLD ENOUGH" AS REASON FOR NOT VOTING AND SAY "DEFINITELY VOTE" OR "PROBABLY VOTE" IN NOVEMBER, SKIP TO Q34. ALL OTHERS CONTINUE.

5. Do you feel things in this country are generally going in the right direction today, or do you feel things have pretty seriously gotten off on the wrong track?

31% = Right direction
58% = Wrong track
11% = No answer

6. What do you think is the most important problem facing this country today? (**DO NOT READ LIST**)

18% = Crime/violence	3% = Congress/government
7% = Economy	3% = Foreign policy
7% = Budget deficit	3% = Health care/health insurance
7% = Unemployment	2% = Social Security/other elderly issues
6% = Drugs	2% = High taxes
5% = Education	1% = Immigration
4% = Ethics/values	1% = Abortion
4% = Welfare	1% = Environment
4% = Homelessness/poverty	1% = AIDS
4% = Race relations	9% = Other
3% = Family breakdown	7% = No answer

7. Thinking about the Democratic and Republican parties, would you say there is a great deal of difference in what they stand for, a fair amount of difference, or hardly any difference at all?

    24% = Great deal of difference
    32% = Fair amount of difference
    32% = Hardly any difference
    12% = No answer

8. I'm going to read you a series of statements, and for each one I'd like you to tell me whether you completely agree with it, mostly agree with it, mostly disagree with it, or completely disagree with it. The first one is . . . (READ EACH STATEMENT). Would you say you completely agree, mostly agree, mostly disagree, or completely disagree with that statement?

	Completely Agree	Mostly Agree	Mostly Disagree	Completely Disagree	No Answer
a. Most elected officials don't care what people like me think.	23%	41%	26%	7%	3%
b. The federal government often does a better job than people give it credit for.	11%	41%	29%	14%	5%
c. Success in life is pretty much determined by forces outside our control.	15%	26%	33%	23%	4%
d. As Americans, we can always find a way to solve our problems and get what we want.	20%	45%	22%	11%	2%
e. It makes no real difference who is elected—things go on just as they did before.	25%	28%	28%	16%	3%
f. The federal government should run ONLY those things that cannot be run at the local level.	29%	38%	18%	7%	8%
g. I'm pretty interested in following local politics.	16%	32%	30%	19%	3%
h. Most issues discussed in Washington don't affect me personally.	14%	23%	37%	23%	3%
i. There should be a limit on how many terms a person can serve in Congress.	48%	26%	11%	9%	6%
j. Government should play an active role in improving health care, housing, and education for middle-income families.	57%	26%	11%	4%	3%

k. A woman's right to decide about abortion should be preserved.	53%	20%	8%	14%	5%
l. Illegal immigrants and their children should NOT be allowed to receive education, health, and welfare benefits.	27%	20%	25%	22%	6%

9. Now I'd like to ask your opinion of some groups and organizations. First, would you say your overall opinion of . . . (**INSERT ITEM, ROTATE ITEM A & B**) is very favorable, mostly favorable, mostly unfavorable, or very unfavorable?

	Very Favorable	Mostly Favorable	Mostly Unfavorable	Very Unfavorable	No Answer
a. Republican Party	7%	35%	28%	14%	16%
b. Democratic Party	9%	39%	28%	9%	16%
c. Congress	5%	39%	27%	8%	21%
d. Labor unions	14%	36%	23%	10%	17%
e. Supreme Court	15%	50%	15%	5%	16%
f. Television news	17%	48%	21%	9%	5%
g. The daily newspaper you are most familiar with	18%	53%	14%	6%	9%
h. Your local school board	11%	38%	17%	9%	25%
i. Your city or county council	11%	44%	17%	6%	23%
j. The religion or religious institution you are most familiar with	37%	40%	6%	4%	13%

10. How closely would you say you've followed news about the terrorist bombing in Saudi Arabia that killed 19 Americans—would you say you've followed it very closely, followed it but not very closely, or haven't followed it much at all?

> 29% = Followed very closely
> 46% = Followed, but not very closely
> 24% = Haven't followed much at all
> 1% = No answer

10a. How did you first learn about the bombing? (**IF "TV" OR "RADIO," PROBE TO DETERMINE IF THAT WAS A NEWS PROGRAM OR TALK SHOW**)

> 78% = TV news   ** = Internet news service
> 10% = Radio news   ** = News magazine
> 7% = Read it in the newspaper ** = Radio talk/call-in show
> 3% = From friend or relative 1% = Other
> ** = TV talk show   1% = No answer

11. How closely would you say you've followed news about the White House handling of FBI files on prominent Republicans—would you say you've followed it very closely, followed it but not too closely, or haven't followed it much at all?

> 13% = Followed very closely
> 31% = Followed, but not very closely
> 53% = Haven't followed much at all
>   3% = No answer

11a. How did you first learn about the story? **(IF "TV" OR "RADIO," PROBE TO DETERMINE IF THAT WAS A NEWS PROGRAM OR TALK SHOW)**

> 73% = TV news   1% = News magazine
> 11% = Read it in newspaper   ** = From neighbor
>   7% = Radio news   ** = TV talk show
>   4% = Friend or relative   1% = Other
>   1% = Radio talk/call-in show   2% = No answer

12. How closely would you say you've followed news about Hillary Clinton's meeting with New Age psychologist Gean Houston—would you say you've followed it very closely, followed it but not too closely, or haven't followed it much at all?

>   7% = Followed very closely
> 19% = Followed, but not very closely
> 71% = Haven't followed much at all
>   4% = No answer

12a. How did you first learn about the story? **(IF "TV" OR "RADIO," PROBE TO DETERMINE IF THAT WAS A NEWS PROGRAM OR TALK SHOW)**

> 72% = TV news   2% = News magazine
> 18% = Read it in newspaper   1% = Radio talk/call-in show
>   3% = Radio news   1% = TV talk show
>   2% = Friend or relative   1% = No answer

13. How closely would you say you've followed news about the Valuejet crash in Florida—would you say you've followed it very closely, followed it but not too closely, or haven't followed it much at all?

> 54% = Followed very closely
> 32% = Followed, but not very closely
> 13% = Haven't followed much at all
>   1% = No answer

NOTE: ** indicates response given by less than .5% of those interviewed.

13a. How did you first learn about the grounding of Valuejet by the FAA?
(IF "TV" OR "RADIO," PROBE TO DETERMINE IF THAT WAS A NEWS PROGRAM OR TALK SHOW)

75% = TV news   ** = Internet news service
 8% = Radio news   ** = Radio talk/call-in show
 8% = Read it in newspaper   ** = From neighbor
 4% = Friend or relative   2% = Other
 ** = News magazine   2% = No answer
 ** = TV talk show

14. How closely would you say you've followed news about an outbreak of an illness associated with strawberries—would you say you've followed it very closely, followed it but not too closely, or haven't followed it much at all?

15% = Followed very closely
22% = Followed, but not very closely
55% = Haven't followed much at all
 8% = No answer

14a. How did you first learn about the story? **(IF "TV" OR "RADIO," PROBE TO DETERMINE IF THAT WAS A NEWS PROGRAM OR TALK SHOW)**

65% = TV news   ** = TV talk show
17% = Read it in newspaper   ** = News magazine
 7% = From friend or relative   ** = Internet news service
 5% = Radio news   3% = Other
 1% = From neighbor   1% = No answer

15. Generally speaking, how many days each week do you read a newspaper?

28% = Six or seven times a week   16% = Once a week
15% = Four or five times a week   17% = Less than once a week
23% = Two or three times a week   1% = No answer

16. Generally, how many evenings each week do you watch a TV news program?

49% = Six or seven times a week   6% = Once a week
19% = Four or five times a week   8% = Less than once a week
18% = Two or three times a week   ** = No answer

17. Do you listen to the news on the radio regularly, or not?

35% = Regularly
64% = Not regularly
 ** = No answer

18. How often would you say you discuss politics and public affairs with members of your family—every day, several times a week, or less than that?

    6% = Every day
    16% = Several times a week
    77% = Less often than that
    1% = No answer

19. How often would you say you discuss politics and public affairs with your friends—every day, several times a week, or less than that?

    7% = Every day
    19% = Several times a week
    74% = Less often than that
    1% = No answer

20. I'd like to know how often you read certain types of publications. As I read each, please tell me if you read them regularly, sometimes, hardly ever, or never. (First,) how about . . . (**READ AND ROTATE**)

	Regularly	Some-times	Hardly Ever	Never	No Answer
a. News magazines such as *Time, U.S. News & World Report,* or *Newsweek*	11%	34%	19%	35%	**
b. Business magazines such as *Fortune* and *Forbes*	3%	14%	15%	68%	**
c. *The National Enquirer, The Sun,* or *The Star*	4%	15%	13%	68%	**

21. I'd like to know how often you watch or listen to certain TV and radio programs. As I read each, please tell me if you watch or listen regularly, sometimes, hardly ever, or never. (First,) how about . . . (**READ AND ROTATE**)

	Regularly	Some-times	Hardly Ever	Never	No Answer
a. News magazine shows such as *60 Minutes, Dateline,* or *20/20*	32%	40%	11%	18%	**
b. TV shows such as *Hard Copy* or *Inside Edition*	23%	38%	15%	24%	1%
c. CNN	24%	35%	10%	30%	1%
d. Programs on National Public Radio, such as *Morning Edition* or *All Things Considered*	8%	16%	13%	64%	1%
e. C-SPAN	5%	21%	15%	59%	1%
f. Radio shows that invite listeners to call in to discuss current events, public issues, and politics	9%	20%	17%	53%	**

22. Which of the following two statements about the news media do you agree with more . . .

>   34% = The news media help society solve its problems.
>
>   OR
>
>   48% = The news media get in the way of society solving its problems.
>   18% = No answer

23. Have you EVER called or sent a letter, telegram, fax, or e-mail message to your congressional representative or senator to express your opinion on an issue?

>   23% = Yes
>   77% = No
>   ** = No answer

NOTE: ** indicates response given by less than .5% of those interviewed.

IF "YES" IN Q23, ASK:

23a. Have you done so in the past 12 months?

>   42% = Yes
>   58% = No
>   ** = No answer

24. Have you EVER called or sent a letter, telegram, fax, or e-mail message to a local newspaper to express your opinion on an issue?

>   13% = Yes
>   87% = No
>   ** = No answer

IF "YES" IN Q24, ASK:

24a. Have you done so in the past 12 months?

>   46% = Yes
>   55% = No
>   0% = No answer

25. Have you EVER called or sent a letter, telegram, fax, or e-mail message to a state representative or state senator to express your opinion on an issue?

>   16% = Yes
>   83% = No
>   1% = No answer

IF "YES" IN Q25, ASK:

25a. Have you done so in the past 12 months?

>   44% = Yes
>   56% = No
>   1% = No answer

26. Have you EVER called or sent a letter, telegram, fax, or e-mail message to a member of your local school board or a city government official to express your opinion on an issue?

    14% = Yes
    86% = No
    ** = No answer

IF "YES" IN Q26, ASK:
26a. Have you done so in the past 12 months?

    61% = Yes
    39% = No
    0% = No answer

27. Have you EVER done volunteer work for a charity or other nonprofit organization?

    60% = Yes
    40% = No
    ** = No answer

IF "YES" IN Q27, ASK:
27a. Have you done so in the past 12 months?

    52% = Yes
    48% = No
    ** = No answer

28. In the past 3 or 4 years, have you attended any political meetings or rallies?

    11% = Yes
    89% = No
    ** = No answer

IF "YES" IN Q28, ASK:
28a. Have you done so in the past 12 months?

    68% = Yes
    32% = No
    0% = No answer

29. Some people say we should have a third major political party in this country in addition to the Democrats and Republicans. Do you agree or disagree?

    46% = Agree
    39% = Disagree
    15% = No answer

30. Over the course of the next year, do you think the financial situation of you and your family will improve a lot, improve some, get a little worse, or get a lot worse?

    12% = Improve a lot
    53% = Improve some
    18% = Get a little worse
     6% = Get a lot worse
    10% = No answer

Finally, I'd like to ask you some questions for statistical purposes only.

31. How long have you lived at you present address?

    11% = Less than 6 months
     9% = More than 6 months but less than 1 year
    12% = More than 1 year but less than 2 years
    66% = More than 2 years
     1% = No answer

32. How would you describe your views on most political matters? Generally, do you think of yourself as liberal, moderate, or conservative?

    19% = Liberal
    39% = Moderate
    30% = Conservative
    13% = No answer

33. In politics, do you consider yourself as a Republican, a Democrat, or an independent?

    17% = Republican   4% = Other (volunteered)
    24% = Democrat   9% = No answer
    46% = Independent

34. What was the last grade in school you completed? (**DO NOT READ RESPONSE CATEGORIES**)

    17% = Not a high school graduate   18% = College graduate
    38% = High school graduate   2% = No answer
    26% = Some college

35. Which of the following age groups are you in—18 to 29, 30 to 44, 45 to 64, or 65 or older?

    39% = 18 to 29   7% = 65 or older
    34% = 30 to 44   2% = No answer
    18% = 45 to 64

36. Are you white, black, or some other race?

    68% = White
    13% = Black
    17% = Other
     2% = No answer

37. Are you of Hispanic origin or descent, or not?

    13% = Hispanic
    84% = Not Hispanic
     3% = No answer

38. Was your total family income in 1995 UNDER or OVER $30,000? **IF UNDER $30,000, ASK:** Was it under or over $15,000? **IF OVER $30,000, ASK:** Was it between $30,000 and $50,000, or between $50,000 and $75,000, or was it over $75,000?

    19% = Under $15,000
    27% = Between $15,000 and $29,999
    23% = Between $30,000 and $49,999
    12% = Between $50,000 and $75,000
     6% = Over $75,000
    13% = Refused

39. Finally, would you mind if one of our reporters called you back to discuss your views further?

    43% = Yes, would mind
    57% = No, wouldn't mind

IF "NO, WOULDN'T MIND," ASK:
39a. In case one of our reporters does need to call you back, could I get your name?

——— ◄o► ———

THANK RESPONDENT WITH:

That concludes our survey. Thank you very much
for taking the time to answer my questions.

Appendix B

No-Show '96: Americans Who Don't Vote

SURVEY METHODOLOGY

Results of the survey are based on telephone interviews conducted July 8 through July 21, 1996, with 3,323 adults, 18 years of age and older, living in the continental United States.

The sample of telephone exchanges called was selected by a computer from a complete list of working exchanges in the country. The exchanges were chosen to ensure that each region would be represented in proportion to its population. The last four digits in each telephone number were randomly generated by a computer and screened to limit calls to residences. This procedure provided access to both listed and unlisted residential numbers.

The sample for each region of the country was released in replicates to ensure that the established calling procedures were followed for the entire sample. This procedure also helped ensure that the appropriate number of interviews would be obtained in each region.

At least four attempts were made to complete interviews at every sampled telephone number. The calls were placed on different days and at different times of the day to maximize the chances of reaching a respondent. In each contacted household, interviewers first asked to speak with the "youngest male 18 years of age or older who is at home now." If no eligible male was at home, interviewers asked to speak with the "oldest female 18 years of age or older who is at home." This systematic respondent selection process has been shown to produce samples that closely mirror the population in terms of age and gender.

Eligible respondents were asked whether they were registered to vote at their current address, whether they voted in the 1992 presidential election, what kept them from voting in 1992 if they did not do so, and whether they intended to vote in the 1996 presidential elections. Respondents who said they currently were registered, voted in 1992, and would "definitely vote" or "probably vote" in November 1996 were included in the pool of likely voters, as were those who said they were registered, didn't vote in 1992 because they were not old enough, and would "definitely" or "probably" vote in November 1996. Once a likely voter was identified, the interviewer collected information on the respondent's age, race, education level, and household income before terminating the interview. A total of 2,322 of these short interviews were conducted.

Respondents who said they were not registered to vote at their current address, who cited some reason other than age for not voting in 1992, or who said they would "probably not vote" or "definitely not vote" in November 1996 were classified as likely nonvoters. These 1,001 respondents then were asked a battery of 64 questions to determine the levels and patterns of their news and information consumption; the extent of their alienation from or affinity for governmental institutions, political parties, and politicians; the extent of their participation in other forms of political behavior (such as attending political meetings or contacting their federal, state, or local representatives); and their attitudes on selected social and public policy issues. Likely nonvoters also were asked 8 demographic questions.

To facilitate our exploration of both the similarities and differences among nonvoters, a typology was constructed by using cluster analysis, a statistical technique that classified respondents into the most homogeneous and meaningful groups possible based on their news and information consumption, the extent of their alienation from government and the political process, their feelings of political self-efficacy, the extent of their participation in other forms of quasi-political behavior, and basic demographic characteristics, including length of time at their current address.

The results of the survey have been weighted to adjust for variations in the sample relating to race, gender, age, and education. For results based on the sample of 1,001 likely nonvoters, one can say with 95% confidence that the error attributable to sampling and other random effects is plus or minus 3 percentage points. However, for results based on interviews with subgroups of respondents, the margin of error is larger. For example, the responses of the 288 nonvoters classified as Doers have a margin of error of plus or minus 6 percentage points.

In addition to sampling error, it should be noted that question wording, question order, and the practical difficulties of conducting any survey of public opinion can introduce error or bias into the findings.

(The survey was conducted by Dwight Morris's Campaign Study Group and the Medill News Service and was a collaboration of Northwestern University's Medill School of Journalism and Chicago public television station WTTW, with funding from the John D. and Catherine T. MacArthur Foundation.)

References

Adelman, K. (1996, November 1). Why worry about voter turnout? *Washington Times,* p. B-8.

Attlesey, S. (1998, April 19). Small voter bang for the electoral buck draws concern. *Dallas Morning News,* p. 46A.

Baker, N. (1997, October 26-28). Beyond the ballot box. *(Portland) Oregonian,* p. 1.

Brown, F. (1996, November 3). Sizzle fizzles for voters: Turnout may drop. *Denver Post,* p. A1.

Bruce, P. (1997, October/November). How the experts got voter turnout wrong last year. *The Public Perspective.*

Burnham, W. D. (1982). The appearance and disappearance of the American voter. In W. D. Burnham (Ed.), *The current crisis in American politics.* Oxford, UK: Oxford University Press.

Carney, E. N. (1998, January 17). Opting out of politics. *National Journal,* p. 106.

Cather, N. (1998, July 10). Officials eye voter apathy. *Daily Oklahoman,* p. 1.

Chapman, S. (1998, July 5). The decline in voting: A sign of sickness? *Chicago Tribune,* p. 13.

Clock ticks on voter registration. (1996, October 1). *Atlanta Journal and Constitution.*

Committee for the Study of the American Electorate. (1998a). *Primary turnout falls to record lows; democratic turnout also at nadir; lower November turnout likely, not certain.* Washington, DC: Author.

Committee for the Study of the American Electorate. (1998b). *Primary turnout reaching record lows; historic lows possible in fall election; 120,000,000 eligibles may not vote.* Washington, DC: Author.

Committee for the Study of the American Electorate. (1998c). *Turnout dips to 56-year low; non-South turnout lowest since 1818; GOP loses more in status quo vote.* Washington, DC: Author.

Cosco, J. (1991, October 23). Ex-marshal back in court, on drug charges. *Virginian-Pilot.*

Cramer, J. D., & Jackson, T. (1998, April 12). Few decide for many during May election about 80 percent of eligible voters in Roanoke do not cast local ballots. *Roanoke Times & World News,* p. B1.

DeLuca, T. (1995). *The two faces of political apathy.* Philadelphia, PA: Temple University Press.

Discovery retrieves Spartan filled with blazing images. (1998, November 4). *Chattanooga Times.*

Dyson, E. (1997). *Release 2.0: A design for living in a digital age.* New York: Broadway Books.

ElBoghdady, D. (1998, July 20). Light vote could help state GOP: State above average in midterm turnout, but numbers falling. *Detroit News,* p. A1.

English, P. (1998, August 27). Spark due for general election governor's race expected to revive turnout. *Daily Oklahoman,* p. 1.

First Lady pays first visit to Lynn: Hillary Clinton campaigns here Friday. (1996, October 2). *Lynn Daily Evening Item.*

Germond, J. W., & Witcover, J. (1996, November 23). Why Americans don't go to the polls. *National Journal,* p. 2562.

Give voters a real choice. (1996, June 3). *Wall Street Journal.*

Haight, R. T. (1983, April 13). Six hours: Gunman holds police at bay. *Grand Blanc News.*

Harwood, J. (1998, July 13). Parties focus on true believers as the few who will actually vote. *Wall Street Journal,* p. 1.

Healy, M. (1996, December 15). New movement plots more civil way of living. *Los Angeles Times,* p. 1.

Ho, A. (1998, May 26). Actions that spoke louder than official words. *South China Morning Post,* p. 19.

Human Serve. (1996, May 30). *Alienation not a factor in nonvoting.* New York: Author.

Jourgensen, T. (1996, October 2). First Lady's visit is first rate. *Lynn Daily Evening Item.*

Kagay, M. R. (1996, December 15). Experts say refinements are needed in the polls. *New York Times.*

Kaplan, R. D. (1997, December). Was democracy just a moment? Governments of the future: The future of democracy. *Atlantic Monthly,* p. 55.

Kondracke, M. M. (1996, October 21). *Roll Call.*

Krauthammer, C. E. (1990, May 21). In praise of low voter turnout. *Time.*

Landay, J. S. (1996, August 20). Voter registration hits high, but will people cast ballots? *Christian Science Monitor.*

Landers, R. K. (1988, February 19). Why America doesn't vote. *Congressional Quarterly.*

Marr, A. (1996, November 6). Message for our leaders: Ignore Clinton's America; Major and Blair have similarities with Bill Clinton. But they should learn no lessons from a mere campaigning machine. *The Independent,* p. 17.

Medill News Service. (1996, August). *No-show '96: Americans who don't vote* (series). Washington, DC: Author.

Medill School of Journalism and WTTW Television. (1996, August 19). *No-show '96: Americans who don't vote.* Washington, DC: Author.

Not registered? Then no letter to editor. (1998, May 17). *Omaha World-Herald,* p. 8a.

Patterson, T. E. (1994). *Out of order.* New York: Vintage.

Pew Research Center for the People and the Press. (1998a, March 10). *Deconstructing distrust: How Americans view government.* Washington, DC: Author.

Pew Research Center for the People and the Press. (1998b, June 15). *Voters not so angry, not so interested, compared to 1994.* Washington, DC: Author.

Piven, F. F., & Cloward, R. A. (1988). *Why Americans don't vote.* New York: Pantheon.

Putnam, R. D. (1995). Bowling alone: America's declining social capital. *Journal of Democracy, 6,* 65-78.

Raasch, C. (1998, January 11). Nonvoters complain about candidates, lack of time. *Gannett News Service.*

The right to vote is a responsibility. (1996, November 6). *Chicago Tribune,* p. 20.

Royko, M. (1996, November 7). If media says it's over, why should voters play? *Chicago Tribune,* p. 3.

Sabato, L. J. (1991). *Feeding frenzy: How attack journalism has transformed American politics.* New York: Free Press.

Schomp, C. (1996, November 8). Should we force people to vote? *Denver Post.*

Schudson, M. (1994, Fall). Voting rites: Why we need a new concept of citizenship. *The American Prospect,* p. 62.

Shribman, D. (1998, September 28). The anesthetic of the masses. *Fortune.*

U.S. Bureau of the Census. (1998). *Voting and registration in the election of November 1996.* Washington, DC: U.S. Department of Commerce.

Vellinga, M. L. (1998, March 8). Someday, ballots may offer "none of the above." *Sacramento Bee.*

Vobejda, B. (1996, November 7). Pilgrimage to the polls is lowest in 72 years. *Denver Post.*

Voting with pride. (1998, September 14). *Boston Globe,* p. A18.

White House Press Office. (1998, October 30). *Transcript of remarks by President Clinton on the economy.* Washington, DC: Author.

Will, G. F. (1996, October 31). Electorate yawns and picks a president. *Chicago Sun-Times,* p. 31.

Will, G. F. (1998, July 5). Americans turn away from politics. *Times Union,* p. B5.

Wills, G. (1998, January 25). Whatever happened to politics? Washington is not where it's at. *New York Times Magazine.*

Wolkow, R. (1990, February 11). Ship safety. *New York Times.*

Other Sources

Albright, J., & Kunstel, M. (1988, October). The non-voting Americans. *Atlanta Journal/Atlanta Constitution.*

Anderson, J. (1996, December 8). YAAWWWNNN! We need to wake up the American voter—here's how. *Dallas Morning News.*

Angelo, L. (1998, June 15). Distrust, apathy grip voters. *The Flint Journal,* p. 21.

Avey, M. J. (1989). *The demobilization of American voters: A comprehensive theory of voter turnout.* New York: Greenwood.

Blakely, M. K. (1996). *Red, white, and oh so blue: A memoir of a political depression.* New York: Lisa Drew Book, Scribners.

Bone, H. A., & Ranney, A. (1967). *Politics and voters.* New York: McGraw-Hill.

Bored to the bone. (1996, November 11). *Newsweek.*

Briggs, J. (1996, December). Voter turnout low, tune out high. *Chicago Reporter.*

Dionne, E. J. (1991). *Why Americans hate politics.* New York: Simon & Schuster.

Doppelt, J. C., & Matusik, K. M. (1991, July). *Blueprint for a comprehensive plan for increasing voter registration and voter participation in Cook County.* Chicago: Clerk of Cook County.

Doppelt, J. C., & Shearer, E. (1997, November 25). How the other half lives without voting. *Chicago Tribune.*

Entman, R. M. (1989). *Democracy without citizens.* New York: Oxford University Press.

Flanigan, W. H., & Zingale, N. H. (1991). *Political behavior of the American electorate.* Washington, DC: Congressional Quarterly Press.

Gans, C. (1997, October/November). It's Bruce who got the turnout story wrong. *The Public Perspective.*

Gant, M. M., & Luttbeg, N. R. (1991). *American political behavior: 1952-1988.* Itasca, IL: F. E. Peacock.

Ganz, M. (1996, September/October). Motor voter or motivated voter? *The American Prospect.*

Gosnell, H. F. (1927). *Getting out the vote: An experiment in the stimulation of voting.* Chicago: University of Chicago Press.

Hasen, R. L. (1996). Voting without law? *University of Pennsylvania Law Review, 144,* 2135-2179.

Janda, K., Berry, J. M., & Goldman, J. (1997). *The challenge of democracy: Government in America* (5th ed.). Boston: Houghton Mifflin.

Johnson, T. J., Hays, C. E., & Hays, S. P. (Eds.). (1998). *Engaging the public: How government and the media can reinvigorate American democracy.* Lanham, MD: Rowman & Littlefield.

Kuttner, R. (1987, September 19-21). Why Americans don't vote. *New Republic.*

Ladd, E. C. (1982). *Where have all the voters gone?* New York: Norton.

Ladd, E. C. (1996, June/July). Civic participation and American democracy: The data just don't show erosion of America's "social capital." *The Public Perspective.*

Lesher, D., & Warren, J. (1998, October 26). How much does low turnout matter? Getting voters to the polls is increasingly difficult. *Los Angeles Times.*

Miller, W. E., & Merrill Shanks, J. (1996). *The new American voter.* Cambridge, MA: Harvard University Press.

Nardulli, P. F., Dalager, J. K., & Greco, D. E. (1996). Voter turnout in U.S. presidential elections: A historical view and some speculation. *Political Science and Politics, 29,* 480-490.

National Commission on Civic Renewal. (1998, June 24). *A nation of spectators: How civic disengagement weakens America and what we can do about it.* College Park, MD: Author.

Nichols, J. (1998, October). Apathy, Inc.: Republicans aim to drive down voter turnout. *The Progressive.*

Page, B. I. (1996). *Who deliberates? Mass media in modern democracy.* Chicago: University of Chicago Press.

Putnam, R. D. (1996, January 4). One nation under apathy. *Rocky Mountain News.*

Putnam, R. D. (1996, Winter). The strange disappearance of civic America. *The American Prospect.*

Ragsdale, L., & Rusk, J. G. (1993). Who are nonvoters? Profiles from the 1990 Senate elections. *American Journal of Political Science, 37,* 721-746.

Reality check: The politics of mistrust. (1996, January/February). *Washington Post.*

Riechmann, D. (1998, June 24). Report: Civic life eroding in U.S. *Associated Press.*

Roper Center Databook. (1997). *America at the polls 1996.* Storrs: Roper Center for Public Opinion Research, University of Connecticut.

Shearer, E., Morris, D. L., & Doppelt, J. (1998). No-show '96: Americans who do not vote. In T. J. Johnson, C. E. Hays, & S. P. Hays (Eds.), *Engaging the public: How government and the media can reinvigorate American democracy.* Lanham, MD: Rowman & Littlefield.

Stanley, H. W. (1987). *Voter mobilization and the politics of race: The South and universal suffrage, 1952-1984.* New York: Praeger.

Teixeira, R. A. (1987). *Why Americans don't vote: Turnout decline in the United States 1960-1984.* New York: Greenwood.

Teixeira, R. A. (1992). *The disappearing American voter.* Washington, DC: Brookings Institution.

Thelen, D. (1996). *Becoming citizens in the age of television: How Americans challenged the media and seized political initiative during the Iran-Contra debate.* Chicago: University of Chicago Press.

Tierney, J. (1998, November 2). The big city; low turnout? Try free food and agitators. *New York Times.*

Tune in, turn off, drop out. (1996, February 19). *U.S. News & World Report.*

U.S. Bureau of the Census. (1998). *Projections of the voting-age population for states: November 1998.* Washington, DC: U.S. Department of Commerce.

U.S. Congress, Senate Committee on Rules and Administration. (1993). *National Voter Registration Act of 1993.* Washington, DC: Author.

Wolfinger, R. E. (1991). Voter turnout. *Society, 28,* 23-26.

Wolfinger, R. E., Glass, D. P., & Squire, P. (1990, Spring). Predictors of electoral turnout: An international comparison. *Policy Studies Review.*

Wolfinger, R. E., & Rosenstone, S. J. (1980). *Who votes?* New Haven, CT: Yale University Press.

Index

About the Authors

Jack C. Doppelt is Associate Professor at Northwestern University's Medill School of Journalism, a faculty associate at Northwestern's Institute for Policy Research, and has served as Medill's acting and associate dean. He is coauthor of *The Journalism of Outrage: Investigative Reporting and Agenda Building in America,* a book on investigative reporting and its influence on public policy, and has published numerous articles on libel, the media's influence on the criminal justice system, and media coverage of the legal system. He is also the author of "Blueprint for a Comprehensive Plan for Increasing Voter Registration and Voter Participation in Cook County," an action plan commissioned in 1991 by the Clerk of Cook County. His expertise is media law and ethics and the reporting of legal affairs. He is a graduate of Grinnell College and the University of Chicago Law School and lives in Evanston, Illinois, with his wife and two children.

Ellen Shearer is Associate Professor at Northwestern University's Medill School of Journalism and codirector of Medill's Washington Program, the Medill News Service. She also serves on the board of the Center for Religion and the News Media, a joint program between the Medill School of Journalism and the Garrett School of Theology. She writes on media issues for several magazines and is a regular contributor to *The American Editor* magazine, writing on topics such as readership and Washington reporting. She authored a chapter in *The Changing Reader—Understanding the Forces Changing Newspapers,* published by Northwestern's Newspaper Management Center. Prior to joining Medill in 1994, Shearer's career was in the news industry, where she served in senior management roles at United Press International and *Newsday,* among others. She is a 1975 graduate of the University of Wisconsin with a bachelor of arts degree and lives in Chevy Chase, Maryland, with her husband and two sons.

Both Doppelt and Shearer vote habitually whether they know enough about the candidates or referenda on the ballot or not.